Between Philosemitism and Antisemitism

Between Philosemitism and Antisemitism

DEFENSES OF JEWS AND

JUDAISM IN GERMANY,

1871–1932

ALAN T. LEVENSON

UNIVERSITY OF NEBRASKA PRESS · LINCOLN AND LONDON

Acknowledgments for the use of previously
published material appear on page 189.
Library of Congress Cataloging-in-Publication Data
Levenson, Alan T.
Between philosemitism and antisemitism : defenses
of Jews and Judaism in Germany, 1871–1932 /
Alan T. Levenson.
p. cm.
Includes bibliographical references (p.) and index.
ISBN 0-8032-2957-7 (cloth : alk. paper)
1. Philosemitism—Germany—History—19th century.
2. Philosemitism—Germany—History—20th century.
3. Antisemitism—Germany—History—19th century.
4. Antisemitism—Germany—History—20th century.
5. Germany—Ethnic relations.   I. Title.
DS141.L6435 2004
305.892'4043'09034—dc22
2003023385

Contents

Preface   vii

Acknowledgments   xv

Part 1. Philosemitism in the Public Arena

1. Philosemitic Discourse in Imperial Germany   3
2. The German Peace Movement and the Jews   21
3. The Problematics of Philosemitic Fiction   44
4. Missionary Protestants and the Defense of Judaism   64

Part 2. Philosemitic Tendencies and Individuals

5. The Gentile Reception of Herzlian Zionism   93
6. Christian Author, Jewish Book?   110
7. An Adventure in Otherness   123
8. The Apostate as Philosemite   132

Appendix: The Case for Philosemitism   143

Notes   149

Selected Bibliography   181

Source Acknowledgments   189

Index   191

Preface

The essays presented here offer an analysis of the arguments used in defense of Jews, Judaism, and Jewishness in the period from the foundation of the German Reich (1871) until the ascent of the Nazis (1932). I am well aware that German philosemitism sounds more like an oxymoron than a subject for study. The enthusiasm for Jews, Judaism, or things Jewish that one finds in the Anglo-American tradition appears only rarely in German-speaking lands. Antisemitism provoked the vast majority of the defenses considered here. It could be argued, therefore, that *anti-antisemitism* rather than *philosemitism* is the better term. I find the latter indispensable for two reasons. First, the vindication of what was a traduced and generally disliked minority entailed defending the shortcomings (imaginary and real) as well as extolling the virtues (real and imaginary) of that minority. Even had the Jews' warmest defenders preferred to avoid those discussions or hewed to more general principles such as civil equality or class interests, they could not, and they were drawn into a discussion of Jewish particularities. Second, some individuals described in this book embraced or identified with at least one dimension of Jewishness in a way that must be called philosemitic.[1] While no philosemitic *tradition* existed in Germany, there were philosemitic individuals who testified to the existence of pro-Jewish attitudes in a generally hostile environment.[2]

Before defining the central term *philosemitism*, a few words about this unlikely choice of topics seem in order. Much of the impetus for the choice came from the glaring contrast between the ubiquity of scholarship on antisemitism and my own upbringing in suburban New York in the 1960s. I cannot recall a single instance of antisemitism from my childhood, although I encountered many instances of philosemitism. I realize, of course, that late-nineteenth-century Germany differs fundamentally from late-twentieth-century America. Still, I find it difficult to imagine a society so completely antisemitic that it admitted no exceptions.

Beginning with Sander Gilman's pioneering study of Jewish self-hatred, the issue of why some German Jews had such a negative self-image reemerged as a scholarly crux.[3] The growing interest in Jewish apostasy only sharpened the conundrum, for surely most Jews could identify the rantings of a Wilhelm Marr or a Theodor Fritsch as totally detached from the actual role of Jews in Germany.[4] How, then, can one situate the negative self-image of some Jews in the concrete realities of German culture beyond the general dynamics of majority-minority relations?[5]

The answer to this question lies partly in the language used by the anti-antisemitic camp. That group, comprised of respected teachers and political leaders of the nation, also wished for the disappearance of a distinct Jewish entity. Even anti-antisemites continued to entertain negative appraisals of Judentum, which can be translated as "Jewry," "Judaism," or "the Jews." Much of what follows is a midrash on Istvan Deák's sage comment, "Jewishness indeed was determined not so much by one's enemies as by one's friends; and it was a source of humiliation, for—all the hypocritical assertions of the courts of the Weimar Republic to the contrary—'Jew' was a pejorative term."[6]

In *Vichy France and the Jews*, Robert Paxton and Michael Marrus proposed that low-level antisemitism must be a precondition for a successful anti-Jewish agenda.[7] Paxton and Marrus posited three discrete levels of antisemitic feeling: ideologically driven, passive-aggressive, and latent. Research done on Nazi Germany in the 1980s and 1990s yielded a more nuanced view of the role antisemitism played in the Third Reich. On the whole, scholars found that while intense antisemitism did not motivate voters for the Nazi Party, sufficient antisemitism existed for Hitler to drive Germany toward increasingly intense antisemitic policies from 1933 to 1939 with minimal opposition.[8] My curiosity was aroused by the thought that Paxton and Marrus—and the aforementioned scholars on German Jewry—seemed to leave those with few antisemitic tendencies or with a preponderance of prosemitic tendencies out of the picture altogether. Where, why, and how, I wondered, did latent antisemitism turn into something that should no longer be called antisemitic?

Two much-discussed works, Paul Lawrence Rose's *German Question/Jewish Question: Revolutionary Antisemitism from Kant to Wagner* and Daniel Jonah Goldhagen's *Hitler's Willing Executioners: Ordinary Germans and the Holocaust*, strengthened my conviction that the topic of pro-Jewish sentiment deserved investigation.[9] Despite the considerable merits of each work, both revert to an earlier idea of national character that must be used far more cautiously than these authors use it. In both works, this national (read: antisemitic) character is "demonstrated" through the undeniable presence of antisemitism in selected highbrow texts and then employed as an explanatory device for nearly all thoughts and actions. Paul Rose, who rightfully calls attention to the presence of Jews in the discourse of German revolutionaries, tacitly ignores those traditions that fit poorly into his understanding of revolutionism as well as developments that occurred outside the realm of the elite documents he analyzes.[10] Rose also forces his evidence to prove the Germans' uncontrollable hatred for Jews. Rejecting Jacob Katz's perfectly sound exploration of Wagner's path from (relative) philosemitism to rabid antisemitism, Rose dismisses even the possibility of philosemitism as a "false category."[11] For Rose, as for Goldhagen, German philosemitism is nothing more than the desire to kill the Jews kindly through radical assimilation rather than annihilation. Although the long-term results of structural assimilation may indeed be disastrous for Jewish continuity, the distinction between those Gentiles who wish to murder Jews and those who wish to marry them is considerable.

In terms of historical accuracy, Goldhagen's opening chapters leave much to be desired. Goldhagen opines, "By the end of the nineteenth century, the Jews' greatest friends, the liberals, had by and large abandoned them."[12] Goldhagen wishes to show a steady and continuous growth in antisemitic sentiment, but he does so at the cost of neglecting the numerous anti-antisemitic petitions, the anti-antisemitic Reichstag speeches of Heinrich Rickert, Ludwig Windhorst, and others, and the creation of the liberal Verein zur Abwehr des Antisemitismus (Association for the Defense against Antisemitism), or Abwehrverein, in 1891. Far from abandoning the Jews, the antisemitic assault engendered a defense, even from missionary Christians. Goldhagen cites a Socialist Party (spd) report from 1936 that antisemitism was on the rise without stating that the socialists officially and publicly opposed antisemitism from start to finish.[13] Sounding more like a prosecuting attorney than a historian, Goldhagen successfully shows a far wider and far more intently evil circle of perpetrators than much recent Holocaust research. But more is not all. Goldhagen does a disservice not only to those who were horrified by Nazi atrocities but also to their precursors, who found the antisemitism of the Wilhelminian and Weimar periods reprehensible and worthy of dissent.

Rose and Goldhagen offer a flawed picture morally, intellectually, and even pragmatically. Morally, the idea of national identity invites abuse, as Jews know all too well. Intellectually, the flattening-out effect of works like Rose's and Goldhagen's erodes any need to make a distinction between levels of intensity of antisemitism. But research on the Holocaust makes it clear that this distinction is simply indispensable. The difference between latent antisemitism, which prepares the ground for acquiescence, and ideologically driven radical antisemitism, which galvanizes antisemitic programs, is considerable. All gradations were needed, ultimately, to carry out the Final Solution. Pragmatically, were one to accept Goldhagen's analysis, the only conclusion would be that certain societies are collectively rabid and that nothing can be done to alter them. That degree of historical determinism simply does not ring true. The Holocaust was neither predictable nor inevitable.[14]

Nevertheless, Rose's dismissal of philosemitism as a "false category" is understandable. If we expect a pure philosemitism, we will not find it easily or often in a basically antisemitic society.[15] But alongside these initially negative images, positive images could and at times did develop. When these became the dominant images, I would argue, we have a philosemite—even if antisemitism prejudices remained. Let me offer a concrete example. In an excellent revision of Thomas Mann's attitude to Jews and Judaism, Alfred Hoelzel concludes, "A strain of negativism, however, remains constant and consistent from first to last. It never truly becomes outright antisemitism—such a charge would be a gross and unfair exaggeration—but neither do the facts confirm the philosemitism that Mann claimed." I could quibble with several of Hoelzel's particulars, and I think the relative weight he assigned to the nadir of Mann's attitudes (*Walsüngenblut*) and the apex (*Joseph und seine Brüder*) is unjustified, but my stronger disagreement is conceptual.[16] It is undeniable that Mann never abandoned describing certain unlikable behaviors and people as Jewish. He thus remained antisemitic. But, far more decisively, Mann spoke out against the persecution of Jews and in favor of Zionism. Socially and intellectually, as Hoelzel acknowledges, Mann admired the Jewish *Geist*, and his reservations about a Jewish state reflect his sense—and not his alone—of what Europe would lose by the departure of the Jews. Mann never became the sort of "pure" philosemite that would pass Rose's test. Relative to his historical context (and what other measure should a historian employ?), Mann at age seventy must be considered a philosemite even if at age seven he could not.

Philosemitism is indeed a term that should be used cautiously. Alan Edelstein's *An Unacknowledged Harmony* alerts us to two likely pitfalls: apologetics and decontextualization.[17] Wittingly or unwittingly, Edelstein engages in apologetics in a number of ways. He tacitly equates, by way of contrast, philosemitism with antisemitism, going so far as to explain the continued presence of Jews in the Christian West as evidence of philosemitism. But of course anti-Judaism and antisemitism have been the mighty streams, while philosemitism has been the trickling brook.[18] To juxtapose the one with the other misrepresents the respective historical importance of movements for and against Jews and Judaism. Nowhere in this book will the reader find the phrase philosemitic movement or tradition because in Germany there was none—there were only philosemitic tendencies that were cultivated or uncultivated to varying degrees. (The various rubrics assigned philosemitism by a variety of scholars [for example, missionary Christian, biblical chiliastic, liberal, economic, humanistic, utilitarian] strike me more as templates than analytical categories. Franz Delitzsch and Hermann Strack, for instance, were missionary Christians with a predilection toward philosemitism, but Johann de Le Roi and Gustaf Dahlman were missionary Christians too, and their attitudes were quite hostile. The same could be said for all the above-mentioned categories.) The apologetics that mar Edelstein's work applies also to Alfred Low's *Jews in the Eyes of the German*.[19] What makes Low's book apologetic is his portrait of a German intelligentsia evenly balanced between pro- and anti-Jewish attitudes combined with his tendency to engage in "cherry picking"—reporting the best and concealing the worst. While making my case as forcefully as possible, I have tried not to gloss over the less savory material.

In previous works on philosemitism, decontextualization often serves as the handmaid to apologetics.[20] The connect-the-dots procedure employed by Edelstein, Solomon Rappaport, and, more recently, William and Hilary Rubinstein yields an impressive number of philosemitic occurrences and expressions but divests them of their larger historical context.[21] Like antisemitism, philosemitism cannot really be understood divorced from a particular time and place.[22] The important studies of philosemitism by Jacob Katz, Todd Endelman, Celia Heller, Dagmar Herzog, and Frank Stern derive their value precisely because they explain the subject in the context of surrounding developments. For that reason, German philosemitism in the period from 1871 to 1933 must be located in the political matrix of German liberalism's declining fortunes after 1879, the unexpected missionary Christian defense of rabbinic Judaism following the Berlin antisemitic debate (*Antisemitismusstreit*) from 1879 to 1881, the marginality of the German peace movement, and the German intelligentsia's profound ambivalence on the Judenfrage (Jewish question). My goal is to avoid both apologetics and decontextualization—how well or poorly I have succeeded in this the reader must judge.

The importance of contextualization forces me to state my expectations modestly. I am more a student of Jewish history than of German. In all chapters of this book I have leaned very heavily on the secondary scholarship and relied mainly on the published and public expressions of philosemitism. These limitations notwithstanding, I believe that much is to be gained by a panoramic overview of the philosemitic discourse common to those derisively called the "Jewish protection guard" (Judenschütztruppe) by their enemies. Exactly how far could the defense of Jews, Judaism, and Jewishness be pushed in an antisemitic environment? How did Germans from a wide spectrum of affiliations and beliefs defend a small but vexing minority? Did continuity or discontinuity prevail in the patterns of defense? To what extent did antisemitism premises hamstring defense efforts? What was the opposite end of the spectrum from the deadly hatred of German antisemites? Within the limits stated above, this book attempts to answer these questions.

The period on which I have focused needs little justification.[23] With the emancipation of the Jews in 1869 and 1871, legal equality became a reality. The contested issue of emancipation was quickly challenged, and the fact that the Jews' supporters were defending the status quo continually imparted a reactive flavor to their efforts, unlike the earliest advocates of Jewish emancipation. The year 1932 offers another obvious terminal point. Under the Nazis, Judenfreundlichkeit (befriending Jews) was no longer a minority position, it was a crime. Opposition to antisemitism in the Nazi dictatorship, therefore, takes on a wholly different aspect from defense efforts undertaken in a "free" society.[24] Efforts at rescuing Jews from the Holocaust have been well investigated and, in any case, seem to be a very different phenomenon.[25]

Dagmar Herzog's *Intimacy and Exclusion* offers a revisionist interpretation of the nexus of politics and gender in the mid-nineteenth century that highlights the inability of liberal Christians to imagine a permanent place for Jews and Judaism in their vision of Germany.[26] Frank Stern's *The Whitewashing of the Yellow Badge* offers a thorough explanation of the functional manipulation of philosemitism in the post–World War II period.[27] For Stern, postwar philosemitism offered a way to ingratiate the German nation to its American conquerors, to assuage guilt, and to help rehabilitate and normalize Germany in the eyes of the world. I have tried not to let hindsight overly determine my analysis. On the other hand, it seems inevitable that the deficiencies of German philosemitism appear more clearly as a result of the Holocaust and because I live in a generally liberal and pluralistic country.

The term philosemitism began to appear about the same time as the term antisemitism—it had already been employed in the Berlin antisemitic debate of 1879–81.[28] At the time, this word meant nothing more than opposition to organized antisemitism. I take philosemitism to mean *any* pro-Jewish or pro-Judaic utterance or act. Conversely, I reject several potential objections to the term. To begin with, I will not hesitate to describe an act or an utterance as philosemitic simply because the actor or speaker would not have.[29] The denial of any philosemitic motive provided a stock rhetorical opening to many anti-antisemitic tracts. Hermann Strack, for instance, declared that he defended the Talmud in pamphlets and in courts of law against misrepresentation out of scholarly considerations. The net effect of these actions certainly redounded to the benefit of German Jewry. Second, I do not require philosemitism to be enunciated as a central principle. Heinrich Rickert championed civic equality (*Rechtsstaat*), explicitly defended Jews as productive members of society, and attacked antisemites as the opponents of legal equality. This strikes me as adequate evidence of a philosemitic stance, even though the philosemitism was ancillary.[30] Third, philosemitic tendencies may proceed from a variety of impulses and coexist with less friendly sentiments. While anti-antisemitism usually provided the first prompting of philosemitic sentiment, that does not mean that all philosemites liberated themselves from prejudices regarding Jews or Judaism. That Wilhelm Marr's failed marriages to Jewish women and Richard Wagner's resentment toward both Jewish patrons and competitors played a role in the genesis of their antisemitism does not diminish it. Conversely, to offer an explanation of an individual's philosemitism does not explain it away—that is a clear-cut genetic fallacy. Fourth, the construct "semitism" has come under assault as inherently prejudicial. In this line of argument, philosemites and antisemites are tainted by their shared premise—that there is a "semitic" essence at all.[31] While this may be true in theory, in practice the historian has a right to distinguish attempts at defense from attempts at defamation. As to the desirability of philosemitism as a phenomenon per se, I will reserve my comments on this touchy subject for the book's appendix.

These chapters began as independent essays; I subsequently realized that this format better suited the episodic nature of German philosemitism than an attempt to create a running narrative. The downside of this organization is that several loci of philosemitism do not get discussed. The Abwehrverein was certainly the most important non-Jewish anti-antisemitic organization in this period. Many Abwehrverein members and pamphlets are quoted in the first chapter of this book, but a reexamination of this organization was rendered unnecessary by the studies of Barbara Suchy and Erik Lindner.[32]

The Abwehrverein reflected genteel, mainstream, aristocratic Left Liberalism. But independent left-wing intellectuals also wrote a great deal about antisemites and Jews. In a seminal work, Istvan Deák called attention to the Jewish descent of many of the contributors to *Die Weltbühne* (The world stage), though he underestimated, in my view, the amount of attention given in this journal to the Judenfrage. I counted fifty-eight articles on Jewish matters (many cultural as well as political, and many unrelated to antisemitism) from 1919 to 1993, most of which were sympathetic and many of which were by non-Jews.

Socialists wrote about the Judenfrage extensively—their record was a mixed one. The enormous popularity of figures such as Eduard Bernstein and Paul Singer; the philosemitic utterances of Ellie Marx and an older Friedrich Engels; the anti-antisemitism of academic socialists (*Kathedrasozialisten*) such as Gustav Schmoller (1836–1917), Lujo Bentano (1844–1931), and Karl Lamprecht (1856–1915); the stirring resolution proposed by August Bebel at the 1893 SPD congress lauding the Jewish contributions to socialism—all suggest that philosemitic sentiments were widespread if tangential to socialist goals. Even the splenetic essays by Franz Mehring linking philosemitism to capitalism, since they present philosemitism and antisemitism as equally bad, should probably be read as protests against the excessive sympathy noted above.[33] Nevertheless, given the investigations of Donald Niewyck, Robert Wistrich, Shlomo Na'aman, Edmund Silberner, and others, it did not seem worthwhile to reinvestigate the specifically socialist manifestations of philosemitism.[34] It certainly pains me to exclude intriguing works such as Rudolf Schay's *Die Juden in der deutschen Politik* (Jews in German politics), a work that celebrated in 1929 the distinctive role Jews played in forwarding Germany's political progress.[35]

Missionary Protestants were not the only detractors of antisemitism from a Christian perspective. Liberal Protestants such as Michael Baumgarten in the 1880s and Eduard Lamparter in the 1920s boldly attacked antisemites. Lamparter—minister, politician, and Abwehrverein stalwart—wrote two positive and respectful books on Judaism, and he deserves more attention than he has received.[36] Jews and Catholics generally found themselves far apart in political, cultural, and religious matters. Still, there were sympathetic voices in the Catholic world. Ignaz Johann von Döllinger (1799–1890), an opponent of the doctrine of papal infallibility, wrote two works in favor of the Jews and against the antisemites.[37] Jacques Kornberg convincingly argues that Döllinger's pro-Jewish position cannot be understood independently of his opposition to ultramontanism and the latter's antisemitic tendencies. Döllinger, Kornberg notes, identified with the Jews "as victims of the same forces seeking to bury liberal Catholicism."[38] The *Antisemitismusstreit* of 1879–81 prompted Döllinger's extraordinary address to the Bavarian Academy of Science on 25 July 1881, later published as *Die Juden in Europa* (The Jews in Europe).[39] Alban Stolz (1808–83), another well-known Catholic cleric and author, praised rural Jews for their abstemiousness and devotion to work and family.[40] However, given the diametrically opposed political, social, and religious tendencies between Jews and Catholics, we should not be surprised to find relatively little evidence of Catholic philosemitism—at least in the public arena. I likewise failed to find an adequate home for the numerous anti-antisemitic pamphlets and for the philosemitic snippets in the *Rundfrage* (round-table forums) for which Germans had such an appetite.

Given the skepticism sure to greet this topic, I would like to emphasize that I have not dumped all my three-by-five cards into this text. Studies of liberal *Vereine* along the line of George Mosse's discussion of the Goethe societies, scientific research institutes, and Weimar period novels in which Jews appear in minor but positive roles (such as Erich Maria Remarque's *Drei Kameraden*) could add much color to the picture I have painted.[41] Two recent histories of this period focusing on Christian-Jewish intermarriage suggest more friendly social interaction than is usually assumed.[42] Despite the attention German Jewry has received from scholars, much work remains to be done on the history of Jewish-Christian relations outside the ranks of the elite.

What remain as discrete topics are the following: a rhetorical analysis of liberal rhetoric in the Imperial period (chapter 1); an inquiry into the advocacy of Jewry by several figures associated with the German peace movement (chapter 2); a survey of fictional efforts at portraying Jews sympathetically (chapter 3); a reappraisal of the missionary Protestant defense of Judaism, especially that of Franz Delitzsch and Hermann Strack (chapter 4); a reappraisal of the non-Jewish reception of Theodor Herzl and Herzlian Zionism (chapter 5); an exploration of the Jewishness of Thomas Mann's novel *Joseph und seine Brüder* (chapter 6); a case study of philosemitism as a path toward conversion to Judaism in the person of Nahida Remy–Ruth Lazarus (chapter 7); and a case study of residual Jewish loyalties in the lives of two apostates from Judaism, Selig Cassel and Edith Stein (chapter 8). This work concludes with some reflections on the nature of philosemitism as manifested in modern Germany and on the role of this phenomenon in the contemporary Jewish setting.

Acknowledgments

Most of this book was researched and written during my sabbatical year in Israel, 1999–2000. I want to thank Dr. David S. Ariel, president of Siegal College of Judaic Studies, for granting me an entire year's leave. Every able-bodied teacher at a small institution is needed to field classes; my sabbatical represented a much larger sacrifice on David's part than it would have for most college presidents. The college has been my home for twelve years, and I continue to be grateful to spend my days with such a wonderful group of colleagues and students. A number of my faculty colleagues—Sylvia Abrams, Moshe Berger, Ron Brauner, Roger Klein, Lifsa Schachter, Jeff Schein—have shown a great willingness over the years to read various essays of mine on this and other subjects. The support staff—especially Sheryl—and the library staff have been there to bail me out of my frequent computer blunders and to locate obscure German-language master's theses, most of which proved only marginally relevant—I thank them. Henry Frank, originally of Chemnitz, helped me decipher handwritten letters and checked many of my translations.

The funding for my sabbatical year was provided by the American Council of Learned Societies and the Vidal Sassoon Center for the International Study of Antisemitism. I am also grateful to the scholars at Tel Aviv University and the Hebrew University of Jerusalem who gave me guidance on this project, including Jeremy Cohen, Shulamit Volkov, Steven Aschheim, and David Zissenwine. Monika Richarz, in 1994 the director of Judaica Germania, arranged my support from the Deutscher akademischer Austausch Dienst (German Academic Exchange). My summer in Cologne convinced me that there would be adequate material to address this subject meaningfully.

A number of other scholars have, over the years, encouraged me to pursue my research and not succumb to the temptation to spend all of my working hours in class preparation. I want to thank David Biale, Marc Bregman, David Brenner, Todd Endelman, Peter Haas, Susannah Heschel, Dagmar Lorenz, David Myers, Keith Pickus, Linda Raphael, David Sorkin, Alan Steinweis, and Kenneth Stow for responding to my modest efforts to say something about the modern Jewish experience. For Marc Lee Raphael, my mentor, no words of thanks could be adequate. Needless to say, despite this abundance of good counsel, many shortcomings remain. They are mine alone.

Since the publication of my book *Modern Jewish Thinkers* (2000), I have lost a grandfather, a father, and a stepfather. May the memory of Bill Goldman, Larry Levenson, and Harlan Hettmansberger be for a blessing. Reading, writing, thinking, and teaching are great ways to make a living, but the love of friends and family is the real consolation for loss and the real reason for getting up in the morning. I am lucky to wake up every day to my loving wife, Hilary, and my adorable son, Benjamin. This book, naturally, is dedicated to them.

Between Philosemitism and Antisemitism

Part 1. Philosemitism in the Public Arena

1. *Philosemitic Discourse in Imperial Germany*

There are many shades of political opinion and the shadiest of these is the liberal.

Phil Ochs, "Love Me, Love Me, Love Me, I'm a Liberal"

In any case, the struggle [between the antisemite and the democrat] is not equal. If the democrat were to put some warmth into pleading the cause of the Jew, he would have to be a Manichean too, and equate the Jew with the principle of the good. But how could he do this? The democrat is not a fool. He makes himself the advocate of the Jew because he sees him as a member of humanity; since humanity has other members, the democrat has much to do.

Jean-Paul Sartre, *Anti-Semite and Jew*

Although Germans adopted the terms Judenfrage and *Emanzipation* in the early decades of the nineteenth century, the debate over the Jewish future began in pre-Napoleonic times under the impact of the Enlightenment's critique of the old regime.[1] The "tolerance debate," as Peter Erspamer terms it, may be dated to Gotthold Ephraim Lessing's plays *Die Juden* (1749) and *Nathan der Weise* (1769). In *Nathan*, Lessing created a pariah figure who served as a trenchant critic of Christian orthodoxy and the feudal order. Christian Wilhelm von Dohm, a Prussian civil servant and the most influential proponent of improving the status of Jews, departed from Lessing's idealized portrait. Dohm's *Über die bürgerliche Verbesserung der Juden* (1781–83) argued that Jews had been corrupted by centuries of persecution and that equality would require their rehabilitation. In Dohm's view, Jews were not ready to serve in positions of authority such as the judiciary, and he did not demand a complete dismantling of Jewish communal autonomy, as Napoleon would at the Parisian Sanhedrin in 1807. The Jewish philosopher Moses Mendelssohn, the third in this trio of German reformers, recognized the dangers inherent in a qualified emancipation and recognized that Dohm (and others) visualized the German-Jewish encounter as a one-way street. The minority would need to conform to the majority: Jews were to become German.[2]

With the unification came the extension of emancipation to all of Germany's Jews. Bismarck united the nation through "blood and iron," but from 1871 to 1879 he ruled the nation with the help of the National Liberals, whose ambivalent views on Jewry descended from Lessing and Dohm. The 1870s saw the beginning of rapid industrialization, urbanization, commercialization, a stock-market crash, and, concomitantly, the breakdown of older folkways. This decade served, in Jacob Katz's phrase, as the crystallization period of modern antisemitism. By 1879 two major developments crucial to our story had transpired. First, antisemitism emerged as a definite force in German life. In that year, a racist pamphleteer (Wilhelm Marr), a Protestant preacher (Adolf Stoecker), and a venerated scholar (Heinrich von Treitschke) all lent weight to the popular swell of anti-Jewish sentiment. Second, Bismarck made a major switch in alliances from the National Liberals to a combination of the Conservative and the Catholic Center Parties, hitherto Bismarck's major foe. From that point on, as Peter Pulzer wrote, "it is difficult to think of a time when German liberalism was not in crisis."[3] Overnight, the majority of German Jews had been cast into the opposition, and there they would remain until the Weimar Republic.

In the Imperial period, opinions concerning the Judenfrage (Jewish question) became a touchstone to identify the bearer with the forces of progress or with those of reaction. In a seminal essay, Shulamit Volkov concluded: "Wilhelminian society underwent a process of cultural polarization. While internal divisions and controversies over principles and tactics continued to preoccupy the activists, two main blocks of ideas[,] . . . two cultures[,] were formed. These were often symbolized by two concepts: antisemitism and emancipation."[4] Volkov delineated the significance of antisemitism as a "cultural code" for the forces of reaction while leaving the other pole—emancipation—undeveloped. Volkov's preference of subjects in this regard mirrors historiography in general. Despite recent attempts to challenge the notion of a German Sonderweg, the concept that Germany's path differed fundamentally from that of Western Europe, the sheer quantity of Holocaust-related literature keeps the spotlight on antisemitism.[5] The liberal bias of modern academics who consider tolerance and diversity the norm rather than the exception also serves to focus attention mainly on developments that diverge from this model. Only the search for altruism in extremis, as in the case of Holocaust rescuers, has produced scholarly investigations of acts that might be called "pro-Jewish."[6]

The asymmetrical political roles of antisemitism and emancipation also explain why pro-Jewish acts have been neglected. Unlike antisemitism, which served as a useful right-wing linchpin, support for Jewish interests never served as an organizing principle for the various groups who opposed organized antisemitism: political liberals, Protestant missionary societies, and socialists. In each of these cases, doctrine supported the equality of the Jew qua citizen, qua would-be Christian, qua worker but never Jew qua Jew. At best, these groups shared the view that solving the Jewish question in an acceptable manner could not include abandoning emancipation. The palpably different agendas of these anti-antisemitic groups might be taken as a sufficient reason why even emancipation (much less philosemitism) did not galvanize them as effectively as antisemitism galvanized their opponents. But this is begging the question. After all, rural supporters of the Agrarian League and middle-class urban advocates of the Naval League managed at times to coop-erate in the cause of ultranationalism despite considerably different interests. No statement supporting emancipation ever garnered 265,000 signatures, as did the 1880 Antisemites' Petition. The Conservative Party's adoption of the 1892 Tivoli Program marked the incorporation of antisemitism into the political mainstream. When antisemites made Judentum the buzzword of overturning the status quo, an apologia for Jews or Judaism unavoidably became part of its defense.[7]

Within the program of legal, economic, and intellectual modernization that led to the emergence of a German bourgeoisie and a unified nation, Jewish equality was regarded as a by-product. Analyzing the nexus of Jews and German liberals, Pulzer concludes that although the Jews "had good friends and allies, few were prepared to put the defense of Jewish rights above all other priorities."[8] Thus the defenders of emancipation engaged in discourse about Jews, but they did so unwillingly. The emancipation of the Jews certainly did not necessitate philosemitism, but neither did it preclude it. Why, then, does "German philosemitism" sound more like an oxymoron than a subject? The answer to this question may be found partly in the nature of the discourse of defense. This chapter elaborates four rhetorical tendencies common to all defenses of Judentum: first, the negative understanding of Judentum implicit in all discussions; second, the lachrymose language regard-ing the Jews' real and purported failings; third, the critical role of Christian or German self-presentation and self-interest that dominated pro-Jewish discussions; and fourth, the ambivalent attitude toward even positive Jewish characteristics.

The Stain of Judentum

The starting point for this discussion must be the recognition that the very word "Jew" has been perceived negatively.[9] The opprobrium attached to Jewry in the course of the Middle Ages never wore off altogether. Of course, emancipation brought an ever-increasing number of Jews and Gentiles into social contact. The rising number of intermarriages, legalized in 1875, and the need for National Socialists to enact Rassenschande (race-shaming) and Judenfreundlichkeit (Jew-befriending) laws sixty years later prove that on an individual basis Jews and non-Jews could achieve amicable relations. Nevertheless, Judentum as an idea retained its stigma, and a low-level antipathy to it pervaded German society. Although his own attitude toward Judentum was far from simple, Nietzsche's statement about his fellow Germans merits examination: "I have never met a German yet who was favorably inclined toward the Jews; and however unconditionally all cautious and politic-minded men repudiated real anti-Semitism, even this caution and policy is not directed against this class of feeling itself but only against its dangerous immoderation, and especially against the distasteful and shameful way in which this immoderate feeling is expressed—one must not deceive oneself about that."[10] While many Germans appraised individual Jews positively, they could do so without compromising a theoretical disdain for Judentum. Gustav Freytag, for instance, evaluated Jews as "allies, friends, fellow workers in every field of our practical and intellectual life," married a Jew, and still disliked the abstraction Judentum. In his response to Richard Wagner's "Das Judentum in der Musik," Freytag, the bestselling author of Soll und Haben, ridiculed Wagner's simplistic dichotomies of German and Jew. Then Freytag delivered his coup de grâce: "In the sense of his brochure, [Wagner] himself appears as the biggest Jew."[11] One waits in vain for Freytag's next sentence declaring that the dichotomy between German and Jew is itself false.

Speaking to the revolutionary situation in the post–World War I era, pioneering sociologist Max Weber opposed the composition of an investigative committee looking into the causes of Germany's defeat: "Gentlemen who are pacifists and who—regardless of how—are considered Jews should not have been seated. I do not think I could be suspected of being anti-Semitic; almost my whole circle of friends is Jewish and a cousin of mine was Felix Mendelssohn's wife. Indeed, I have been charged in a letter by an officer of being a Jew."[12] Even as Weber distanced himself from antisemitism with the stereotypical disclaimer "some of my best friends are Jewish," he accepted that Jewishness was a condition that could compromise the representation of purely German interests.[13] A more prosaic detail but one that acquires significance in the context of repetition is Weber's thinly veiled umbrage at being taken for a Jew. In fact, few Gentile authors declined to declare themselves non-Jews and, therefore, disinterested parties in the debate. In the Kaiserreich, the need to "clear" oneself of undue Jewish loyalties began with the disavowal of Jewishness itself. Count Heinrich Coudenhove-Kalergi's Das Wesen des Antisemitismus (The essence of antisemitism) announced: "Whoever says or writes the slightest thing about the Jews which is not unfavorable will be decried equally as a Jew and a Freemason. Certainly in my case this means will not work. In my family tree one finds not the slightest trace of Jewish blood."[14]

This standard disclaimer by anti-antisemitic authors recognized a real problem: being tarred as a member of the Judenschütztruppe (Jewish protection guard). The very existence of a work like Semi-Gotha, an antisemitic publication that tracked down real and purported Jews with the zeal and accuracy worthy of a Joseph McCarthy, showed how damaging some quarters regarded this libel. But the Jews' champions failed to take issue with the dubious premise that a Jewish author's views not only on "purely German matters" but even on Judentum were somehow suspect. Hellmut von Gerlach, an antisemitic, right-wing Junker turned left-wing activist, wrote, "I would not consider it the slightest blemish if I were entirely or a certain percent Jewish. I know what a noble role the Jewish grandmother played in the refreshing of the intellect in many noble families. But to the best of my ability, I cannot come up with any Jewish ancestors."[15] Gerlach, like many liberals, coupled his denial of Jewishness with a narrow justification of Jewry on the basis of what it contributed to German life. Coudenhove-Kalergi goes beyond the standard disclaimer: "Were this the case, however [that he was partly Jewish], not only would I not deny this but rather I would recognize it happily, because I would be proud of a possible relation with the most holy men and women who have wandered on this planet."[16]

In Weber's formulation, by far the most typical, the notion of being taken for a Jew is comical but insulting. Gerlach denied that being a Jew was shameful; Coudenhove-Kalergi went further still, imagining Judentum as a positive albeit idealized state of being. But Friedrich Engels may have been unique when he stated: "I myself have been made a Jew by the *Gartenlaube* [a satirical newspaper], and in any case, if I had to choose, I would rather be a Jew than 'Herr von . . .'!"[17] Just as the Jews' supporters never failed to remove suspicions of Jewish lineage, they persistently declared themselves "neither antisemites nor philosemites." In order to present one's credentials in a debate about Jews, honesty demanded that Jewish failings be acknowledged (as if any human grouping could somehow be without them). When the Socialist Party made that declaration, the motive was clearly electoral; all parties to the left were susceptible to the charge of being Judenschütztruppen. But when an explicitly anti-antisemitic organization like the Verein zur Abwehr des Antisemitismus, or Abwehrverein, scrupulously avoided citing *Im deutschen Reich*, the paper of the Centralverein deutscher Staatsbürger jüdischen Glaubens (German Citizens of the Jewish Faith, CV), and buried the fact that it received material aid and information about Jewish life from Jews, it was a concession that the slightest Jewish contact devalued a defense of Judentum.[18] The Abwehrverein's concern proved partly justified. When antisemites uncovered evidence that its leader of many years, George Gothein, had Jewish ancestors, the scandal was considerable.[19] Both the right-wing Christian missionary Franz Delitzsch and the left-wing Christian Carl Scholl were "slandered" as being Jews.

Only rarely did anyone attack the presupposition itself: "The main thing is, all battles of opinion—in the name of reason and in the name of the law—must be removed from the untenable terrain of Jew or non-Jew."[20] Responding to the antisemitic protests against a Heine memorial, Ernst von Wildenbruch championed the cause of individualism in the weekly *Nation* as follows: "Therefore, the cultivated of Germany must be clear about it. The question is handled entirely falsely if one considers it from the narrow pro- or antisemitic standpoint. It should be made clear that a far greater, weightier question stands as the decisive one."[21]

The denial of Jewishness or the denial of affection for Judentum unquestionably served some writers merely as a rhetorical device, a way of establishing credibility in the Judenfrage debate. But more than rhetoric motivated the following statement: "I am no anti- and am no philo-. I stand as an observer of the phenomenon. . . . The task of the researcher and observer in this matter is not to love and not to hate but to recognize."[22] Anti-antisemitic authors who trumpeted their scientific objectivity conceded a great deal to their opponents when they tacitly accepted the proposition that affection for a particular group was as unjustified as aversion. Nor was this sort of statement limited to political liberals. Gustaf Hermann Dalman (1855–1941), an important figure in the missionary movement, wrote, "From the antisemitic and philosemitic battlegrounds I distance myself completely." Dalman favored Jewish equality in order to ease its disappearance into Christianity through a "fair fight" rather than through compulsion.[23] Those Germans who denied being philosemites acceded to the chimerical desire for a "monolithic culture" (*Einheitskultur*). The nationalist Treitschke expressed his detestation of a "German-Jewish mixed culture" (*Mischkultur*), but so did his most formidable opponent, Theodor Mommsen, when he publicly pronounced that "entry into a great nation exacts a price" and privately encouraged secularized Jews to become Christians.[24]

Within the Abwehrverein the desire for an *Einheitskultur* conflicted with the task of aggressively defending the civil equality of the Jews. When Prof. Albrecht Weber called for a wide-ranging mixture of religious, social, and economic reforms in Jewish life in order for Jews to achieve social acceptance, he sounded perilously close to a demand for forced assimilation. Embarrassed, the Abwehrverein published anti-antisemitic letters from Weber to Freytag showing his detestation of antisemitism. That Weber continued to work with the Abwehrverein demonstrates how aptly the organization's name delimited its liberalism. Even in a private letter to Moritz Lazarus, historian Karl Hillebrand complained of the loss through emigration of the "half-Germanized" Jews and the arrival of the un-Germanized Ostjuden (Eastern European Jews) in their stead. Hillebrand clearly regarded Judentum as an "indigestible quantum" (Nietzsche) and resented the efforts Germany needed to make in order to make the Ostjuden even "half-Germanized."[25]

The Jews were not the only minority affected by the Prussian domination of Imperial Germany's political culture. Poles, Danes, Alsatians, and ethnic Germans who were Catholics also had to resist pressure to merge into an *Einheitskultur*. A comparative study of German minorities on this point would undoubtedly be a significant contribution. Based on the Jewish example, the German view of what constituted "special pleading" on behalf of a minority was a broad one. When one writer contended that the "Jewish poor deserve more compassion than the [poor people] of other nations" because their poverty was externally imposed by discrimination, he was staking out ground that nobody wanted to walk on or even approach with respect to any marginalized group within the Reich. [26]

If denying Jewish origins proved independence from Judentum, then acknowledging Jewish deficiencies was the most efficacious way of proving independence from philosemitism. Wilhelm Schirmer, a pastor from Düsseldorf who found Christian hatred of Judaism inexcusable, began his plea for tolerance with this concession: "It is true that many Jews are usurers. We condemn this as strongly as the most rigorous antisemite." [27] Schirmer accepted that getting a serious hearing on this issue necessitated some concession to the opponents of Judentum. That some antisemites were honorable men and that some Jews were flawed turned out to be something that had to be repeated. One politician-author who departed from the ranks of the antisemites reassured his readers as follows: "I have absolutely not turned from a Saul to a Paul overnight. I have also not sold my conscience, as many believe; I still maintain that parts of the antisemitic reproaches against Judentum are fully justified. I contend, however, that the antisemitic parties and the agitators who march at their head do not have the right to attack them." [28] Because Jews were citizens of the *Rechtsstaat*, their physical safety and the rule of law had to be preserved. But far from championing Judentum per se, this sort of spleen supports Richard Wagner's characterization of the Jews' place in the liberal equation: "the subjects of our forcible sympathy." [29]

This ingrained German antipathy toward Judentum also tended to limit the opposition to antisemitism to a narrow political format. Heinrich Rickert, an important Left Liberal Party figure, explained his opposition to antisemitism in an 1880 Reichstag debate as follows: "The Jewish question is not a question of sympathy or antipathy. It is demanded of nobody that he should be forced to have personal relations with Jews if it is not according to his tastes or that he must find those Jews in his circle worthy of love and praise. Everyone should use his own tastes and his [own] spiritual and social demands as a plumb line [to character]." [30] Rickert's words echo the official position of the Abwehrverein, to which he belonged. Neither the defense of the *Rechtsstaat* nor the defense of Jewish rights necessitated liking Jews. Remarkably, many Gentile calls for intermarriage as a means of solving the Jewish question demurred from arguing the desirability of social contacts with Jews, presumably a prerequisite to exogamy. Intermarriage represented the favored means of settling the Jewish question in liberal quarters, but this view seems not to have engendered any social conclusions. [31]

One might, as many German Jews did, find the position of Rickert and the Abwehrverein admirable and sensible. I do not question the reality of positive Jewish-Gentile relations in the private and even organizational realms. But the political nature of anti-antisemitism proved ill-equipped to deal with antisemitism in Wilhelminian Germany, which despite limited electoral success proved essential to the "cultural code" of reaction and noticeably influenced social relations beginning in the 1890s.[32] Max Spangenberg, student leader of the nondenominational Freie wissenschaftliche Vereinigung (Free Scholarly Association, FWV), described the politicization of social life in Berlin as follows: "In obscure corners of the Wiener Cafe, on the open promenade of the Unter den Linden, wherever one goes, the first question on seeing an acquaintance is: 'Is he Christian? Is he Jewish? Is he pro-Semitic? Is he anti-Semitic?' "[33] The FWV did more than most groups to counteract the attempts to turn Jews into pariahs, including celebrating Jewish-Christian intermarriages of university students. Yet even Spangenberg bridled at the "villainous misrepresentation of our organization as being *prosemitisch* or *philosemitisch*."[34] As a response to the antisemitic "cultural code," which affected not only politics but also social relations, philosemitism—not merely emancipation—was a necessary response. Paradoxical as it may seem, in order to voice plausible pro-Jewish arguments, a denial of philosemitism, comprehended as the irrational antonym of antisemitism, was a desideratum. German philosemites did not launch a challenge to the fundamentally negative penumbra of associations surrounding the term Judentum. Wherever possible, they attempted to make antisemitism, not Judentum, the issue. Given the vituperation and ubiquity of the antisemitic assault, however, discourse about Jews was unavoidable.

The Misery of Judentum

In the opening salvo in his lifelong battle to legitimize diaspora existence, Salo Baron criticized previous Jewish historians who presented their past as being composed exclusively of material suffering and cultural creativity. Not only Jews found that a useful tack. Beginning in the Enlightenment, the current (read: decayed) state of Judaism was painted in the darkest colors in order to make the future shine more brightly. Dohm's tract offers a representative example: "I can assert that the Jews are more morally depraved than other nations, that they are guilty of a disproportionate number of minor offenses, that their character in the main is more given to usury and deception in business, that their religious prejudices are more divisive and antisocial. But . . . the great depravity of the Jews is a necessary and natural result of the oppressed condition in which they have been for so many centuries."[35] By the 1870s, Dohm's appeal to patience had lost all force in antisemitic eyes. Berlin University's eminent historian Heinrich von Treitschke insisted, "Emancipation has been carried out so fully as to preclude every ground for further Jewish demands."[36] But while antisemites reckoned that the Jews had had their opportunity and squandered it in tribal bad faith, their opponents tended to concede Jewish deficiencies and make excuses for them. Jewish deficiencies, the staple of so many antisemitic tirades, provided the bulk of the material for pro-

Jewish discourse as well, even though it was presented in an exculpatory manner. The picture of suffering and scholarship, already a distortion in Baron's view, became even more skewed by a nearly exclusive focus on Jewish suffering.

In the Judenfrage debate during the Kaiserreich, antisemites possessed a rhetorical advantage as opponents of the status quo. They could pick areas of Jewish-Gentile tension (especially economic) and force a response from the Jews' defenders. These defenders, however, proved unable to stand outside the debate and appreciate just how deeply they shared the regnant anti-Jewish stereotypes. In 1893, for instance, Freytag again took on antisemitism in Vienna's *Neue Freie Presse*. He began with a four-page analysis of why the Jews have their particular failings, including sagacity and wit ("Scharfsinn und Witz"), which some writers might actually consider to be assets. Only then did Freytag speak of the duties of Christian love, having already provided a detailed set of reasons why Christian love, when it comes to Jews, will be a real trial.[37] Franz Delitzsch defended Jewry against August Rohling's slanderous misrepresentations of the Talmud. Yet Delitzsch regarded the de-Christianization of oath, marriage, and school as something undertaken for the Jews' benefit.[38] The embers of resentment against Judaism flared up even among some of antisemitism's most trenchant and knowledgeable critics.

Nearly all philosemitic authors gave full play to the theme of Jewish suffering through the ages. In a savagely sarcastic essay, "Der Jude wird verbrannt" (The Jew must burn), Wilhelm Schoppe devoted the first forty-one of forty-six pages to a chronicle of Christian oppression. Almost as an afterthought, Schoppe added, "We also should not undervalue the Jewish sense of charity."[39] Apologizing for Jewish deficiencies rather than celebrating Jewish contributions seemed to be the anti-antisemitic weapon of choice. In effect, negative details of Jewish life and history comprised the bulk of Germany's anti-antisemitic literature. Steven Katz's verdict on the achievements of racist antisemitism during the Weimar years applies to undifferentiated antisemitism in the Kaiserreich: "And even before this final deadly transformation of the political landscape of Germany and her allies, this racial perspective would have scored a notable success in setting a good deal of the political agenda—even for those in the political center and left. The universally heightened sensitivity to Jewish issues caused by the unrelenting propaganda of the extreme right forced the shape of political debate into contours constructed out of, even if opposed to, this racial program."[40]

There were exceptions to this rule. *Der Juden Anteil am Fortschritt der Kultur* (The Jewish contribution to the progress of culture), a pamphlet published by the Abwehrverein, listed Jewish luminaries, with the author's disclaimer that German Jews did not figure prominently in certain fields such as diplomacy and statecraft only because Germany had not followed the example of Westernized nations.[41] This focus on positive Jewish achievement contrasted with the usual procedure in the Abwehrverein's publication, which included snippets on positive Jewish themes but buried them near the back of the paper. The bulk of the *Mitteilungen* comprised reports of antisemitic developments. Clearly, chronicling the continued oppression of Judentum struck defenders as more effective than proclaiming Jewish contributions. During the Weimar period, the philosemitic camp seems to have recognized the necessity for such a line of argument. In Prague in December 1931 a journal called *Der Philosemit* appeared. Edited and written by Jews and non-Jews, this journal celebrated Jewish life and culture. It also ceased publication after a year for reasons I have been unable to determine.[42]

A passage from the memoirs of Hellmut von Gerlach reflects this concession to a lachrymose view of German Jewry. In a series of apostrophes, he rebutted the deprecation of Jews in Germany as follows:

- Why are [Jewish] lawyers only lawyers and almost never judges? Only because the few Jews who are allowed to enter the judicial positions are unfailingly kept on the lowest step.

- Why are the Jews so unwarlike? Because in Prussia not only the officer corps was shut to them but also [because] they could not become reserve officers.

- Why were so few Jews artisans? Because until the emancipation they were shut out of these guilds.

- Why were the Jews not farmers? Because until 1812 they were not permitted to own land.

- Why do they deal so often in moneylending? Because under the authority of canon law only they were permitted to deal in moneylending.[43]

My argument is not with Gerlach's good intentions or with the (overall) factual accuracy of the causes of Jewish particularism. My point is, first, that the rhetorical point of departure is Jewish defects; second, that Jewish life in Weimar hardly supported these outmoded generalizations; and third, that the exceptional status of Judentum is never really questioned here or elsewhere in Gerlach's memoirs. The popularity of a Gentile version of the lachrymose conception that adduced more suffering than scholarship dovetailed with the liberal hostility toward the articulation of an internally driven, specifically Jewish agenda.

The Reproach of Judentum

In 1882 the empress Augusta, wife to Wilhelm I and mother of Friedrich Wilhelm III, wrote to Frau von Bonin attacking antisemitism as an impediment to integrating Jews through baptism. Augusta demonstrates the ability to formulate an anti-antisemitic position without any fondness for Jews (implicit in much of the evidence adduced thus far) and introduces a new theme: anti-antisemitism as a Christian agenda item: "I have naturally no tendency to get heated up about specifically Jewish matters, but I disapprove of antisemitism, because it is a thoroughly un-Christian phenomenon. We damage our perspective [through antisemitism] and bring ourselves under the suspicion of religious intolerance. Where remains, then, the possibility to lead even a few individual Jews to Christianity? Does not the Jewish mission also count among the Christian organizations?"[44] What the empress, like most other anti-antisemitic opponents, fails to do is imagine the Jew as the actual target of antisemitism. It may be that only after the Holocaust do we recognize, as Jean-Paul Sartre wrote, that "the antisemite desires the death of the Jew."[45] Certainly, some Gentiles fully confronted the idea that Jewry faced the principal danger from the rise of antisemitism. Bertha von Suttner, who had witnessed the victims of Russian pogroms, insisted that antisemitism aimed at the physical destruction of the Jews. Dr. Hermann Nothnagel, like Suttner a founding member of the Austrian branch of the Abwehrverein, feared that the rise of Herzlian Zionism would lead to pogroms.[46] Within the Reich proper, a teacher in Neuwied's gymnasium warned against underestimating the threat to Jews caused by the dissemination of ritual murder charges.[47]

Thus a sense of antisemitism as a physical threat to Jewry existed, but often one finds formulations such as the following: "Whoever in the name of Christianity strikes the Jews shames the name Christian and strikes at the Church of Jesus Christ in its pure form."[48] The author continued to attack antisemitism, rather vaguely, as a betrayal of justice, humanity, and spiritual culture. One Austrian woman warned that "antisemitism is a teaching that no true Christian can follow: every antisemite is a sinner. . . . Antisemitism makes the bestial in man come alive, and if the shackles are taken off the bestial, there are no more restraints. Then law and rights will be blown in the air, and there will no longer be antisemitism but anarchism!"[49] Without the pyrotechnic language, the consistory of Hesse, prompted by Otto Boeckel's antisemitic movement, voiced a similarly vague note of concern: "The antisemitic movement poses a serious danger for the peace of the population."[50] These anti-antisemitic expostulations find some victim of antisemitism beyond Judentum, in short, some more worthy object of defense. One detects an unconscious shifting of the focus of the antisemitic threat from Judentum to Christianity or *Rechtsstaat*. This indifference to the fate of Judentum itself derived from the liberal view that Jewry must eventually disappear into the wider German culture, but it inevitably blunted the defense of German Jewry.

Long-suffering Judentum played an important role in Christian anti-antisemitic rhetoric. Authors pressed the Jewish question into the service of showing how far Germans were from realizing the ideals of Christianity, Christian love in particular. In a statement beginning, "Antisemitism denies the essence of Christianity," the author continued: "The Jews are a living reproach to us, that we did not meet them as Christians, but through our pride, misled them into becoming what they have become."[51] Locating the problem exclusively in the Christian camp, Pastor Wilhelm Schirmer proclaimed from his pulpit that heathens and Mohammedans may have hated Jews but that he expected more from Christians.[52] Even without the invocation of Christian ideals, anti-antisemites employed Judentum in the role of tribune: "Are we in Germany already so commercially bankrupt that we combat Semitism by Pharaonic means?" Another anti-antisemite accepted Jewish shortcomings but pointedly placed the blame with the antisemites: "The oppressors of Judaism have sowed what they have reaped. Just give the Jews social equality too, and all results of the former servitude will quickly disappear."[53] By imagining German Jewry as a living reproach—perhaps even as a punishment—to an incompletely realized Christianity, authors vented their resentments against the antisemitic perversions of Christentum or Deutschtum.[54] But one can easily imagine how unlikely it would be for this sort of rhetoric to lower the level of resentment toward Judentum. Blaming the victim is always an attractive option, and German philosemites could not always resist the temptation: "Every German who revels in the distinction between Semite and Aryan falls into the same significant error for which the Jews have paid so heavily. For the pious madness of being the chosen people, [which] was certainly the initial cause of their getting ahead[,] . . . later degenerated in their imaginations [into] fanaticism [and] obscurantism and thus became the basis for their nameless suffering."[55] Neither the recognition of Jewish suffering nor the rejection of antisemitism masks the sneaking suspicion that at root the Jews are ultimately to blame for antisemitism.

Defenders of Judentum combined reproaching antisemitism with a positive assessment of what Jews have to offer Germany. Is the Jew not sober and moderate? Is he not a good family man? Does he not hold loyalty high? Without the Christian overtones, the same line of thought is found in discussions of the health of the German nation: "In these things we have much to learn from him!"[56] Non-Jewish proponents of intermarriage, taking Bismarck's famous comment praising the expected benefits of "crossing the German stallion with the Jewish mare" hyper-literally, frequently listed contributions (lower tuberculosis and alcoholism rates; a preternatural ability in musical, mathematical, and commercial arenas) that Jews could make to Germany's racial makeup. The pioneering scholar of Jewish mysticism, Gershom Scholem, denied a German-Jewish symbiosis on the grounds that there were never two partners to the dialogue: "To the infinite intoxication of Jewish enthusiasm there never corresponded a tone that bore any kind of relation to a creative answer to the Jews; that is to say, one that would have addressed them with regard to what they had to give as Jews, and not what they had to give up as Jews."[57] Sobriety, family orientation, and gratitude were regarded as Jewish qualities that could improve the German national character but only in the course of a total amalgamation. Scholem's judgment, with respect to the philosemitic camp, creates a false dichotomy: giving as Jews and giving up as Jews were seen as one process.

The discourse that judged the worth of Judentum on the narrow standard of what it could impart to Deutschtum needs to be contrasted briefly with that of Friedrich Nietzsche. In an oft-quoted passage from *Beyond Good and Evil* he writes:

> *That Germany has simply enough Jews, that the German stomach, the German blood has trouble (and will still have trouble for a long time) digesting even this quantum of Jew—as the Italians, French, and English have done, having a stronger digestive system—that is the clear testimony and language of a general instinct to which one must act. "Admit no more Jews! And especially close the doors to the east (also to Austria!)"—thus commands the instinct of a people whose type is still weak and indefinite, so it could easily be blurred or extinguished by a stronger race. The Jews, however, are the strongest, toughest, and purest race now living in Europe.*[58]

Nietzsche invoked Jewish purity, vitality, and strength as a reproach to German weaknesses, beginning with antisemitism. In this way, Nietzsche "belongs" to this discourse. Moreover, Nietzsche also imagined a Judentum to suit his fancy. His dichotomy of Jew and German withstands scrutiny no better than his dichotomy of Greek and Jew. But Nietzsche—and this is critical—wrote as a self-willed, self-imposed outsider. The status of the outsider, generally understood as a stain on Judentum, Nietzsche regarded as Judaism's best feature. To the extent that Judaism allowed itself to be co-opted and mainstreamed by Christianity, the former became "an ill-smelling Judaism of rabbinism and superstition." Since few Germans shared Nietzsche's affection for the status of the outsider or his unbounded contempt for Christentum, we can ask, How did the Jews' supporters deal with this generally recognized outsider status?[59]

Possibly the most disturbing method of championing the Jews' right of inclusion in Germany was to locate a different Other. I quote the following passage at length:

> *Will one deprive the Jews places and offices and so forth? How comical. If the noble Abraham Lincoln, president of the United States, still lived, he would clap his hand against his head. "What," would he say, "are*

the Jews below the Negroes [Niggern]? We have done everything for their freedom, and they have been raised to our equals, and Christians and Jews have unified for that noble work. Now, thirty years later, do the Christians persecute the Jews [their equals] again?" The Negroes themselves, who name Lincoln their savior, their Christ, occupy positions of value in America. There are among the Negroes lawyers, doctors, and artists! Will one permit to the Negroes what is denied to the Jews?[60]

Note that Schoppe dwelt as much on the originally debased status of African Americans as on their current accomplishments. His argument implied that any group, however degenerate, can contribute to a nation, not that every group that makes up a nation deserves consideration as a matter of principle. Of course, the real appeal of this argument rests on the simple assertion: there are people even less Westernized than the Jews. Lest the reader think this tactic unique, Carl Friedrich Heman's pro-Zionist book *Das Erwachen der jüdischen Nation* (The awakening of the Jewish nation) executed the same maneuver with respect to Islam. Supporting the emergence of a Jewish state in Palestine as an outpost for European Christianity, Heman denigrated Islam at every turn. Skewering both monotheistic competitors, Heman noted that the Reform proponents of a Jewish "mission" had nothing to brag about: "Here also it would be better for the rabbis to keep silent. Judaism certainly has no reason to be proud about the daughterhood [*Tochterschaft*] of Islam. . . . [T]he morality of Christianity and Judaism are more closely related than the Muhammedan, which stands far below both."[61] Such proponents could not deny the Otherness of the Jews, but they could find still more foreign elements to contrast with the Jews. A variation of this theme, favored by the Abwehrverein's *Mitteilungen*, was to report on the abuse German Jews received as Germans while abroad.[62] By imagining a situation in which Germans and Jews would be lumped together as the Other, the *Mitteilungen* pointed out the injustice of regarding German Jews as non-Germans at home. Consistently, the Ostjuden, the Jews of Eastern Europe, proved the most convenient group with which one could favorably compare German Jews. Ignaz von Döllinger, Catholic theologian and historian, friend of Moritz Lazarus, and an oft-quoted philosemitic author, wrote: "The strongest accusation and the principal root of the popular hatred against the Jews are the economic harm, especially in the Slavic lands, carried out with their still-existing predilection for the interest and usury trades. In the East one calls this disgrace, especially in Galicia, a devastation. The guilt is undeniable, and our Israelite citizens deplore it as do we."[63] Döllinger, a good liberal, believed that the German Jews could set an example for the Ostjuden. As a matter of fact, German Jews were uniquely placed to make others in their image. And what was that image? "The German Jew thinks essentially German in all areas of spiritual and social life."[64]

A Few Good Jews, a Few Good Jewish Qualities

Professor Otto Caspari of Heidelberg, a regular contributor to the Jewish question debates in Imperial Germany and a member of the Abwehrverein, admitted that there were many "Shylocks" among the Jews but pointed to the larger group: "The second, better, and predominant group is represented and characterized through Jesus, who as a martyr developed a series of psychological properties that, like noble suffering and meek patience, are outstanding properties that the intellectually gifted of this tribe [*Stamm*] do not lack."[65] The acceptance of Shylock (the creation of an English Christian) as a Jewish archetype is surely uncritical, but no more so than the philosemitic Pastor Schirmer's acceptance of Ahasveros, the wandering Jew, as a good representative of Judentum.[66] Caspari's assumption that the very best Jew, Jesus, abandoned Judaism was also standard for the times, albeit historically untrue. That aside, it may strike the reader as rather silly that Germany's six hundred thousand Jews could be neatly divided into two basic personalities.

But Professor Caspari meant what he said; indeed, he reflected a hoary tendency to pigeonhole Jewish types and Jewish qualities, good as well as bad. In his groundbreaking work *Aussenseiter*, Hans Mayer noted the tendency in the novels of Freytag, Raabe, and Dahn to oppose an entirely stereotyped Jewish character with the "exceptional" good Jew who broke ranks and ventured all for the attainment of Deutschtum.[67] The exceptional popularity of *Soll und Haben*, *Hungerpastor*, and *Kampf um Rom* extended to Jewish households, but one can hope that Jewish readers recognized these figures as fictional. Undoubtedly, many Gentile readers also recognized this, but evidence suggests the easy distinction of good Jew–bad Jew could be seriously broached in a political context. Treitschke's frequent lauding of one or two good Jews to highlight the unrepentant majority provides a striking example: "A certain number of European Jews have, as a matter of fact, succeeded in really adopting the nationality of the people among whom they live. . . . The history of our own literature affords instances of some Jews whose characteristics are essentially German; this is pre-eminently true of Moses Mendelssohn. [But] it is equally certain that in Berlin, and eastwards from that city, there are many Jews who are inwardly real Orientals, in spite of the language they speak."[68]

Of course, Treitschke cannot be adduced as evidence for this tendency among philosemites any more than Wagner, who had room for both Ludwig Börne and Heinrich Heine in his German pantheon, though never at the same time. Nevertheless, the assumption of the empress Augusta and Theodor Mommsen that the cultured "good" Jew would become Christian if the antisemites would let him expressed a more subtle version of the same train of thought. Even on a private level, memoirs attest to the tendency to regard upstanding Jews as exceptions rather than as challenges to the stereotype. In his memoir "Wie ich als Jude in der Diaspora aufwuchs" (How I grew up as a Jew in the Diaspora), the Socialist leader Eduard Bernstein recalled his neighbors' praise, "You Bernsteins are not really Jews."[69]

Curiously, personal testimonials attest to the greater willingness of ordinary Germans to challenge the prevailing stereotypes. Jan Cronje's *Ich werde nie Anti-semit* (I would never become an antisemite) reflected a working-class Catholic set of values that discredited antisemitism on Christian grounds alone. But Cronje tackled one of the most negative stereotypes head-on when he held up the Polish pants-selling lad as a model of hard work, fidelity, domesticity, and self-improvement. True, Cronje did not neglect to use this image as a reproach to fellow Germans ("Isn't such an immigrant an example that puts the native to shame?"), and he expended several pages defending the Jewish use of garlic, abstention from pork, and circumcision. But to focus on the very target stigmatized by Treitschke as the essence of the Jewish problem went beyond the public defenses of Cronje's more prominent counterparts.[70]

Franz Kramer's *Wie Ich die Juden sah. Aus den Erinnerungen eines 78 jahrigen Katholiken* (How I saw the Jews: From the memoirs of a seventy-eight-year-old Catholic) described his childhood experience as a Sabbath goy. Kramer emphasized the Jewish charity, kindness, and piety he witnessed as a boy, claiming, "[W]ere the character of Jewry [des Judentums] really comprehended, the entire scandal of antisemitism would be undone." Praising the Jews' contribution to German culture, their loyal service in war, and the Jewish rituals he witnessed firsthand, Kramer complained that the antisemites did not appreciate the "inner Jew," a criticism that could also apply to the lachrymose discourse used by Jewry's proponents. That Kramer found a few Jews worth praising is nothing unusual: after all, Himmler himself conceded the fact that each German knew "one decent Jew." But the working-class Kramer took the initiative to argue that the "decent Jew" represented most Jews, not one in eighty million.[71]

The tendency to separate good from bad Jews complemented the desire to distinguish good from bad Jewish qualities. In light of the antisemitic tendency to find something malignant in even positive qualities, the Jews' protagonists were correct to proceed with caution. After retelling a long history of both the Jews' originally productive economic role and the subsequent medieval oppression that reduced them to moneylending and peddling, Döllinger turned his attentions to the present situation:

> In the majority of states [the Jews] provide a relatively slight number of the judicially handled cases of criminality, and [they] constitute in property and wealth, even in life duration and propagation, outstanding segments of the population. The old virtues of frugality and abstinence, the well-ordered family life, the piety of the children toward their parents,

which did so much, in the difficult times of the Middle Ages, to preserve
this people from dissolution have also not departed from them. Family
ties and conversion to Christianity are more frequent than previously; in
Berlin one counted in the previous years 2,000 proselytes.[72]

Döllinger's consideration of the inner virtues of the contemporary Jew contrasted
with his historical survey, a typical dismal presentation of events. But this can be
reconciled in light of Döllinger's comment that "the German Jew thinks essentially
German in all questions of spirit and social life, which was not the case in previous
centuries."[73] This line of reasoning did not press Jewish virtues into the service of
the German nation at the immediate cost of Jewish existence. Döllinger made a
case for the compatibility of certain Jewish virtues (sobriety, frugality, filiopietism)
with German society in the context of what might be called civil religion. He looked
forward to intermarriage, conversion, and the ultimate disappearance of the Jew.
Döllinger did not go as far as Pres. Dwight David Eisenhower's famous dictum:
"Our government makes no sense unless it is founded on a deeply felt religious
faith—and I don't care what it is."[74] Still, something of the notion of civil religion
remains: the Jew's Jewish tradition makes him a better, if transitional, German.
But the following contradiction philosemites never recognized or reconciled: if
Jewish virtues make a good German, why must Judentum disappear as a distinct
unit?[75]

The liberal philosemitism that existed in Imperial Germany emerged out of an
anti-antisemitic imperative. Nietzsche's view that the protest against antisemitism
was driven by the immoderation of antisemites seems incontrovertible. The defense
of Jewish emancipation relied on the proposition that there was something wrong
with antisemites, not that there was something right with Jews. Antisemitism as
social antipathy stirred hardly an objection. Liberal secularists and Christian missionaries alike employed a lachrymose language that served to distance the defender
from the Jewish defended. One could go further and argue that a transference took
place in which the *Rechtsstaat*, or Christianity, or German *Kultur* took precedence
as subjects needing defense against antisemites. The proponents of the emancipation found nobler grounds for opposing antisemitism than its threat to Judentum.
When the defenders of Jews located good Jews, they were termed exceptional;
when positive Jewish qualities were cited, they were treated as inherent assets that
could be transferred to the account called Germany. A small handful valued distinctly Jewish contributions to German life, appreciated the color Jews added to the
German mosaic, defended communal Jewish interests, and accepted a continued
Jewish presence in Germany. These few self-selected outsiders were open to the
transformative encounters with individual Jews that carried them beyond anti-
antisemitism and into more pronounced forms of philosemitism. Even among the

defenders of the Jews, they were the exceptions (and they will be treated separately in chapters 5 through 8).

The foregoing analysis further suggests that antisemitism successfully determined the parameters of plausible "Jew-talk." Most proponents of emancipation never contemplated extending their definition to make room for Judentum as a distinct element in German life. Jews qua Jews were far from gaining unqualified acceptance from their friends as well as their foes. No tactical choice on the part of the Jews' defenders made emancipation rather than philosemitism the shibboleth in their cultural code. In Imperial Germany the alternative never received serious discussion. Of course, only in light of the Third Reich do the failures of liberalism during the Imperial period—the failure to develop a sympathy for pluralism, to recognize the personal as political, to allow low-level prejudices and outmoded stereotypes to go unchallenged—strike us as tragic flaws. Nor, in the absence of a comparative study, can we be confident that at the turn of the last century matters were different in Western European countries or in the United States.

We should also remind ourselves that the proponents of Jewish emancipation would have been horrified by subsequent developments; they were often shocked by the relatively restrained antisemitism of the pre–World War I period. It may be worth recalling that in Imperial Germany the battle for Jewish rights seemed victorious compared to the struggles for the rights of women and of workers. Would most Germans have recognized Jews as a more beleaguered minority than ethnic Poles or Alsatians? The absence of a more persistent philosemitic discourse was indicative but hardly decisive in determining the cultural code of emancipation or in mediating the struggle between liberalism and reaction. Ultimately, Sartre was right: in modern times the liberal has had—and continues to have—much to do. One item on the progressive agenda was controlling the nationalist and militaristic impulses of the Great Powers. To this effort in German-speaking lands we now turn our attention.

2. The German Peace Movement and the Jews

Until very recently, Jewish support for the American peace movement was proverbial if anecdotal.[1] Like many historical phenomena, this one appears to be overdetermined. To begin with, the left-of-center orientation of the majority of American Jews makes them better candidates for a left-of-center movement. The overwhelming majority of Jews who arrived in the United States from czarist Russia were poor, and many found industrial work in the large cities, a breeding ground for labor unions, socialism, and the peace movement. An adage has it that New York Jewish politics came in two colors: pink and red. Jews also played an active role in the 1960s counterculture, an important breeding ground for the contemporary peace movement. Idealism and self-interest worked together, since a tiny and historically oppressed minority has good reason to champion the cause of right versus might. All of these reasons probably have some merit, but they fail to account for the little-known fact that Jews played a disproportionately great role in European peace movements too. One additional factor, therefore, needs emphasizing. Jews have been made to feel welcome in the peace movement, which has opposed antisemitism since its inception.

This chapter examines four founders of the peace movement in German-speaking lands: Bertha von Suttner (1843–1914), Ludwig Quidde (1858–1941), Count Heinrich Coudenhove-Kalergi (1859–1906), and Friedrich Wilhelm Foerster (1869–1966). My focus will not be on their peace activities, an area that has been well researched, but on how these non-Jewish peace activists thought about Jews and Judaism. Three observations will be elaborated here. First, the peace movement in Germany was home to a number of outspoken anti-antisemites. Second, the peace movement created an institutional culture in which Jews and Gentiles collaborated freely and as equals. Third, German peace activists favored a progressive and at times radically progressive resolution to the ubiquitous Jewish question.

Before investigating these activists, the level of Jewish involvement in the peace movement needs to be addressed. Nobody in Germany kept statistics on this, but Jews were identifiably active at the leadership level. The organizational spirit of the Deutsche Friedensgesellschaft (German Peace Society) was Alfred Hermann Fried (1864–1921), a dynamic bookseller and publisher. Fried was born, bred, and buried in Vienna, but he was the son of two Hungarian Jews. When Bertha von Suttner engaged in a correspondence campaign to get the Berlin chapter of the German

Peace Society off the ground, Max Hirsch (1823–1905) and Gustav Karpeles (1848–1909) served as her whips. Hirsch, elected three times to the Reichstag, was a nephew of the famous rabbi and journalist Ludwig Philippson (1811–89). Hirsch belonged to several organizations, none of them Jewish. Karpeles, a well-known journalist and literary historian, belonged to a family active in many areas of Jewish life and played an important role in the Jewish Society for Jewish History and Literature.[2] Suttner's diary entry of 10 September 1892 approved of Karpeles's desire to work behind the scenes lest the initiative for a Berlin chapter appear "too Jewish."[3] Despite the tacit agreement between Christian and Jewish supporters of the peace movement to underplay the Jewish role, the list of prominent Jews was still a long one: Eduard Löwenthal, Leopold Sonnemann, Lina Morgenstern, W. A. Berendsohn, E. J. Gumbel, Bernhard Dernburg, Heilberg, Arnhold, and Bloch.[4] *Die Friedensbewegung* (The peace movement), a 1922 publication, contained sixty-four contributors, at least nine of whom were Jewish and five of whom were non-Jews who had publicly opposed antisemitism. Just over half the contributors came from German-speaking lands (*deutsches Kulturbereich*). All of the German contributors were liberals, several were feminists, and a dozen emigrated in 1933.

The contributors to *Die Friedensbewegung* were patently among the organization's most famous members. Were Jews in the German peace society's rank and file similarly represented as in the leadership? There seems no way to know for certain, but circumstantial evidence inclines us toward this conclusion. Studies of the Liga für Menschenrechte (League for Human Rights) and the Bund neues Vaterland (Union of the New Fatherland), peace society splinter groups, demonstrate that these organizations had many members of Jewish descent.[5] Roger Chickering's detailed examination of the Frankfurt, Königsberg, and Danzig peace societies indicates that *Kaufleute* formed the single largest group, followed by the intelligentsia, while "[c]lergymen and blue-collar workers were conspicuous chiefly in their absence."[6] Like Chickering, Karl Holl, the leading scholar on German pacifism, describes a group suspiciously similar in composition to that of German Jewry: "Although the masses of members remain generally anonymous in the sources, the independent entrepreneurs, albeit of lesser success, and the small salespersons made up the greatest percentage. Following that, academic or nonacademic educated [*gebildet*] intellectuals, among them several writers and journalists—a diffuse category that also included a number of teachers in the adult education movement [*Volkshochschüle*]. To the third largest group belonged those occupied in the free professions, above all doctors, lawyers, and pharmacists."[7]

While the xenophobic ranting of German nationalists who derided the Peace Society as Western, un-German, and Jewish cannot be taken at face value, the theme of Jewish participation is so consistent that it should not be dismissed altogether as negative evidence.[8] As a matter of fact, most of the peace activists who wrote against antisemitism were less chauvinistically German and more cosmopolitan in orientation than the average German. Since global disarmament and restraining nationalist excess were central to the program of the peace movement, it comes as no surprise that the movement regarded itself as international in orientation. Although it seems odd given Germany's role in initiating two world wars, German pacifism played an important role in Continental pacifism in the nineteenth century. Immanuel Kant, probably the Christian philosopher most venerated by German Jewry, authored the seminal pacifist tract *Zum ewigen Frieden* (Toward perpetual peace). The leaders of the German peace movement in the Wilhelminian period emanated from the Left Liberal parties, which also commanded the loyalties of many German Jews. In a society that was becoming more antisemitic, especially in the social arena, from the 1890s onward, the German peace movement went against the general current of the era. To put it more pointedly, participating in the German Peace Society meant collaborating with Jews as allies and as equals. While this prospect might have been revolting to some "Aryans," to others it seemed quite a natural, even positive development. A German reactionary would have felt as out of place at a German Peace Society meeting as a Jewish tailor at a meeting of the nationalistic Alldeutscher Verband (Pan-German League).

Bertha von Kinsky, brought up in an impoverished Austrian aristocratic family with a tradition of military service, rejected her conventional background early in her life. Turning down a marriage proposal by the poet Heinrich Heine's younger brother, she worked briefly as a secretary to chemist Alfred Nobel. After Bertha married the relatively unsuccessful novelist Arthur Gundaccar von Suttner against the wishes of his family, the couple became part of the impoverished nobility who did not quite rank in the social circles of the Hapsburg court. After several early failures to establish a career, Bertha found her vocation as an author. Her novel *Die Waffen nieder!* (*Lay Down Your Arms!*), published in 1889 and an international best-seller, inspired many figures in the peace movement. One of these, her old employer, Alfred Nobel, endowed the prize that bears his name at her suggestion. Alfred Fried, another admirer, became the organizational head of the movement until his death in 1921 and served, to some degree, as Suttner's public relations agent. *Lay Down Your Arms!* made Suttner a celebrity. Showcased at every important peace conference, she enjoyed the admiration of world rulers, including Czar Nicholas II. At the first International Peace Congress in The Hague in 1899 she was the undisputed star of the show. Although peace activism took up the best part of her efforts, Suttner supported herself through her writing and promoted a variety of unpopular causes, including feminism, anti-antisemitism, animal rights, and Zionism.

Her support for Zionism, quite an unusual stance for someone also associated with the liberal Abwehrverein, emerged from her friendship with the Viennese journalist who brought Zionism to political life: Theodor Herzl. Suttner and Herzl, authors of utopian novels and champions of unpopular causes, were kindred spirits.[9] Herzl's particular brand of Zionism—liberal, modern, and culturally European rather than specifically Jewish—help explain their affinity. In any event, the goals of European Jewry, whether liberal or nationalist, could be reconciled to Suttner's vision of a league of nations, all guided by progressive principles. This goal made it possible for her to fight for Jewish equality within Europe and also support Herzl's concept of a Jewish state. Bertha von Suttner won the first Nobel Peace Prize in 1903 and lost her husband in 1906. Somewhat out of place in a peace movement that had become increasingly based on grassroots organizing instead of dramatic personal appeals, Suttner died just seven days before the outbreak of the Great War she had tried to prevent.

As Steve Beller has demonstrated, there were few areas of cultural life in Vienna in which Jews did not participate heavily. The liberal intellectual circles of Vienna, the Suttners' social sphere, forged their outlook on the Jewish question.[10] Bertha von Suttner's connection with the journal *Nouvelle Revue* put her in contact with the well-known authors Max Nordau and Lucienne Halevy. Brigitte Hamann's excellent biography of Bertha von Suttner does not dwell on the impact of these Jewish contacts, but it is a fact that she reacted stridently to the pogroms that began in Russia in 1881. Closer to home, the rise of Karl Lueger (Vienna's antisemitic mayor) provoked Bertha to a fictional response. In 1886 Suttner had skewered antisemites in her novels *Daniela Dormes* and *Schach der Qual*. Baron Arthur and Baroness Bertha von Suttner shared the aspirations of Viennese liberals: they aimed at creating a rational, lawful society in which each person would be judged equally. But that universal goal did not stop Suttner from taking up particularist causes, feminism and anti-antisemitism among them. Her outlook on the Jewish question in the early 1890s can be seen in the preface she wrote for James F. Simon's aggressive call for Jewish self-defense, *Wehrt Euch! Ein Mahnwort an die Juden* (Beware! An appeal to the Jews).[11] "The main thing is, all conflicts of opinion must—in the name of reason and in the name of law—be removed from the untenable terrain of Jew or non-Jew. No one should ignore the vague reproach launched against him, 'You are a Jew,' no one should let it go without a response, but rather, one should force the assailant to the wall: 'Yes, I am, just as you are a Christian. . . . What of it?' "[12]

Bertha von Suttner consistently avoided the stereotypical dichotomy of "Jew" and "Aryan." She also refused to enter into the rhetorical game of conceding Jewish defects and demanding improvement in exchange for equality. Like most liberals (Jewish and Christian alike), the Suttners tended to underestimate the centrality and utility of antisemitism to the forces of reaction. Still, Suttner refused to underestimate the viciousness of antisemites, contending that they intended the physical destruction of Jews.[13] In a biting comment, Suttner noted that the political economists who blamed everything on the stock market wished to solve the problem by "hanging 3,000 Jews. Or better yet, turning all the Jews into artificial fertilizer. The last [proposal] was only meant in jest. The gentlemen also have a sense of humor."[14]

For Bertha von Suttner, the connection between anti-antisemitism and peace activism was obvious: "I fight against antisemites even as I do against war, for they represent the same spirit."[15] The "spirit" Suttner attacked was militarism, brutality, and cruelty, the weapons employed by the antisemites in their disappointingly successful campaigns. Suttner criticized fellow liberals—Jewish colleagues included—for not being aggressive or insistent enough in forwarding their basic principles. Appalled by the Russian pogroms, the Liberal disaster in the elections of 1891, and the continued success of Karl Lueger, the Suttners helped establish an Austrian branch of the Verein zur Abwehr des Antisemitismus (Society for the Defense against Antisemitism). The German branch of the Abwehrverein had been founded in 1890 as a response to a wave of antisemitism that swept over Germany. The German Abwehrverein allied itself solidly with the Left Liberals. The Austrian branch also comprised left-of-center figures, though without direct connection to a particular party. Both branches of the Abwehrverein comprised a high-class membership: scholars from all disciplines, well-known jurists and physicians, the mayor of Berlin, for example. Collectively, the Abwehrverein disseminated anti-antisemitic propaganda, reported on antisemitic outbreaks and the governmental responses, and took antisemites to courts of law.[16] Given the Suttners' pivotal role, it comes as no surprise that membership in the Austrian Abwehrverein and in the Austrian peace movement overlapped considerably.[17]

Ludwig Quidde, the son of a well-off Bremen merchant and a well-educated mother, overcame a serious speech impediment and became a distinguished student at the gymnasium. Quidde attributed his political views to his parents; his beliefs were clearly well formed by the time he arrived at the University of Göttingen. Despite a very small Jewish student body (1–2 percent), Göttingen became a hotbed of antisemitism. Although Göttingen lagged behind the University of Berlin, the center of the antisemitic movement, 400 Göttingen students signed the antisemite petition. Quidde organized a counterpetition that garnered 168 signatures. As the student body seethed, university officials did not hesitate to take sides; they disbanded the committee against antisemitism on 25 June 1881. Liberal students responded by forming a Freie wissenschaftliche Vereinigung (FWV). These free fraternities, open to all religious denominations, became an important chapter in the lives of many liberally inclined Christian and Jewish students throughout

Germany. Quidde played a significant role in establishing the Göttingen model.[18] His advocacy of Jewish-Christian amity did not end with his role in the FWV.

Quidde's anonymous 1881 pamphlet, *Die Antisemitenagitation und die deutsche Studentenschaft* (The antisemitic agitation and German students), caused an enormous stir.[19] When Quidde's authorship was revealed, he was challenged to several duels, one of which he accepted despite his moral opposition to dueling. He survived the ordeal and received his doctorate the next year with a thesis on the fifteenth-century Prussian king Sigismund.[20] The pamphlet, his only extended statement on antisemitism, proved that the twenty-three-year-old Quidde appreciated the dangers of the new movement better than the majority of his elders. Quidde warned that the ideals of the collegiate generation were no longer framed by the expectations of 1848 but by the bloody successes of Bismarck in the 1860s and 1870s. He pointed to a generation gap that led older liberals to underestimate the strength of the antisemitic movement and overestimate the powers of progress and education (*Bildung*). For Quidde, a generation of nationalist-chauvinists had come to maturity, and the antisemite petition represented a preview of other, greater demands to come.[21] Quidde explained the antisemitic movement primarily as a varied reaction to the excesses of the 1870s: "It [the antisemitic movement] is a reaction against the economic and therefore also against political and religious liberalism."[22] Quidde recognized that religious prejudices had been transformed into hostility against skepticism, materialism, cosmopolitanism, and a secular spirit in general, even by people who themselves were products of those transformations.

Quidde proposed stealing the antisemites' fire, combating the negative developments in Germany derisively called "Judaized" (*verjudet*) by the reactionaries. This anti-antisemitic tract steered clear of any expressions that could be called philosemitic. Quidde engaged in the standard liberal explanation of Jewish concentration in finance as the product of Christian compulsion in the Middle Ages, but he also denied that the demonstration he helped organize should be considered pro-Jewish. He distanced the goals of liberalism from the defense of Jewry as such, recognized the undeniable racial difference between "us and our Jewish fellow citizens," and ended his essay by calling antisemitism the new Pharisaism.[23] Quidde also noted the rising number of Jewish students as a cause for tension without mentioning that the number of Jewish students at Göttingen was minuscule.[24] Quidde clearly had rhetorical considerations on his mind when he took care not to appear too pro-Jewish: Paul Dulon, the organizer of the petition at Göttingen, derided the opponents of the petition as philosemites. Although Quidde disdained antisemites, nobody reading his pamphlet would have been struck by signs of his empathy for Jews. In 1881 Quidde on the Jewish question sounded very much like a member of the liberal mainstream.

Eighteen eighty-two was a momentous year for Quidde. In addition to completing his doctorate, he married Margarete Jacobson (1858–1940), whose Jewish father was the prominent ophthalmologist Julius Jacobson (1828–89).[25] Quidde, now blessed with a talented wife and handsome dowry, became deeply involved in liberal politics in Munich, where the young couple settled.[26] Quidde's association with the myriad of Left Liberal parties began in the first decade of the twentieth century and lasted until the Deutsche demokratische Partei fused with the antipacifist and antisemitic Jungdeutschen Orden in 1930.[27] The Left Liberal parties in Munich before the war enjoyed the support of the influential *Frankfurter allgemeine Zeitung*, published by Leopold Sonnemann (1831–1909), one of a trio of important liberal Jewish newspaper publishers.[28] Quidde was an important figure in Bavaria's Left Liberal politics, pushing the party toward pacifism and, no doubt, supporting its anti-antisemitic inclinations. In 1895, three years after the Conservative Party adopted the Tivoli Program, which gave an antisemitic orientation to a major party for the first time, the German People's Party (Deutsche Volkspartei) declared itself to be a party of peace.[29] That same year, Quidde's career as a mainstream politician and as an academic with professional standing came to a dramatic end with the publication of his biting satire *Caligula* (1894). Ostensibly a study of Caius Caligula's brief reign of terror, the thinly veiled target of Quidde's work was none other than Kaiser Wilhelm II. Quidde's notoriety (and subsequent jailing for lèse-majesté) consigned him to the role of outsider, a role not unsuited for participation in Germany's marginalized peace movement.

Despite his long association with Left Liberal parties, Quidde's principal energies were devoted to the German peace movement. Quidde clearly considered antisemitism a less critical enemy than militarism, but he never lost his early contempt of the former: "Antisemitism and pacifism are mutually exclusive. Absolutely. The Peace Society is the sworn opponent of any form of racism, also of antisemitism."[30] More revealing than these occasional anti-antisemitic comments is the fact that Quidde worked with Jews throughout his decades-long career as a peace activist. Alfred Fried disagreed with Quidde's conception of pacifism, but the Bremen merchant's son and the irascible Viennese Jew seem to have worked together without problems. Quidde participated in the Bund neues Vaterland, an association of antiwar intellectuals who banded together in 1914. The two most prominent members of the Bund were Albert Einstein, already famous for his contributions to physics, and Eduard Bernstein, the formulator of Revisionist Socialism. Both men were assimilated Jews but with pronounced Jewish loyalties. (Bernstein spoke movingly of the Jewish spiritual contributions to socialism. Einstein became an avid Zionist and was offered the presidency of the state of Israel.)

The German government disbanded the Bund in 1916, adding another mark of disrepute to Quidde's name.

Times of war have been a challenge to the modern German peace movement, forcing difficult choices between principles and popular opinion as the nation redefined dissent as treason. When World War I broke out, Quidde lost much respect in the international peace community for denying that the Central Powers bore sole responsibility despite the invasion of neutral Belgium. Quidde, furthermore, defended military service as a patriotic duty. He insisted that the movement should focus on a postwar settlement that would render future conflict impossible. Trying to force this issue, Quidde used his years of service to call a meeting in Berne, but the results were the exact opposite of what he had expected. Sandi Cooper writes, "Quidde's hope that a meeting of the Berne executive board would produce a joint statement on the war backfired. In many ways, the meeting was the epitaph of the peace movement in Europe that flourished in the nineteenth century."[31]

Quidde's postwar career as a peace activist proved even more frustrating. Younger men such as Friedrich Wilhelm Foerster found Quidde antiquated, still committed to the defunct ideals of 1848, and not nearly confrontational enough for the rougher era of the 1920s. Although he won a Nobel Peace Prize in 1927, Quidde was marginalized in the German peace movement he had done so much to found. Quidde reacted to the rise of Nazism with horror but also with desperation, naively clinging to Hitler's specious claims about desiring peace and earning Quidde the contempt of old friends such as the Junker conservative–turned–Left Liberal Hellmut von Gerlach. Quidde's thoughts on Hitler's antisemitism can be imagined, but despite Quidde's partly Jewish wife, none of his biographers have much to say about the dilemma of being married to a first-degree *Mischling* in the 1930s.[32] Perhaps, as Count Harry Kessler suggested, Quidde was watching his words for his wife's sake. As in 1914, Quidde faced the pacifist's dilemma of confronting a powerful and immoral ruler. Kessler entered this note in his diary on 6 April 1933: "Breakfast with Quidde. He is not a fugitive and wants to return to Germany. He told of the truly horrible flight of [Hellmut von] Gerlach from Berlin and then through Munich over the Swiss border without a passport. He is of the opinion that only a military overthrow [*Militärputsch*] can free us from the brown pest. It is a remarkable transformation of the situation, that he, an old pacifist, must place his hopes on the military."[33]

What can be inferred regarding Quidde's personal "comfort level" with Jews? Family and institutional contacts suggest that Quidde had no Jewish problem whatsoever: he collaborated with Jews personally and politically for sixty years. Letters to and from Albert Einstein in 1930 and 1931 regarding Oscar Wasserman, the director of the Deutsche Bank and a peace proponent, highlight Quidde's comfort with enlisting Jewish support.[34] Nevertheless, it is also worth noting that the Jewish question remained a peripheral one to Quidde. Only rarely in 1928, on the occasion of numerous interviews on his reception of the Nobel Peace Prize, did Quidde bother to mention antisemitism as a prompt to pacifism or democracy. Quidde reacted viscerally against antisemitism but appears to have regarded the Jewishness of so many collaborators as incidental to their common goals. Formally, Quidde's position on the Jewish question was classically liberal; informally, he moved in a mixed social circle with apparent ease.

Like Ludwig Quidde, Friedrich Wilhelm Foerster was a product of the educated middle-class (*Bildungsbürgertum*). Born in Berlin to a Frisian mother and a Silesian father, he was brought up by his parents in the classical German spirit of Alexander von Humboldt and the early Goethe. Despite his mother's family connection to Count Helmuth von Moltke, Foerster's parents were opponents of Bismarck's "blood and iron" politics and opposed to the Prussianization of Germany. Wilhelm Foerster (1832–1921), Friedrich's father, was a famous astronomer, a founder of the Society for Ethical Culture, and a sympathizer with Bertha von Suttner's peace activities. He was also a signer of the 1914 "Manifesto to Europeans," a counter-manifesto to the nationalistic "Manifesto to the Civilized World," in which ninety-three intellectuals defended Germany's invasion of neutral Belgium. The "Manifesto to Europeans," brainchild of Georg Nicolai, garnered four signatures in all, including Albert Einstein's and the elder Foerster's.[35] Friedrich Wilhelm seems to have imbibed the political convictions of his parents. Shortly after his promotion in Freiburg, Foerster spent three months in jail on a charge of lèse-majesté.

By the outbreak of World War I, Foerster had received his doctorate, his *Habilitation*, and had taught in Zurich, Vienna, and Munich. He emerged as one of the leading voices of German pacifism, an opponent of the war; afterward he became a proponent of accepting the Versailles Treaty. He defended the Jewish-born Kurt Eisner, the idiosyncratic and controversial ruler of the Bavarian Republic. Foerster denounced the Jew-baiters who sought Eisner's ruin as deflecting the true responsibility for the German tragedy—a willingness to worship political and military power, a new paganism without the tolerance or universality of the paganism of antiquity.[36] The 1920s and 1930s saw Foerster's emergence as a leading figure among the radical peace activists, a champion of the unpopular cause of admitting Germany's war guilt, and the editor of the left-wing journal *Menschheit* (Humanity). From the outskirts of the German academy, Foerster was also an important contributor to what would become the field of philosophy of education. Foerster fled to the United States in 1933, ultimately settling in Switzerland until his death.

Quidde's anti-antisemitism stemmed from a visceral revulsion against reaction and his unfashionable association with the classic liberalism of the 1848 generation. Foerster's initial orientation toward the Jewish question may have been similarly shaped by classic liberalism, but his mature perspective was stamped by his deep-seated Christian convictions. Rejecting the archrationalism of his parents' household, Foerster embraced religion, though he stayed clear of any institutional association. As to Foerster's early relations with Jews, they cannot be reconstructed. He attended a gymnasium in Berlin with a high percentage of Jewish students and in 1913 and 1914 recorded his disgust at the ultranationalism of German students at the University of Vienna, where he was then teaching.[37] Opportunity to befriend Jews was not lacking, therefore, in his school years in Berlin and Vienna. Foerster's only specific remarks about his personal encounters, however, are found in his largest and most problematic work, *Die Juden* (*The Jews*, 1959). Foerster announces in his introduction to *The Jews*: "Throughout his long life the author has had exceptional opportunities of working with Jews: German, Slavonic and American. He has enjoyed relations of close friendship with them and shared with them in a community of cultural work. When, therefore, the anti-Semitism which broke out at the end of the last century proved to be a phenomenon of cumulative intensity, he could only regard it as something that went utterly contrary to his own feelings—feeling of friendship for Jewry and of admiration for the ethical principles that guided Jewish life."[38] That Foerster failed to write anything similar to the above-cited lines before World War II is not that surprising—next to being Jewish, having Jewish friends was the surest way to disqualify any entry into the Jewish question as philosemitic. As noted above, understating the Jewish factor served an important role even in a dissident liberal group like the peace movement. Foerster's chronology in this passage deserves comment. Not unlike Jews who found their identity with the rise of antisemitism ("Jews by the grace of Stoecker"), Foerster connected his own pro-Jewish feelings to the resilience of antisemitism in the 1890s.

Whenever and however the groundwork had been laid, Foerster's first published analysis of the Jewish question appeared in his *Politische Ethik und politische Pedagogik* (Political ethics and political pedagogies, 1913).[39] Stressing that no European peoples have been in as symbiotic a relationship as Aryans and Jews, Foerster adopted the almost irresistible German urge to divide Jews into two groups: the admirable pious and "religiously highly disciplined Jew," and the uprooted modern Jew. Foerster's preference for the first category, obviously driven by his own religious convictions, would prove to be problematic. The Jews whom Foerster collaborated with in the peace movement were, overwhelmingly, the secular Jews that Foerster described in this essay as guilty of either overbearing egotism or cringing. Foerster ultimately managed his awkward categories by assigning all idealistically motivated Jews to the category of the admirable and "highly disciplined." Thus the Jews within the peace movement, though hardly traditional, were dubbed authentic Jews by Foerster by dint of their idealistic fidelity to the peace movement.

Foerster employed other dichotomies besides pious and impious, arrogant and servile. Contemporary Jews, opined Foerster, had learned a sense of competition, a productive sense of honor (*fordernde Ehregefühl*), but not yet a sense of sacrificial honor (*opfernde Ehregefühl*).[40] The Jews could climb higher than all other peoples, but they could also sink lower, and so on.[41] Foerster's tendency to dichotomize established a language of difference that he consistently employed when discussing Jewry; this language remained unaffected by the events of the following forty years. His "dichotomitis" did not appear to have been a malady in his own eyes—on the contrary. Antisemitism's failure to understand these competing tendencies in the Jew precluded it from apprehending the true solution to the Jewish question: an alliance with the best part of Jewry to convert the degenerate part. Foerster's Christian beliefs claim center stage, but the vocabularies of liberal assimilationism and even of racial thinking inject themselves into his 1913 solution to the Jewish question: "Only through Christ and in Christ will the Jewish question be solved. Neither expulsion nor ghettoization nor mere assimilation and sham conversion can resolve the terrible intrinsic difficulties of this problem. Only when both, the Jew and the Christian, 'assimilate' with their entire souls to the spirit of Christ will the true assimilation of the Jewish people and the Aryan race become possible and capable of life."[42]

In *Mein Kampf gegen des militaristische und nationalistische Deutschland* (My struggle against a militaristic and nationalistic Germany, 1920), Foerster assessed the possibilities for a more pacific Germany in the wake of Versailles. One key to Germany's future, in his view, would be found in the treatment of the Jewish question. Citing Paul Seippel's words that the Dreyfus affair was the overture to the French victory on the Marne, Foerster pronounced, "How we treat the Jews will be the way that we are judged [by the world]."[43] The Eastern European Jews (Ostjuden), in particular, would be a critical testing point. Germany, Foerster maintained, could handle the problem in a way that would make all of Europe grateful or in a way that could poison the international atmosphere. Practically, it seemed like the purest German suicide not to align Germany's economic reconstruction with the energy and practical nature of the Jews.[44] Foerster once again divided Jews into good and bad. He contrasted the degenerate ghetto Jew (the Ostjude) with the noble and inwardly free acculturated German Jew. He seemingly had no awareness that the Ostjuden were patently closer to the "religiously disciplined" Jew he had praised in his *Politische Ethik und politische Pedagogik*. In any case, Foerster believed that the Judenfrage would be a gauge of Germany's post–World War I identity and warned against allowing the antisemites to set the agenda. Rather than allow the antisemites to define the problem, Foerster insisted that Christians of good will should ally themselves with progressive Jews to advance the Ostjuden. Foerster viewed German Jews as partners in the colonializing enterprise of civilizing Ost-juden, not an unheard-of theme for anti-antisemites.[45] Other than the references to postwar conditions, this work mainly repeats his earlier analysis. The language of difference remains predominant; perhaps even more insistently than before the war, Foerster linked Germany's future with that of European Jewry.

Foerster's opposition to antisemitism clearly preceded the Nazis. It cannot be grouped with the sort of ex post facto philosemitism that stemmed from a bad conscience and a desire to demonstrate repentance to the Allied powers.[46] Precisely this track record of anti-antisemitism and his accompanying self-identification as pro-Jewish are what make Foerster's post–World War II reflections on the fate of German Jewry so troubling. Regarding the Jews, Foerster did not learn much from World War II: the events from 1939 to 1945 confirmed rather than shook his opinions. In Foerster's case, this confirmation occurred despite his insistence on the enormity and uniqueness of the crime and his own profound feelings of remorse. Relating a medieval prophecy that Germany would be a land in which a great crime would one day be perpetrated, Foerster wrote in his memoirs:

> *Must I disclose to my countrymen when and where this deadly crime actually took place? It was committed in Auschwitz, where millions of Jews were gassed. They were not millions of victims that resulted from a German Jewish war, no, it was a great murder that had never before been committed in the entire history of the world. Who can take away from me the consciousness of this great guilt? . . . We Germans benefited [from Jews] for hundreds of years, in our culture, in our economy, in our scholarship, in our medicine, and in the world of friendship. No one can do it. But even worse is the fact that this great guilt has been submerged in silence.*[47]

Despite these moving words, Foerster's *The Jews* offers a good example of what troubles many Jews, scholars and laypersons alike, about philosemitism. Published in 1959, *The Jews* attempted to be a spiritual reparation for the indescribable wrong suffered by the Jewish people.[48] Given that intention, it is not surprising that the glorification of Jewish culture and a tragic presentation of the external history of the Jews dominated Foerster's presentation. Foerster warmly praised the piety of the Jews from time immemorial, devoting a chapter to the medieval Pietists. He quoted the many admonitions from Judah the Hasid's moral classic, *Book of the Pious*, at length. The reasons for this choice of Jewish texts, the only text to be discussed at length in *The Jews*, seem apparent. First, the medieval Hasidim were German, allowing Foerster to stress the antiquity and earnestness of the German Jewry. Second, the religious thrust of the *Book of the Pious*, or at least those sections that Foerster read in German translation, was moral. Contrary to the typical presentation of Judaism as mired in legal technicalities, *Book of the Pious* evidences an acute moral sensitivity toward Jews and Gentiles.[49] Equally impressive to Foerster, as to many well-meaning Gentiles and Jews, was the Jews' willingness to commit martyrdom for their beliefs.[50] The long history of Jewish suffering, which culminated in what Foerster called "the National Socialist epilogue," demonstrated the tenacity with which Jews clung to the Ten Commandments and God's kingship.

The history of Jewish suffering, standard fare for anti-antisemites, did not lead Foerster to a deep reappraisal of Christianity. Foerster acknowledged that the Church's record of anti-Judaism had been "not consistently reassuring" but safely categorized the transgressions of the past as not truly Christian in spirit.[51] This rhetorical maneuver, well honed by Christian apologists, failed to do justice to both the ancient past (for example, the demonization of Jews beginning in the Gospels and carried on by the patristic fathers) and also the recent past (for example, the German Christians who sought to eradicate Jewish influence from Christianity under the Nazi aegis). Einstein, an admirer of Foerster who helped secure him entry into the United States and a pension, chided Foerster on this point: "Christianity—taken abstractly—may rightly be considered as a principal moral good of real human progress. The Church, however, in the name of Christian principles, has served apocalyptic darkness more than the eternal goals of humanity."[52] Foerster eagerly acknowledged that the Jewish question was really a Christian question. But this seems to have meant little more to him than that Christians ought to stop blaming Jews for "faults for which they themselves [Christians] bear ultimate responsibility."[53] A really thorough consideration of the role played by Jews and Judaism in mainstream Christian thought does not take place.[54]

There is something terrifyingly unsurprising about the Nazi Holocaust in Foerster's analysis. Despite Foerster's terming it the "epilogue" of Jewish persecution, it appears as another in a long line of martyrdom suffered willingly by the Jews for their faith. Inadvertently, Jews become objects acted upon in the moral history of progress and regress, a theme Foerster had already developed before World War I. In a metaphor that Foerster used in 1913 and repeated in 1959, he wrote, "They [the Jews] were like penguins on some uninhabited island which sailors can kill by the thousands for no better reason than the prompting of an evil whim."[55]

The sociologist Zygmunt Bauman has employed the neologism "allosemitism" to describe the allocation of a special vocabulary to address the radical otherness of the Jews. For Bauman, discussions of Jews are thus supercharged before a particular valence, either positive or negative, is assigned. Allosemitism is radically ambivalent, for it can manifest itself as hatred or love of Jews but tends to be intense and extremely malleable.[56] In Foerster's case, the prevailing tendency is philosemitic, but the negative potential lies just beneath the surface. Discussing

Walther Rathenau and Albert Ballin, two very prominent figures in Wilhelminian Germany, Foerster criticized their German nationalism as a betrayal of their Jewish mission: "Both, in one way or another, lived to see that their treason to their own best principles had been completely in vain. Both were to live through the hour when they received their parting kick and when it suddenly became plain to them that they had consecrated their brains and strength to a Germany that did nothing but squander its enormous moral and spiritual inheritance."[57]

One may find Foerster's antimilitarism admirable and still recognize that he ultimately validated the shabby treatment Rathenau and Ballin received on the basis of some reputed "treason" to Jewish values. But how could either Rathenau or Ballin betray a Jewish tradition that was really no part of their assimilated upbringing? And how could Foerster really expect highly assimilated German Jews to be free from the flaws that plagued Germany in general? The very subtitle of the chapter, "Jews and Christians Give Way [weichen] to Nationalism," shows a lack of proportion on Foerster's part, as if the two groups were equally important in determining Germany's course. Bauman's words about the unbridgeable divide between "the Jew as such" and "the Jew next door" apply nicely to Foerster. However well Foerster knew German Jewry from his youth in Berlin, studies in Vienna, and activities in the peace movement, he was able to disconnect that knowledge from some ideal, abstract, essentialized Jew constructed out of his own private theology. How else to account for the damning discussion of Ballin and Rathenau, the citations to the deeply ambivalent novelist Gustav Freytag, the metaphor of penguins done to death, and the persistent dichotomy between "good" and "bad" Jews? As Bauman suggested, the language of radical difference (allosemitism) invited the segregation of the facts of history, which Foerster recognized, from a construction of Judentum that Foerster had forged nearly half a century earlier.[58]

A similar balancing act between praising and damning can be found in Foerster's discussion of modern Israel, found near the end of The Jews. Foerster noted the extraordinary practical difficulties involved in the building of a new Jewish nation and then took a different tack: "Yet all this can do no more than serve the purpose of re-creating the material conditions of a new Israel. By this I mean a Jewish nation, which, in the midst of a world concerned almost exclusively with materialistic things, will remain faithful to its historic mission, a Jewish nation, in a word, which will provide within itself the political center where its religious and ethical vocation will be turned into a lasting reality."[59] Casting the mantle of the prophets upon a new, weak, tiny, and beleaguered nation made sense given Foerster's idealization of the powers inherent in the individual Jew and collective Jewry but, of course, hardly corresponded to reality. Foerster engaged in the typically modernist gesture of overloading the entity Jew with whatever significance he wanted. What makes

Foerster unusual, in the modern setting, is the generally positive valence to which he assigns the ideal Jew. Nevertheless, the scene is set for deep disappointment should the Jews fail to live out their divinely appointed role.

Fundamentally, this combination of high expectation and anticipatory disappointment stems from Foerster's traditional Christian soteriology. He criticized Christianity's failure to incorporate the Jewish legacy appropriately—its ignorance of Christianity's Jewish roots, ignorance of Judaism's ethical and spiritual qualities, too much focus on the person of Jesus, and not enough commitment to the Old Testament idea of God as judge. Ultimately, however, Foerster bounced the question back to the Jews: "How can we explain the fact . . . that the Jews for centuries unhesitatingly chose death for themselves, for their wives and for their children, rather than embrace the Christian Faith?"[60] Foerster wished to highlight the affinity of Judaism and Christianity, yet he seemed strikingly unable to imagine Judaism's ability to be spiritually adequate on its own. Once again, Foerster intended the following statement found in *The Jews* to be philosemitic: "Now it is a very extraordinary thing that the greatest counterpoise to this Aryan split between spirit and life should be found in the particular genius of Jewry. Because of this it is only through the conjunction in Christianity of Semitic and Aryan elements that something truly human could come into existence. Naturally I am speaking here of the earthly and cultural foundations of the life of Christianity."[61]

When Christianity succeeds fully in being Christian, the Jew will cease to be a Jew. This was Foerster's initial solution to the Jewish question in 1913, and it was his solution in 1959.

More than any other figure examined here, Heinrich Coudenhove-Kalergi belongs to a bygone era. A Bohemian nobleman with ancient lineage on both sides of his family, Coudenhove received a Jesuit education, earned a doctor of laws, and entered the Austrian diplomatic service. At thirty-six, married to a Japanese woman and the father of two boys, he retired from public service to manage the family estates left to him by his father. Besides the considerable practical demands of running a manorial estate, Coudenhove educated his children, composed bedtime prayers for the family, engaged in eclectic correspondence, and studied religion and philosophy. He also supported the nascent Austrian peace movement and prohibited his sons from playing with toy soldiers, quite a statement for a former big-game hunter who appeared in the Austrian equivalent of *Sports Illustrated*. An uncommonly energetic scholar, Coudenhove earned a second doctorate (in philosophy) from the University of Prague at age forty-two, mastered sixteen languages, and produced a considerable literary legacy. *Das Wesen des Antisemitismus* (The essence of antisemitism, 1901), begun as Coudenhove's doctoral thesis at Prague, became his most successful work. It was reissued in 1923 with a biographical sketch; reissued again in 1929 with a long afterword by son Richard; and reissued three times between 1932 and 1935, with a total printing of twenty-two thousand copies. Translated into English as *Antisemitism through the Ages* in 1935, *Das Wesen des Antisemitismus* was reissued once again in 1992 in German with a new introduction by Coudenhove's granddaughter Barbara. With the possible exception of Jean-Paul Sartre's *Réflexions sur la question juive*, no single nonliterary anti-antisemitic work can claim such a successful publication history, certainly none in the German language. Coudenhove's premature death in 1906 at the age of forty-five silenced the voice of a promising progressive.

Coudenhove was a private scholar without many Jewish contacts, and he was distant from the daily politics of the Jewish question. He was, in his son's words, a conservative in his respect for tradition, a liberal in his advocacy of tolerance, and a socialist in his hatred of social injustice.[62] Coudenhove was an unusual man, and *Antisemitism* has more than a few quirks. Despite a deep study of Western and Eastern religions, Coudenhove commenced his work with an impassioned defense of Catholicism as the best of all religions, totally irrelevant to the theme and incongruous with the tone of the remainder of the work. The original 1901 edition also contains a long poem devoted to religious toleration, excised in succeeding editions. For all its many peculiarities, *Antisemitism* is a remarkable work. Coudenhove began with the standard denial of Jewish ancestry but with a twist: "Anybody who writes or utters the slightest word about Israel which is not unfavorable is at once cried down as a Jew or as a freemason. This expedient will have no effect in my case. There is not the slightest trace of Jewish blood in my genealogical tree. Had this been the case, instead of concealing the fact, I would candidly and most joyfully have proclaimed it, because I would have felt proud of a possible kinship with the noblest men and women who ever wandered on this planet."[63]

Denial of Jewish roots, as I noted in chapter 1, served as a necessary patent of reliability when discussing the Jewish question. Coudenhove subverted that shibboleth with the unabashed Judeo-enthusiasm of a convert. As he wrote at the conclusion of the work: "I confess that among my Christian friends and acquaintances I can call to mind only three who were inspired by Philo-Semitism. I confess that I have myself been a theoretical Anti-Semite. . . . Had I been asked a few years ago, when I decided to study the Jewish question and to write a book on it, whether this work would turn out Anti-Semitic, my answer to this question would most probably have been in the affirmative. A serious and, as I believe, a thorough study of the subject has taught me better."[64] Coudenhove's study of antisemitism was as he described it: serious and thorough and, one could add, written with verve and passion. These were the features that made *Antisemitism* an anti-antisemitic "classic," despite its profound inconsistencies.

Coudenhove's principal thesis is that religious intolerance lies at the root of the phenomenon of antisemitism. He proved this point directly, through an historical inventory of Christian-Jew hatred, and indirectly, through a variety of claims. He laid special emphasis on the first (negative) exposure to Judaism through early religious education and very ostentatiously walked out of the Ronsperger Church every Good Friday when the service reached the passage regarding the perfidy of the Jews.[65] For Coudenhove, racial differences were a fraud; the Jews comprised many different races, as did contemporary Europeans. One could speak of semitic languages but not of semitic peoples. Even in the Greco-Roman past the Jews' minority religious beliefs and practices caused the social animosity of pagans, but only with the advent of Christianity did this hatred exceed the normal limits of xenophobia. Other nations such as the Parses and the Armenians have also survived through the ages without a state; Jews in non-Western parts of the world have been treated more or less like any other minority. Coudenhove's rational analysis contained a distinct demystifying tendency, but the contrary tendency is just as strong. Coudenhove seems to have gotten stuck between what he says he was trying to do (engage in an empirical investigation into the nature of antisemitism) and a deeply seated traditional religious vantage point on Jewish difference. The first contradiction, therefore, is a common one in philosemitic discourse: whether to describe Jews and Judaism in natural or supernatural terms. Coudenhove described Jewish martyrdom as a "supernatural divine greatness."[66] He followed Renan's verdict that "the best of all men have been Jews and the most wicked of men have also been Jews." He noted that "[a]nybody who remembers that the Lord Jesus Christ was born among this nation will not wonder at its differing so greatly from all other nations."[67] Coudenhove thus replaced Jesus' death at the hands of Jews with Jesus' birth from the womb of a Jew. Accepting Jewish difference as a reality, Coudenhove gave it a positive spin.

Ultimately for Coudenhove, antisemitism had been a pan-Christian phenomenon, cutting across denominational borders. Coudenhove clearly objected to the widespread tendency to equate antisemitism with medievalism and medievalism with the Catholic Church, thus letting other Christians off the hook. Although he devoted several pages to indicting the Dominicans' role in Jew hatred from the thirteenth century until the present day, he defended the popes as posting a generally favorable record in opposing antisemitic assault.[68] Regarding Protestant antisemitism, Coudenhove uttered a judgment that would probably have been rejected by most contemporaries but that seems more plausible in light of the Holocaust: "If we compare the attitude of Luther and of the Protestant Church in the Middle Ages [sic] toward the Jews with that of the Roman Church, it becomes strikingly evident that the latter behaved towards this unfortunate people comparatively more humanely and tolerantly than did the Protestant Church. Nothing is more unjust than the assertion that strict Protestantism is more enlightened, progressive and tolerant than the Roman Church."[69]

Religious intolerance in all its forms drew sustenance from monotheism and the Hebrew Scriptures. Thus Judaism, in its more Orthodox forms, initially created the intellectual climate for oppression and martyrdom. Although Coudenhove did not have a positive view of Orthodox Judaism, he did not take this potentially antisemitic turn of argument very far, nor did he suggest that Jews were responsible for their own suffering. Individuals and institutions carry the responsibility for their deeds. Coudenhove concluded that there needed to be a move back to an Ur-religion that preceded these visions and that recognized that love of one's neighbor is the true basis for faith. His introductory poem, "Enoch," imagined a pre-Judeo-Christian figure as a potential basis for a common religious faith without the intolerance that monotheism inevitably bred. Spinoza's influence on Coudenhove appears very pronounced here on several counts. Coudenhove prescribed philosophy for the elite and religion for the masses; argued that there can only be one universal truth overarching all religions; and "proved" Catholicism's superiority by showing that no other religion had performed so many deeds of "charity, pity and compassion."[70] Here is the second contradiction: a committed Catholic convinced of his tradition's superiority, on closer inspection, turns out to share the views of a renegade Jew from Amsterdam.

Spinoza considered Jesus the most perfect representative of the human being. So did Coudenhove, for whom Jesus epitomized the moral imperative to love one's neighbor. Both Christians and Jews needed to be led in that direction. How will the modern Jew be led to Jesus? By Reform Judaism, answered Coudenhove, "the noblest, and most beautiful rejuvenation of Judaism and the greatest imaginable simplification of monotheism." Coudenhove did not expect religious conversion. Indeed, he thought the talmudic doctrine that the pious of all the nations would have a share in the world to come superior to the doctrines of Christianity and Islam. Nevertheless, Jesus represents a religious ideal that will ultimately win over Jews, precisely because they are so smart and admirable. "It is my firm conviction that it is only a question of time when all educated Jews with their capacity of education and their love of knowledge will hail and adore Christ, our Lord as one of the best, greatest and holiest men of their nation, while persisting at the same time their aversion for Christianity."[71] Reform Judaism, to Coudenhove, was everything religion should be: ethical, universal, international, and cosmopolitan. The Reform Jewish mission, as Coudenhove saw, would be to cure humanity of the poison of religious fanaticism.[72] In a view both pluralistic and ironic, Coudenhove concluded that the world needed Jesus Christ and Reform Judaism for its salvation. Coudenhove thus combined traditional Christian supersessionism regarding Jesus as a religious archetype with a Reform view of "mission."

Reform Judaism and Zionism, bitter enemies in 1901, were considered by Coudenhove as partners in the solution to the Jewish question. Reform, as noted in the preceding paragraph, had a role to play in the bridging of the remaining gaps between Jews and Christians in Western Europe. With the vast exodus carried out by Zionists, Coudenhove expected the remaining Jewish population to be small and easily assimilable. But Zionism had a critical role to play: rescuing Eastern European Jews from the clutches of the czar. However much the Christian states would be impoverished by a Jewish exodus (and Coudenhove listed the impressive contributions made by Jews in all fields), Christians had a moral duty to help the Zionists along. Eastern European Jews, Coudenhove held, would be prepared to emigrate. "It is not true what the Anti-Semites say that the Jews would not go, because they would as committed then be reduced to the necessity of cheating each other. . . . Try it[,] gentlemen, work for Zionism, and you will soon see how crowds of Jews will emigrate."[73] Sympathy with Zionism from the antisemitic impulse of getting the Jews out of Europe was not a new phenomenon. Helping Zionism out of a moral impulse to aid in solving the Jewish problem, despite the loss it would entail for Christian Europeans—that was something unusual. For a committed Christian like Coudenhove to be both pro-Reform and pro-Zionist on the basis of what each movement could contribute to furthering an internal Jewish agenda was unusual in the extreme.

If empathy with the Jewish condition was one of the lessons Heinrich Couden-hove-Kalergi and Mitsu Aoyama of Castle Ronsberg, Bohemia, wished to teach their children, they succeeded admirably. Count Richard Nikolaus Coudenhove-Kalergi (1894–1972) founded and inspired the Pan-European League, a forerunner of the contemporary European Community. His activism in the peace movement began before World War I. In the 1922 collection *Die Friedensbewegung*, mentioned above, Richard contributed the article on Judaism in the section "Wege zum Pazi-fismus" (Ways to pacifism). (That a Catholic should be chosen to write this section probably says something about both the secular loyalties of Jews in the movement and their Judaic limitations. In the same section, Albert Einstein contributed the essay on science and Ernst Toller the one on revolution, so suppressing the Jewish involvement in the movement could not have been a motive here.) Coudenhove's remarkable confession probably expresses what several non-Jewish peace activists thought about Judaism. The "text" Coudenhove used was not the elite texts of Judaism but the history of the Jewish people. A believer in Jewish "world mission" like his father, Coudenhove argued that the realization of Jewish justice was socialism; Jewish abstention from power politics was pacifism. Jews, claimed Coudenhove, were the first European people to disarm, albeit unwillingly. The most ancient cultural people (*Kulturvolk*), Jews were more mature. Like adults, Jews resorted to words; like children, Europeans resorted to violent conflict. In Richard Coudenhove's estimation the Jews, to use an analogy employed by Disraeli and Nietzsche on earlier occasions, were a second European nobility. His conclusion is a remarkable statement that takes many antisemitic imputations and boldly calls them virtues. It is doubtful that the following statement would have been penned in his father's day by a supporter of Jewry. World War I had made the Jews' enemies bolder but, in this instance, had also made them the Jews' friends:

> *The diaspora made the Jews into an international people. From this curse came a blessing. Excluded from narrow nationalism, the best among the Jews found their fatherland in the world, their patriotism in humanity. The world mission of the Jews is the rebuilding of a destroyed world community through a new cosmopolitanism, pacifism, and socialism. They are precursors of a coming denationalized humanity. Their goal is to love together instead of hating each other, to build rather than to destroy, to unite instead of dividing. Under the sign of their prophets humanity will be led out of the Egyptian bondage of capitalism and militarism into the praiseworthy future land of freedom and peace.*[74]

Richard Coudenhove continued his contribution to anti-antisemitism with the updating and republishing of his father's work in the 1920s and 1930s. Richard's revisions of *Antisemitism* were really independent essays, one of which was published by the Paneuropa Press in 1937 under the title *Judenhass!* Although Richard Coudenhove shared his father's detestation of religiously based antisemitism, his appraisal of postwar antisemitism forced him to emphasize other factors and new realities. The mass emigration of Eastern European Jews, the rise of Bolshevism, and the impoverishment of Europe, Coudenhove sensibly argued, created the context for antisemitism in the postwar period. Germany, not Russia, had become the world capital of antisemitism, to his deep dismay. Following in his father's footsteps, Coudenhove urged Western Jews to support Zionism. Contrary to their fears, the exodus of Eastern European Jews would make the Jewish question easier to resolve by reducing the number of Jews who would remain in Europe and become fully integrated into their respective nations.

A progressive to the core, Richard Coudenhove believed that a solution to the plight of the Jews could be found. Coudenhove considered the persecution of Jews the "essence" of the Nazi revolution. He recognized that the churches' opposition to the Nazis was driven mainly by Nazism's anti-Christian, not anti-Jewish, implications. Nevertheless, Richard Coudenhove, as late as 1935, still saw assimilation and national exodus as the two alternatives to solving the Jewish problem in Germany. Physical annihilation was as unthinkable for this conscientious and cosmopolitan Christian as it was for European Jewry.

The following table may help to emphasize our first conclusion:

Ludwig Quidde:	Bremen *Bildungsbürgertum*	marginalized academic,	secular, liberal, assimilationist
Bertha von Suttner:	Austrian aristocrat,	novelist,	secular, liberal, Federation of Nations
Friedrich Wilhelm Foerster:	Berlin *Bildungsbürgertum*	marginalized academic,	Christian, assimilationist
Heinrich Coudenhove-Kalergi:	Austrian aristocrat,	marginal academic,	Christian, Federation of Nations

The variety of anti-antisemitism evidenced by the figures discussed above was considerable. Foerster and Heinrich Coudenhove were deeply influenced by their Christian beliefs; Quidde and Suttner, deeply moral individuals, were resolutely secular. Suttner and Coudenhove, aristocratic inhabitants of the multinational Austro-Hungarian Empire, envisioned a solution that gave play to Jewish contributions within both the land of their birth (assimilationism) and the Jewish homeland (Zionism). Quidde and Foerster, middle-class North Germans, ultimately endorsed assimilationism, though without the impatience and intolerance of diversity typical of most German liberals. The three men held doctorates; Bertha von Suttner, as a woman, was excluded from attending university. Quidde married a Jew; Suttner had many Jewish friends; Heinrich Coudenhove knew Jews mainly through an exchange of letters. Suttner, Quidde, and Foerster collaborated with Jews in the German Peace Society and other organizations, as did Richard Coudenhove. What seems less important than the precise positions held on the Jewish question by these figures is their very participation in a movement that offered a haven for Jewish-Christian collaboration.

Christians (by birth and by conviction) constituted the majority of the German Peace Society and, with the exception of Alfred Fried, the bulk of its visible leadership. Nevertheless, scholars have neglected the presence and significance of the large number of Jews in the movement.[75] Consequently, scholars have failed to sufficiently acknowledge the nexus between peace activism and anti-antisemitism, although that nexus seemed obvious to the four figures discussed above. The casual way in which both Arthur von Suttner in 1894 and Hellmut von Gerlach in 1937 equated the two positions is telling:

> Before we will be able to achieve peace from the outside, we must produce peace within. For this work, we [the Abwehrverein] and you [the peace movement] work entirely on the same side.[76]

As a younger man I was an antisemite because I knew no Jews, so was I,
until about 1900, a militarist because I knew no pacifists.[77]

The names on peace publications, the socioeconomic composition of the movement, the prominence of Jewish peace activists in the public arena, the presence
of such outspoken anti-antisemites must have made it clear to contemporaries,
friends and foes alike, that here was a place that welcomed Jews as Jews.

What role did the German Peace Society play as a vehicle for Jewish identity? An
investigation into this matter would be well worth undertaking. I would conjecture
that a wide and imprecise range of Jewish identity could probably be found among
Jewish members. Just as the precise view of non-Jews on the Jewish question
mattered less than their possessing a generally anti-antisemitic outlook, I suspect
that Jews who shared the basic goals of the German Peace Society would have been
welcome whatever their own brand of Jewishness. No doubt the highly acculturated
Jews were more represented than the highly observant, who tended to be less
political than the Jewish mainstream. The Jews in the German Peace Society may
not have been crackerjack Talmud scholars, but figures such as Albert Einstein,
Eduard Bernstein, and Gustav Karpeles certainly had healthy Jewish identities. But
again, this should not be overemphasized: just as the Christian anti-antisemites
differed in their view of Jewry, so, probably, did the Jewish members. The German
Peace Society offers support for George Mosse's claim that German Jews developed
a left-wing identity in organizations that, prima facie, were not Jewish at all.[78]

What does this investigation suggest about placing the German Peace Society within the framework of German Left Liberalism? The consensus is that
nineteenth-century liberalism defended Jews qua citizens-in-general, not qua Jewish citizens. In Germany, leading liberals such as Theodor Mommsen spoke out
against a German-Jewish *Mischkultur* and rarely deviated from a projection of
complete Jewish assimilation: German Jews were ultimately expected to become
indistinguishable from other Germans. That position, publicly, was the bottom
line. This "ideal" liberal ideology, however, needs fleshing-out in a social context. Dagmar Herzog's *Intimacy and Exclusion* and Keith Pickus's *Constructing
Modern Identities* present two examples (the Mannheim Monday Club and the
Freie wissenschaftliche Vereine) of settings where Christians and Jews socialized
as equals.[79] Certainly, the Christian (and many Jewish) members of these organizations expected complete assimilation and entertained ambivalent views about
Jewish difference. Nevertheless, I would conclude that how these organizations
functioned mattered more than what they said. The German Peace Society offers
a third example of a liberal context in which the term *neutral society* is justified.[80]

I hope that a final thought on the contemporary application of this study will not
be inappropriate. In the modernist mindset, one's religious and ethnic community

was supposed to be irrelevant to one's political affinities, and a political organization felt compelled to fight for the good of society, often at the expense of being able to fight openly for the particular segments of that society. In the postmodern era that we now inhabit, a progressive movement can oppose antisemitism, racism, and sexism without fear that it compromises its avowedly universal mission. Naturally, this freedom of expression has its own pitfalls. In the wake of 11 September 2001 and the ongoing war in Iraq, the peace movement has sharpened its criticisms of America's Middle East policies. Whether the various peace organizations can champion the legitimate rights of the Palestinians without opening the door to Israel bashing and charges of a Jewish conspiracy in Washington remains an unsettled question. On this issue, the American peace movement could do far worse than to emulate its predecessor, the German Peace Society.

3. *The Problematics of Philosemitic Fiction*

The role of fiction in propagating and updating antisemitic stereotypes in modern Germany is widely acknowledged. Few would deny that the popular image of the Jew was fixed in popular imagination more by the novels of Gustav Freytag and Wilhelm Raabe than by antisemitic polemics such as Wilhelm Marr's *Der Sieg des Judenthums über das Germanenthum* (The victory of Judaism over Germanism) and Hitler's *Mein Kampf*. The racist, *völkisch*, and paranoid trilogy of novels by Arthur Dinter probably exerted more influence on the masses in the 1920s than any political tract published by the Nazis. Dinter and Freytag have generally been assumed by scholars to represent the two poles defining the range of fictional Jewishness. Dinter portrayed "the Jew" as irredeemably vile.[1] Freytag poses far greater difficulties of interpretation. Beginning in the 1880s, Freytag spoke out against antisemitism, raised his stepson (from his third wife) as a Jew, and regarded himself as a stalwart liberal. Nevertheless, George Mosse and Hans Mayer have convincingly argued that Freytag's *Soll und Haben* perpetuated negative stereotypes about Jews and upheld the "good Jew" versus "bad Jew" dichotomy so characteristic of German literary representations of Jewishness.[2]

While historians have paid too little attention to the political defenses of Jews and Judaism, scholars in German studies appear to have neglected literary philosemitism almost entirely.[3] This chapter demonstrates that several non-Jewish authors succeeded in creating positive Jewish characters and narratives. These works clearly exerted less influence than those of either Freytag or Dinter. Nevertheless, it would be imprudent to dismiss them as aberrations. The authors discussed below may not have been famous, but neither were they unknown scriveners without a readership. All of these works take the Jewish question as their principal subject.[4]

My use of the term philosemitic fiction is qualified. First, I do not claim that these authors were free from all anti-Jewish prejudices. When determining the presence or absence of literary antisemitism, those who argue that the text rather than the author should be the decisive factor make the better case.[5] Second, even these texts display considerable ambivalence, both confuting and perpetuating Jewish stereotypes. The minimizing of distinctively Jewish realities and the trivializing of antisemitic impulses tended to denude these works of fictional power. I pass no judgment here on the effectiveness of philosemitic elements, only on their existence. Third, I am aware that the literary construction of a "semitic essence" may be considered inherently antisemitic. Recent scholarship indicates that various authors assumed a "semitism" notwithstanding widely divergent views as to what "semitism" entailed, overemphasis on the topic being the sole constant in this discourse.[6] Literary philosemitism is both place-specific and time-specific. Religious conversion, the balancing of tradition and reform, and the endless debate between Hebraism and Hellenism loomed large in British representations of the Jew but played only a minor role in German fiction. Political emancipation, economic embourgeoisement, and intellectual *Bildung* served as critical themes for the contemporaries of Lessing and Dohm. By the end of the nineteenth century, pro-Jewish German authors explored other matters.[7]

What themes drew the attention of sympathetic authors in Imperial and Weimar Germany? What issues touching Jews and Jewishness did they write about? Three themes emerged persistently in my reading: the definition of homeland (*Heimat*), the nexus of love and death, and the relationship of power and powerlessness in German-Jewish interaction. My chosen themes are tentative and subjective—other readers could conceivably identify other themes of greater centrality. Nevertheless, I think the historical context makes the prominence of these three themes more than arbitrary and less than surprising.

Although the German Reich granted formal recognition to Jews as citizens entitled to equal rights under the law, a mere legal pronouncement did not make the Jews into Germans. As Peter Pulzer nicely comments, most Germans did not share this ultimately French understanding of belonging. Germans defined their *Volk* more by blood ties, kinship, and a near-mystical connection with a particular place than by formal decrees.[8] As Celia Applegate has demonstrated, *Heimat* provided a crucial component of German identity.[9] Applegate notes the degree to which a conscious sense of *Heimat* was cultivated as a result of the national unification of 1870. The more the Bismarckian settlement forced Prussian leadership into every area of life, the more necessary was a sense of local belonging as a means of validating the heterogeneity of actual Germans. When Germans reflected on the feeling of belonging, their thoughts turned often to the romanticized notion of *Heimat*. Christian authors who championed German Jews as an integral part of Germany naturally turned to the concept of *Heimat* for support, but the tension between formal equality and the informal quality of "belonging" posed a problem for Gentile authors sympathetic to the Jewish condition.

The connection between love and death has been a perennial theme in Western literature, but in these philosemitic novels this connection is obsessively linked to Jewish endogamy versus Jewish exogamy. Jewish-Christian intermarriage became a legal possibility in 1875, and by World War I as many as ten thousand Germans lived in a mixed marriage. This reality provided cannon fodder for the Judenfresser (Jew haters; literally, Jew eaters), who alternated between disparaging Jewish incest and warning against Jewish-Aryan racial pollution. Jewish periodicals fudged on this issue. As members of a small minority, Jewish authors recognized endogamy as a critical tool for group survival. As newly enfranchised citizens, they realized intermarriage was a powerful proof (really and metaphorically) for ultimate compatibility with non-Jewish Germans.[10] Non-Jewish authors also grasped this nettle hesitantly, generally finding it easier to kill their protagonists than to marry them off successfully. Another maneuver that we will turn to presently in *Die Juden von Kronburg* was to imagine a successful Jewish-Christian relationship, find an improbable reason for its nonculmination, and then marry the hero off within his ethnic group. Jewish women, as Ruth Klüger pointed out, were a different matter and could join the majority culture through exogamy, though rarely without complications, principally, the complication of sexual power.[11]

Power, as even the most elementary student of Foucault knows, is fundamentally a relationship, never completed and always threatened by change.[12] Here again, while the detractors of Jewry always knew just how much Jewish power was acceptable (none), Jewry's proponents had a more difficult time imagining the proper power relationship between Jew and Christian, majority and minority. (Even that early champion of Jewish *Verbesserung*, Christian Wilhelm Dohm, explicitly rejected the idea of Jews occupying important civil service or judicial positions.) However insignificant in the grand scheme of things, Jews wielded more power in Imperial and Weimar Germany than they had at the beginning of the era of emancipation. The writers considered below found Jewish economic power easier to imagine than political power, and sexual power was nearly inconceivable, at least for Jewish males. Although these works kept admirably clear of the paranoia so typical of antisemitic representations, the initial success of the Jewish characters, especially when they enter the public domain, inevitably led to disaster.

The following three pairs of authors demonstrate an increasingly problematic treatment of the three themes explained above.[13]

Heinrich Siemer	Novel, contemporary setting	several positive Jewish types	very well-versed in Jewish matters explicit, apologetic
Emil Felden	Novel, contemporary setting	several positive Jewish types	very well-versed in Jewish matters; explicit, apologetic
Ernst Pueschel	Novel, past & contemporary setting	Jewish tragic hero	familiar with Jewish matters; apologetic
Alfred Knobloch	Novel, past & contemporary setting	Jewish tragic hero	familiar with Jewish matters; apologetic

Wilhelm von Scholz	Play, medieval setting	*völkisch* Jewish hero-apostate killed	not well-versed in Jewish matters; highly ambivalent
Herman Jaques	Novel, contemporary setting	*völkisch* Jewish "hero" stymied	not well-versed in Jewish matters; highly ambivalent

Heinrich Johann Siemer (1886–1936), author of *Judah und die Andern* (Judah and the others) was a prominent labor leader, an SPD activist, and a prolific author who won Max Brod's plaudits for his reflections on his five-year stint in a monastery.[14] Siemer's *Judah und die Andern* offers a coming-of-age novel about four lads before, during, and after World War I. The opening begins by contrasting the earliest days of Hansgeorg Weete, the blond, handsome, earth-bound child of the German border (*Wesermarch*), with Samuel Goldstein, the brilliant but troubled scion of Eastern European Jews who moved to Oldenburg from the Jewish ghetto of London's East End. While Hansgeorg's mother sings him a lullaby, "In allen Idiomen der deutschen Heimat" (In every idiom of the German homeland), Samuel's mother's tune (in Yiddishized German) extols the virtue of Torah study and implores him to remain "un ehlicher Jued / Wet er af tomid verbleiben" [a true Jew / Which he should always remain]. In case we do not grasp this contrast, Siemer informs us, "So early began the division between Hansgeorg Weete and Samuel Goldstein."[15] By the end of the book, Weete has become a right-wing fanatic, and Goldstein, a socialist agitator, has been murdered by the comrades of his childhood friend.

Weete, initially bound to the *Heimat* more completely than the others, loses his way through the insidious Dr. Zett, an antisemitic agitator, and through his infatuation with Hilde Hoyer, a medical student. In his extremely misogynistic portrait of Hoyer, Siemer inverts the *schöne* Jüdin (seductive Jewess) topos, which combined sexuality and danger in the person of the seductive Jewish woman. When Hansgeorg refuses to heed his sister's plea to return home to attend to his dying father and gets involved with a "big-city girl," it symbolizes Hansgeorg's detachment from the life-giving *Heimat*. In the course of tormenting the sexually inexperienced Hansgeorg, Hoyer alludes to this inversion directly: "'Hansgeorg, were Jews among your lovers?' 'You must never, never kiss a Jewish girl!' she said. 'Oh, have you indeed done so? Have you smelled them? Come, kiss me! I smell like ripe peaches.'"[16] Hansgeorg, with the half-awareness of a young man heading toward disaster, falls for both Dr. Zett (who gives Siemer a chance to parody antisemitic tirades) and Hoyer. The themes of *Heimat*, love and death, and power come together when Hansgeorg and Hoyer culminate their relationship. Reminding Hansgeorg of a time when he killed a snake in his native forests, Hoyer implores him to kill again.

This time, in Berlin, not Oldenburg, he kills a man, not a snake; rather than evidencing his manly prowess as a hunter, it represents his total manipulation and leads to his subsequent suicide.[17]

Goldstein, the dominant figure in the novel, embodies many stereotypical Jewish features. His thought and speech are punctuated by endless questions, his great but overly rationalistic intellect is noted at every turn, his deep sense of non-belonging and quest for significance torment him until his socialist epiphany. The omniscient narrator has Goldstein ponder his friends' banter: he is less open and less forthright, a perfect exemplar of the "restless Jewish intellect." Goldstein can be an exasperating figure—his friendship with the others stretches the bounds of plausibility—but ultimately a sympathetic one. Rejecting the parochial Jewish loyalties of his uncle and aunt (Goldstein's parents die in the opening pages of the novel), he looks for a mission among humanity that will be more than a merely Jewish, Maccabean act.[18] Goldstein embodies what the Jewish Marxist Isaac Deutscher once called "the non-Jewish Jew," the Jew whose own background propels him beyond the pale of Jewish life in search of universal truths. On the eve of being executed, Goldstein tells his would-be murderers that he is an internationalist and a revolutionary though neither a Bolshevik nor an anti-German.[19] Goldstein dies bravely as an idealist, a public leader, a father, and a husband. Goldstein finds his *Heimat* in the masses, love with a fellow Jew and revolutionary (Baila Rosenbluth), and power as a leading figure in the workers movement. In an allusion to the murder of Walther Rathenau, Siemer rejects political violence, but one can hardly overlook the subtext warning against the acquisition of Jewish authority. Goldstein's martyrdom arrives as a natural resolution of his elevated status.

The second pair in Siemer's novel, Gerd Jürgens and Benno Kahn, represent the opposite of fanaticism. Gerd is described, too often, as beyond all particular regions and religions.[20] Friendly and open-minded, he seems to be a stand-in for the author's own views.[21] Siemer did some extensive digging into Jewish life and Judaic teachings. Several places in the novel offer long explanations of contemporary Jewish realities or Jewish texts. These digressions add about one hundred pages to the novel and indicate Siemer's didactic intent.[22] In a typical philosemitic speech Gerd tells Benno that the key is justice—one does not need to overlook the faults of individual Jews. In a case of fact and fiction meeting, Benno warns his friend, " 'Gerd, they will call you Jew-lover, an advocate for the Israelites.' "[23] Gerd experiences no real character development or sudden enlightenment; he simply accepts that Germans should be judged on their deeds rather than their background. Goldstein's highly dramatic figure dominates the novel, but Gerd's quiet friendship stands at the center: he is the character around whom the others revolve.

Benno, the son of South German farmers who had tilled the soil for ages, offers the diametric opposite of Samuel Goldstein: "In Benno Kahn remained hardly a

THE PROBLEMATICS OF PHILOSEMITIC FICTION

ghetto memory, the holy and healthy power of the earth had almost entirely effaced it."[24] Benno's first love is machinery. Serving with distinction as a fighter pilot in the war, Benno becomes an upstanding member of the Jewish community, marries Goldstein's sister, a stereotypically Jewish beauty with dark skin and big eyes, and tries, with Gerd's help, to keep their childhood chums from inevitable disaster. In Benno's case, *Heimat* and sexuality do not pose problems for Siemer, but the issue of power does. Siemer gives his character a distinguished war record and describes him as a brave fighter, but Benno acts like a Jewish "Uncle Tom," either laughing off or half-agreeing with antisemitic characterizations of Jewish qualities. Having created a Jewish hero, Siemer does not quite know what to do with him. Tellingly, Benno engages in two episodes of violence, both aimed at fellow Jews, first with a Russian Jewish soldier whom he kills in the war and second with a German Jew who sympathizes with the British cause whom Benno pummels. Giving Jews power (at least in a male and German context) means giving them the potential for violence; this was a difficult nut for even the most philosemitic author to crack safely. Siemer did it by displacing this violence onto other Jews.

Emil Jakob Felden (1871–1959), born in Metz, was an Alsatian patriot and champion of German culture. Felden studied theology, philosophy, and economy at Strasbourg University. An ordained Evangelical minister who was also active in the Socialist Party, Felden authored a slew of books. Leaving Alsace in the wake of the Versailles Treaty, he continued his political and pastoral activities in Bremen. Active in the Verein zur Abwehr des Antisemitismus, Felden survived the Nazis.[25] His *Die Sünde wider das Volk* (The sins against the people) rather obviously borrows its title from Arthur Dinter, but, unlike Hans Reimann's pseudonymous parody, *Die Dinte wider das Blut* (The sins against the blood, 1922), Felden earnestly, even didactically, attacks antisemitism as the national disease. These biographical details are relevant to Felden's novel, because after the Franco-Prussian War Alsatians were treated like outsiders by Prussian officials. Felden thus identifies Jews and Alsatians as two kinds of unjustly suspected Germans. Consistent with those (see below on Pueschel and Knobloch) who regard antisemitism as an imposed and false phenomenon, Felden portrays Jewish-Christian relations in Alsace before the advent of Adolf Stoecker's Berlin-based antisemitism as idyllic, a fact that is hard to square with historical reality.[26]

The development of Friedrich Becker, a working-class Alsatian who becomes a professor of semitics and defender of Jews and Judaism, occupies the best part of the novel. The text itself and the thirty-two tightly spaced pages of endnotes offer ample evidence of Felden's scholarly immersion in Jewish matters; making Friedrich a professor of semitics gave Felden a natural vehicle for conveying much of that knowledge to the reader. At every juncture, Felden lectures us through the

49

person of the likable and winning Friedrich about the teachings of Judaism and the absolute compatibility of those teachings with the modern demands made upon Jews to be good citizens and good neighbors.[27] In the course of Friedrich's budding friendship with Jakob Loeb, he discovers a range of Jewish virtues: Jews work hard in every area of life. Jews are very generous with their friends and coreligionists. They are very grateful for good deeds—Friedrich and his whole family benefit many times over from his schoolyard defense of Jakob. Jews have practical solutions to life's problems. When Friedrich's father dies, the Jew Loeb proposes that Friedrich's widowed mother earn a living as a greengrocer.[28]

Friedrich enjoys close social relations with all the Jewish characters, not an exceptional one or two, in the book and falls in love twice with Jewish women. The first, Miriam, becomes a lifelong friend; the second, Elfriede, becomes his wife. A few mildly flawed Jewish characters are thrown in for verisimilitude, but Felden clearly wants the reader to accept the Other and accept him or her without reduction to a single stereotype. The erotic attraction to Miriam, Jakob's sister, contributes to Friedrich's increasing identification with the Loebs: "Jakob's sister [Miriam] had developed from a young girl into a young woman, with dark eyes like glowing coals and blue black shimmering hair that enwrapped her oval face with finely cut features like a crown."[29] Friedrich would marry Miriam without either of them having to change religions, but Miriam thinks it will cause her father hurt, and neither of the young pair wants to do that. This sort of treatment of a rejected intermarriage—absolutely feasible yet honorably rejected—was standard fare for Jewish periodicals such as the *Allgemeine Zeitung des Judentums* and the *Israelitische Wochenschrift.*[30] The second, consummated relationship with a Jewess, therefore, comes as a bit of a surprise. Loeb arranges for Friedrich to meet Prof. Ferdinand and Frau Professor Lewandowski of the University of Strasbourg. Professor Lewandowski's children, Elfriede and little Gustav, offer Felden a second chance to show a Jewish family, this time *gebildete* (educated, cultivated, and acculturated) but otherwise possessing the same virtues as the Loebs. Gustav becomes Friedrich's very willing Hebrew pupil and his admirer; Friedrich sees in Gustav the little Jakob whom he lost to influenza and antisemitism long ago. Elfriede, a bloodless character compared to Miriam, wins Friedrich's heart when Dr. Hans von Artenburg, who terminates their engagement because of racial differences, breaks hers.[31] Interestingly, Friedrich marries the weaker and less "Jewish" of the two women, judging by name and by appearance. Perhaps Felden, consciously or unconsciously, wished to avoid stretching his reader's credulity or evoking the destructive *schöne* Jüdin topos.

Little needs to be said about the novel's villain, Adolf Finster, son of a Prussian official and a prototypical antisemite. Finster is wholly ignorant of Jews and Judaism, and his hatred stems from his father's xenophobia and his jealousy of the hero's academic and romantic success. On hearing of Friedrich's engagement to Elfriede, he reacts angrily, terming Friedrich judaized (*verjudet*) and attributing his success to the influence of the Jews.[32] Finster, like Ernst Pueschel's Martin Otto Kraft (below), seems completely asexual or latently homosexual, since both men's cliques appear as exclusively male. Felden resolves the issue of *Heimat* easily: Alsatians and Jews belong to the German people. The true outsiders are the intolerant North Germans who have no appreciation for the Alsatian brand of Deutschtum and contribute nothing but malice to the public arena.[33]

The closing section of the novel takes place after World War I, revolution, and the return of Alsace to the French. Friedrich and his family leave his birthplace rather than live under French rule. Prof. Friedrich Becker returns to a Germany infected by antisemitism. Disempowered by the armies of the entente, Finster and his cronies press their attack on German Jewry, continuing an assault begun against Jakob Loeb, Friedrich's weak and defenseless childhood friend. In a veritable page out of Ruth Klüger's essay "Die Leiche unterm Tisch" (The corpse under the table), Jakob Loeb's curious schoolmates file by the bier to see the dead Jew-boy laid out. Jewish figures such as Papa Loeb and Professor Lewandowski are wholly benign but powerless in the face of external events. Miriam is a strong character but is isolated by the end of the novel by her spinsterhood and the death of her family and best friend.

Despite the pleas of both the women who love him, Friedrich enters the political fray. The climactic scene pits Friedrich against Finster at a public meeting, where Friederich is bludgeoned by an antisemitic hoodlum and then nobly dies as Miriam and Elfriede minister to him during his last moments, patently recalling the two Marys of the crucifixion. Intellectually and socially, Felden's Friedrich offers us a remarkable fictional reconstruction of how a Christian becomes a defender and friend of German Jewry. If we judge Felden as an Evangelical minister, we are struck by how he emphasizes the role of Judaism in creating upstanding and moral characters without supersessionist condescension. If we judge him as a member of the political Left, we note that hard work, reliability, and responsibility are the defining characteristics of Jews as citizens. A more pro-Jewish novel one could hardly hope to find. Regrettably, what makes the philosemitic Friedrich's identification with Jewry complete is all too clear: he joins Siemer's Moritz Goldstein, Ernst Pueschel's Siegfried Meyer, and Wilhelm von Scholz's Nasson as martyrs to the spirit of intolerance.

The tantalizingly brief entry in the *Deutsche biographische Index* informs us that Benjamin Corda (1859–1916), an *Oberbürgermeister* in East Prussia, used the pseudonym Alfred Knobloch for his literary endeavors. Knobloch's *Gläserne Wände* (Glass walls, 1914) relates the rise and fall of Michael Eli Lesser, the only child of poor but upright village Jews from Zagora, located somewhere in East Prussia, presumably Posen Province.[34] The Lessers, Ruben Eli and Rahel, married for love but otherwise comport with the positive stereotypes of small-town Jewry. Rahel is industrious, competent, and clever. Ruben, though without any driving ambition, has a head for business. His greatest pride, however, is his family, his Jewish-looking wife and his tall, handsome son, who enjoys success, both social and academic, in school from the start. The town of Zagora (eighteen hundred inhabitants) is without significant social tensions despite its being divided between German, Poles, and Jews.[35] Zagora's business world in the 1860s, the decade of the protagonist's birth and childhood, is oriented westward toward Leipzig. Ruben Eli is a moderately successful porter who depends on the Leipzig fair (*Messe*) for his income. All this is threatened by a plan to build a railroad line through Zagora. The sixteen-year-old Michael Eli, realizing the implications for his family's livelihood, determines to make money—lots of it. This is the real beginning of the novel, a rags-to-riches story of a Jew's commercial success and human alienation comparable to Abraham Cahan's *The Rise of David Levinsky* and Mordechai Richler's *The Apprenticeship of Duddy Kravitz*.[36]

Financial success forms the main story of Michael Eli's life, but his German patriotism provides an important leitmotiv. The eighteen-year-old, above whose writing table loom pictures of both Bismarck and Moltke, receives the crushing blow that he is too near-sighted to serve in the military. He responds by writing the kaiser a personal appeal to serve. Successfully inducted into the Prussian army, Michael Eli meets a distant relative, Major Pfeiffer, an oddity in an antisemitic officer corps:

> *Major Pfeiffer was the pride of the family and even, in a certain sense, of the Jews in the entire city. He wasn't baptized, he made it as a Jew to major in a distinguished regiment in which Leeser served, he was called up eight weeks every year, commanded a front-line battalion, ate in the officers' mess [Kasino], and was loved and respected by the officer corps. He bore an Iron Cross first and second class from the French war. . . . [H]e was a natural leader of men. . . . [H]e rode horses perfectly. He had much semitism in his expressive and clever traits such that the ancient race was recognizable. But he carried himself in such a military manner; he lived only in the army and probably knew . . . the army manual almost by heart.*[37]

Major Pfeiffer gives Knobloch an opportunity to discuss antisemitism in the German army, and he has Pfeiffer tell Michael Eli that in 1880 the army is no career for a Jew. Having no children himself, Pfeiffer leaves his young relative the sub-

THE PROBLEMATICS OF PHILOSEMITIC FICTION

stantial fortune of three hundred thousand marks. On the disbursement of this endowment, Knobloch tells his readers about the excellent customs "bei Juden" to endow local charities. For the remainder, "Pfeiffer had left his money for [Michael's] business, not for his enjoyment."[38]

Michael Eli's childhood love, the Christian daughter of the local pharmacist, became a nun.[39] Since he cannot marry for love, as did his parents, Michael Eli decides to marry for money. Since Michael Eli cannot acquire honor through an army career, as did Pfeiffer, he pursues wealth. Michael Eli concludes a successful marriage with Sidonie Silberstein, a town beauty with a handsome dowry. Michael attends to his construction business, Sidonie to running the household and raising two children, Wilhelm and Susannah. Within a few years, Michael achieves financial success and general approbation.[40] He remains the hard-working boy from Zagora: "His table remained the same as in Zagora, a simple old-Jewish kitchen, not kosher (his father already had not kept kosher because of his occupation) but entirely simple. Although he was a healthy eater, he needed and wanted only one special course, rare fruit. That was all. If he scored some success, he would have a glass of light beer first. Wine did not grace his table. A good cigar was his only luxury."[41]

Lesser's friendship with the mayor becomes a partnership of long duration. The mayor, presumably a stand-in character for the author, gives some impassioned speeches for the need for German unity. There is no Polish question, he tells an admiring Lesser, but, rather, a German question.[42] Their friendship also serves as a vehicle for Lesser to explain why Jews go into business so often: no other avenue of employment was open to them. "'Look where you will, in the government, in the railroads, in the courts, in the officer corps, even in parliament, nowhere will you find Jews. Pure Christians. Here and there a so-called Jew who has become a Christian.'"[43] The mayor accepts Lesser as a man of quality without qualifications, noting that the luxury of antisemitism could not be maintained at any rate in the eastern parts of the empire, although many Christians, openly or secretly, are antisemites. When Lesser points to the success of Pfeiffer, the mayor repeats what Pfeiffer told Lesser years before, that his career could not be duplicated in the current atmosphere.

Gradually, Lesser returns to his Jewish roots. As a self-made man he did not have time to visit synagogue often and like his father was forced by business to replace the Sabbath with Sunday for a day of rest. He did not incline to deep piety but respected the traditions of the past: "Now he felt the synagogue a source of Jewish strength, from primeval times forward. . . . What one named European culture [*Abendland*] was a branch from the tree of Israel."[44] While Lesser turns back to tradition, his son, Wilhelm, moves away from it, informing his father that he will not enter the family business but prefers to study law. (We may question whether a Jewish father would be disappointed at having a lawyer for a son.)[45] Their conflict accelerates, and by the end of the book the estrangement between father and son is total. Wilhelm greets his father with a scantily clad blond whom he introduces lasciviously as "my friend."[46] Lesser, shocked, realizes that his relationship with Wilhelm is over. Daughter Susannah deals Lesser his deathblow when she falls in love with one of Wilhelm's friends, refuses to consider a Jewish mate, and elopes to be married in a country church.[47] Lesser pursues the couple, intending to break up the ceremony. But he gets lost, wanders in the cold wet weather, and contracts a fatal illness. As he approaches death, bereft of friends and family, his last bequests are to a Jewish community with which he has had but a formal relationship: "For his gravestone he ordered a simple stone, as was common in earlier times, no costly monument. His entire name, Michael Eli Lesser, with birth and death dates appeared on the obverse. On the converse, however, stood the words: 'I was a German and I became a Jew.' A few weeks later he died."[48]

The epitaph and the title of the novel remain ambiguous. Do the glass walls separate Jew from German, rendering a complete synthesis impossible? Perhaps, but Knobloch presents Lesser as a good German and seems to approve of his reacquiring Jewish loyalties. Even at his most assimilated, any Jew who paid his communal taxes and brought respect upon the community by his success and probity would hardly have been considered as marginal as Knobloch imagines. But if Lesser remained a good Jew and a good German, what went wrong? Perhaps nothing more than the inevitability of dynastic decline, a theme in any era and one in which the bourgeois era excelled (see, for example, Thomas Mann's *Buddenbrooks*). Perhaps the "Jewishness" is extrinsic here, a shorthand for the original bourgeois virtues that the founding dynast possesses and his epigones do not? But I suspect Knobloch intended to say something particular to the Jewish situation, namely, that the flight from Jewishness or, at any rate, the distancing of the Jew from his ancestral traditions leads to disaster. If I am correct, the glass walls separate the alienated Jew from the grounded Jew—Michael Eli Lesser from Ruben Eli Lesser. But if so, why such an unhappy ending?

Ernst Pueschel (1881–1941) authored over thirty books, including the very successful *Die neue Heimat* (The new homeland, 1924).[49] Pueschel's *Die Juden von Kronburg* (The Jews of Kronburg) relates the rise of antisemitism at the end of the nineteenth century and beginning of the twentieth century and its tragic results in a previously peaceful town some fifty kilometers from Berlin.[50] Pueschel painted pre-antisemitic Kronburg as an ideal example of the German homeland (*Heimat*), where Jews and Christians lived without any friction whatsoever. When childhood friends Siegfried Meyer (Jewish) and Gottfried Menzel (Christian) hear antisemitic agitation for the first time they are astonished, having been brought up without class or racial antipathies and accustomed to respect each person according to his convictions.[51]

Pueschel pushes this theme: Jewish *and* Christian merchants who practiced their businesses too sharply were made unwelcome, and no difference whatsoever in lifestyles between Jews and non-Jews can be discerned anywhere in the novel. Pueschel underscores the improbability of a local drama: "One would relate ever so little about Kronburg as about many other similar or equally large cities in Germany if fanatical antisemitism, if fraternal hatred [*Brüderhass*] had not planted its flag within Kronburg's walls!"[52]

One man, the Berlin born and bred Martin Otto Kraft, a preacher under the spell of Adolf Stoecker, bears responsibility for turning utopia into hell. Named after the spiritual father of Germany (Martin Luther) and the father of German political unity (Otto von Bismarck), Kraft represents the reversal of their monumental efforts.[53] In an early interchange between Kraft and the Christian hero, Oberpfarrer Menzel, Pueschel notes the various (usual) antisemitic themes that Kraft employs to win over the mob, including the Jews' domination of the press, their presence in revolutionary movements, and their disproportionate concentration in free professions. This interchange, of course, allows Pueschel to present explanations of the Jews' special role in the German economy.[54] All in all, Pueschel fails to presents a very convincing picture of how antisemitism first took hold in the 1880s and 1890s. Why Kraft's rhetoric initially appealed to Kronburgers makes little sense in the context of the novel, since Pueschel neglects to link antisemitism to any of the deeper unsettling currents within German life (modernization of the economy, technology, economic fluctuations, reactionary modernism, *völkisch* nationalism, and the like). Jewish behavior during World War I was exemplary, with Jews fighting and sacrificing on a par with non-Jews. Pueschel's read on postwar antisemitism seems more compelling: "Then came the breakdown, then came the revolution! The Jewish question returned. A sinner for the monstrous misery of the German people must be found! The Kapp Putsch worsened the suffering. The Jewish question rose, rose ominously. Healthy human understanding was gagged: In [Kaiser] Wilhelm the Second's veins—so one said—Jewish blood flowed, otherwise he wouldn't have brought such misfortune to Germany! The people had learned nothing from the war; the ancient German tragedy of fraternal hatred took command."[55]

Antisemitism, as it appears in Kronburg, is an aberration that succeeds only by the initiative of Kraft, whose name ("power" in English) captures his goal and the amoral battery of techniques he uses to attain it. Beyond the rambling about a de-Judaized Germany, Pueschel denies Kraft any positive program. His cultish male henchman presents a sharp contrast to the two balanced, bourgeois, intimate families in the novel, the Menzels and the Meyers. Pueschel intentionally makes the philosemitic camp the inheritor of the bourgeois traditions that he obviously champions, yet he seems uncertain about what his "good" characters should do about antisemitism other than bemoan it. The Jews of Kronburg move bravely but reluctantly to their own defense, assuming that their virtues are self-evident. One character exclaims, "'I reject the word "defense." We do not need to defend ourselves, certainly not here in Kronburg! Our life and deeds suffice to prove that the antisemites have made false claims!' "[56]

The brunt of anti-antisemitic activism in Kronburg centers on Oberpfarrer Menzel and his like-minded family and friends. The antithesis of his fellow churchman, Kraft, Menzel represents the older traditions of Kronburg, religious tolerance, brotherhood, and love. Menzel opposes the emergence of the German Christians (Deutsch Christen) led by Kraft and the spineless Archdeacon Bange. Pueschel's portrait of Menzel draws on a venerated literary tradition—the cleric who serves as a mouthpiece of humanity rather than as a mouthpiece of Christian dogma.[57]

The theme of love and death surfaces in the courtship of Siegfried Meyer and Elizabeth Menzel, the pastor's daughter. Elizabeth becomes the focus of a romantic competition between Meyer and the ironically named Treuenfeld, who later joins the antisemitic agitators. Siegfried Meyer, ostensibly one of the novel's heroes, is a one-dimensional character, as are the remainder of Pueschel's Jews. Siegfried's speech to Elizabeth rejecting conversion to Christianity could easily have been cribbed from any number of antiapostasy polemics by Jewish authors: "'Were I to become a Christian one would object that I was a hypocrite. I could not even respect myself. Denial of my religion is denial of myself, of my people, it is a sign of despicable cowardice! I am a German, and an outstanding German virtue is faithfulness. I will not break faith against myself and against my people. It would be un-German!' "[58] Equally one-dimensional and admirable is the Jewish doctor, the black-bearded and bespectacled Levysohn.[59] Frau Meyer, Siegfried's mother, offers the completely predictable stereotype of the doting Jewish mother. The rabbi, a somber figure, goes about bemoaning the dangerous turn taken by Kronburg's increasingly antisemitic populace. Elizabeth comes closest in this novel to showing signs of character development. Initially, she refuses to see why Siegfried cannot be baptized a Christian in order to enable their marriage. Elizabeth confesses that having been brought up Evangelical, she regards Protestantism on a higher step than Judaism and sees no reason why she should move backward. The barriers that specific religions place against intermarriage seem to her foolish considering that they are in all essentials equal.[60] Having come to agree with Siegfried that apostasy would be cowardly and with the rabbi that a *Confessionslos* existence for people who believed in God was empty, Elizabeth decides to convert to Judaism. She determines to become a Jew and help her husband struggle against intolerance.[61] Elizabeth's decision takes place on page 223; by page 240 Siegfried has been stoned to death by a Christian mob. At the Menzel family doorway, Elizabeth stands over Siegfried's body screaming and is abused by the crowd as a Judenschickse (Jew lover). Siegfried posthumously finds "acceptance" in a Christian shelter: "Siegfried

Meyer was carried into the Pfarrer's house. Dr. Levysohn could only certify the death of the young man."[62]

Despite the eulogies delivered by Menzel, the rabbi, and Siegfried's regimental commander, the novel ends on an unconvincing note. The reader does not really feel that Siegfried's death has served as the cathartic release of anti-Jewish animus or that the Kronburgers will heed Menzel's words to make Siegfried a cause to rally around. Elizabeth, transformed into the "Jew's bride," is an object of local curiosity. Siegfried's former commander delivers the novel's closing speech, a eulogy:

> *Comrade Meyer, your old commander and comrades in war want to say farewell. I do not need to praise you; your deeds testify to your worth. You were a German in your heart and in your actions. You stood in the front lines in highest danger for our Germany when others folded—your Germanness we now praise! You have proven that also in German Jewry live a love of the fatherland and a willingness to sacrifice. These deeds, which you have sown, must bear fruit! Live well, you German hero, and greet your comrades above by the Great King. . . . We say: There still live people who know what heroism is, who work for unity.*[63]

Siemer and Felden succeeded in creating informed, passionate philosemitic novels. The novels of Knobloch and Pueschel rendered a sympathetic, if ambivalent, picture. The two works considered below straddle the borderline of philo- and antisemitism. Wilhelm von Scholz (1874–1969), whose breakthrough work was *Der Jude von Konstanz* (1903), became a leading member of the Prussian Academy of Arts and a supporter of the Nazis. Scholz later repented, though he never regained the popularity he had enjoyed in the 1920s and 1930s. He set his five-act play in fourteenth-century Switzerland. Death surrounds the title character and tragic hero of *Der Jude von Konstanz*. Nasson, an apostate physician in the century of the Black Death, cannot heal himself, his community of birth, or his community of faith. Corpses populate the beginning and end of the play. Violence and death triumph over Nasson's patently eighteenth-century Enlightenment perspective on life. The Jews defame Nasson as an apostate to Christianity; the Christians persecute him as a closet Jew. Azarijah, a Jew, pays no attention to Nasson's repeated plaints regarding the common humanity of Jew and Christian.[64] Azarijah considers such sentiments childish, as he does Nasson's view of human progress. The blood-and-death motif reaches a climax with Simlai's call for an armed insurrection against Christians: "'Jehovah's enemies must bleed!'"[65] Scholz presents Christian intolerance as equally objectionable. Overhearing Azarijah's berating of Nasson, Cyprianus complains that the Jews are the lords, the Christians are the slaves, that Jews enjoy their bread from the sweat of Christian brows, that Jews price everything too high for the Christian inhabitants of the city. As the insurrectionary Jews are brought in chains before the bishop and the *Burgermeisters*, Nasson, who tried to warn the Jews to flee, falls under suspicion. Azarijah delivers the coup de grâce, denouncing Nasson as a "seeming Christian" (Scheinchrist). Nasson refuses to deny Azarijah's charge and, despite the cajoling of the bishop, chooses death at the hands of the Inquisition.

Given this play's opaque hostility toward Jews, I would not consider this a "pro-Jewish" work were it not for the fact that Nasson is the hero of the piece—though that heroism involves a rejection of normative Judaism. The good Jews in this play are either apostate Jews or Jews without any power—Jewish women. Nasson's conversion certainly seems more germane to nineteenth-century than fourteenth-century conditions. Nasson makes pragmatic considerations the keystone of his argument, proclaiming, "'I must work . . . Jewishness bars my way,'" as if there were no Jewish doctors in the medieval world.[66] In a speech to Azarijah, Nasson insists that he never felt himself to be a wanderer or part of the Jewish community. Azarijah warns Nasson that denial of the Jews would be part of the price Nasson would have to pay to become a Christian and that complete acceptance would always elude him.[67] This caveat certainly reflects a nineteenth-century concern—quite a few Jews refused to have themselves baptized on exactly the grounds that it was cowardly to abandon a defamed community. Supporting Nasson's religious conversion with the theme of *Heimat*, Scholz has Nasson declare, "'Homeland signifies a wife, a house, a circle in which I can work.'"[68] Despite his ability to feel as they do about Constance, Christians regard Nasson as an outsider:

> CRISPIN: "You said: Here will be my homeland."
> NASSON: "Yes, my homeland, I thought."
> CRISPIN: "Your homeland is indispensable like light is indispensable for the blind, about which he cannot dream. You don't recognize homeland, you'll never feel it. Homeland is—I cannot tell you—it is like love, a quiet peace."
> NASSON: "Seek not! Seek not! Homeland is the ability to die, to sink into familiar soil."
> CRISPIN: "That's it! Who has homeland dies easily."[69]

Love and death figure prominently in *Der Jude von Konstanz*. Nasson did not convert in order to win himself a Christian girl—his beloved is the Jewess Bellet, who implores him to reconvert so that they can marry. In the end, she converts in order to marry Nasson. Racial and religious endogamy, therefore, are preserved, appropriately, by the Jews. The sexual threat in this play does not come from Nasson, it comes from impudent Christians who threaten the honor of Jewish girls.[70] The murder and revenge of Blarer, a young patrician and womanizer, propel the plot forward to a violent confrontation between Jews and Christians.[71] The theme of the Jewish femme fatale is hinted at here, but the dominant maneuver is the inversion of the antisemitic theme of the lecherous Jew who preys on Christian women. Blarer is the predator, and he pays for it with his life. But Nasson pays too, dearly. The bloodthirsty Simlai stabs Bellet before his own death sentence is carried out to ensure that she dies as a Jew. In short order, Nasson loses his love, his homeland, and his life.

Scholz displayed little real interest in medieval Jewish life. The names of his Jewish characters seem picked out of a hat, not at all the familiar names of medieval Ashkenazim.[72] Anna, Nasson's servant, counsels him to cut off all contact with Jews after his apostasy—as if a medieval Jew in Germany had any choice in the matter. Nasson's oath that the Christians are contemplating mayhem, sworn to the Jewish leaders of Konstanz in the name of "Adam, Henoch, Abraham, and Moses," legitimately mentions Gehinnom but otherwise contains a confused babble.[73] Nasson's interchange with Bellet when she agrees to convert lacks all probability; it sound like a cross between Mr. and Mrs. Spinoza contemplating a honeymoon and Rodgers and Hammerstein's *Oklahoma*: "'Bellet, I have you and hold you. We'll build us a homeland somewhere in a foreign land, we alone, you and I.'"[74] When speaking of *Heimat*, Scholz neglects the fact that many medieval Jews were comfortably well settled in their locales and were even local patriots and that many Jews were doctors, tradesmen, and agriculturists, animal husbandry being a particular specialty of German Jews. The solitary exception to this lack of knowledge is Scholz's citation (significantly, placed in the mouth of Bellet, a woman) to the famous midrash in which God reproaches the angels for celebrating while the Egyptians drown. Why this one snippet caught Scholz's attention cannot be determined—certainly *Der Jude von Konstanz* evidences no hint of the thorough encounter with Jewish sources found in Siemer, Felden, and, as we shall see, Thomas Mann.

The themes of love and death, homeland, and power merge at the end of the play. Imperial intervention spares the Jews, but to the crowd's displeasure. The bishop, who proclaims himself Nasson's physician (of the soul), continues the failed-physician motif: Nasson, refusing to declare himself either Jew or Christian, is condemned to the flames. *Der Jude von Konstanz* visualizes nothing but death and frustration for the relationship of German and Jew. Despite the nobility and best efforts of Nasson to remain faithful to both communities, he winds up cursing both and is cursed by both in return.[75]

Hermann Jaques's *Das Kreuz des Juden* (The cross of the Jews) contains numerous anti-Jewish stereotypes, fails to realistically consider Jewish existence, and is animated by a *völkisch* sensibility. The novel presents Jewish assimilation into German life as impossible and a bad bargain for Jews. Despite this, the Jewish hero, Moritz

Hardenstein, comes out as an honest, sincere fellow, while Sennitz, introduced sympathetically, betrays his university chum, sells his own sister's future short, and becomes an antisemitic hatemonger for the Agrarian League. *Das Kreuz des Juden*, a sort of *Family Carnovsky* without I. J. Singer's ability, relates the rise and fall of three generations in a Jewish family. The founder of this ill-starred dynasty came as a wandering Polish Jew, poor and *heimatlos*, in the early nineteenth century and settled on the outskirts of Berlin, as do many of the Jewish families in these philosemitic fictions. Jaques approvingly notes that despite being a pig farmer [*sic!*], the grandfather remained Orthodox. His son, Samuel Hardenstein, in a step as improbable as his father's occupation, marries the Christian daughter of a shopkeeper. Their marriage proved less than ideal, as his wife grew fat and ugly, but Samuel took great pride in having won a Gentile.[76] The Jews' sexual power is vitiated here by misogyny—Jaques presents the conquered Christian in as unflattering a light as possible. Samuel Hardenstein has great business sense (another stereotype) and, defying his father's dying instructions to take care of the land and the pigs (the *Heimat* theme redivivus), sells his property to a real estate developer for a phenomenal sum.

The conflict between the generations continues with Samuel's son, Moritz, who seeks social entry into the Junker aristocracy. Within a short period Moritz has become the prototypical self-hating Jew, informing the unimpressed Sennitz that he despises Jewish materialism and frivolity as much as any antisemite.[77] When Moritz returns from university he meets his father in the Tiergarten villa the latter has constructed in fashionable Berlin and is shocked by the transformation of Samuel into a man of the world: "[Samuel] sported a lightly graying beard, which, formerly looking like a primeval forest, was now cut in the Parisian manner of Henry IV; his hair was ordered, and instead of the mass of hair, the big clever eyes and the long fine nose now ruled his face. He thoroughly looked the part of the millionaire."[78]

The novel follows Moritz Hardenstein's stifled advancement: frustrated friendship, frustrated love, and the failure to win acceptance. Jaques treats all these issues with a heavy hand. Moritz's first love, Ella von Hernborg, the daughter of an army major who befriends Moritz, initially assures him that his ancestry does not matter, only his character. When Ella grows older her self-awareness of the comical contrast between the short, long-nosed, dark-skinned Moritz and her classically German beauty leads to his peremptory dismissal.[79] More sensitive to Moritz but equally immune to his advances is Hilda von Sennitz, the sister of Moritz's university friend. She represents the love of *Heimat* and the wholesome decency of German womanhood, totally at home in Gross-Sennitz—tall, blond, and borne aloft by grateful horses.[80] Hilda advises Moritz to enjoy his youth and find a wife, but

Moritz rejects the only viable romantic candidate, Ada Salanda, a wealthy, solitary heiress who lives near the Hardenstein estate in the Tiergarten.

The most interesting figure in the novel, Salanda represents the authentic Jew, grounded in her *Volk*, a Zionist enthusiast. Salanda agrees with the other characters in the novel that Moritz is Jewish despite his Christian mother and despite his baptism. Salanda's dark, exotic beauty recalls Sir Walter Scott's Rebecca, and Jaques portrays her as if he had just completed a seminar on Edward Said's *Orientalism*: "Blood hammered in his ears; the beauty of this woman robbed him; an aroma rose from her, possibly that of a French perfume or of her chestnut brown hair. It stopped his speech. She spoke, and the words rang soft and dreamy as distant rushing water of southern nights, and in her Oriental, blazing eyes glowed a strange light."[81]

Salanda is Orientalized and eroticized, but when she speaks a very unpleasant Jewish superiority complex shows itself in full bloom. She tells Moritz that the Jews waste their energy revolving in a foreign solar system when they have intellect and wealth, the two main factors of earthly power. Salanda contends that with organization and commitment the Jews will no longer be at the mercy of the nations and that the states will no longer dictate Jewish desires.[82] Jaques's ambivalence here could hardly be more complete. While clearly siding with Salanda that the Zionist option would be better for the self-hating Moritz, his vision of Zionism projects a threatening Jewish lust for power and domination. Jaques resolves this threat by making Salanda a solitary woman and by having Moritz reject her political plans and sexual overtures, reaffirming Jewish powerless and impotence (via infertility).

If the self-affirming Jew is hostile, the self-denying Jew is pathetic. Moritz buys a title (*Rittergut*) so that he can become a reserve officer. (On hearing the news, Salanda sends him a letter—with an exotic, Oriental aroma—with an imaginary bill telling him how much money his various attempts at assimilation have cost him.) Thinking that his title will endear him more to Sennitz, Moritz instead finds his friend growing continually colder. Traveling to Gross-Sennitz to reconcile, Moritz discovers a cynical letter from Sennitz telling Hilda that she should consider marrying Moritz in order to bolster the family fortunes. Betrayed by the Sennitz clan yet convinced that Zionism speaks in a hateful tone, Moritz Hardenstein takes his leave of Europe in a ship dedicated to scholarship, a bizarre cross between Darwin's *Voyage of the Beagle* and Theodor Herzl's *Altneuland*.

Johann Ferch's revealingly titled *Mensch, nicht Jude! Roman* (Man, not Jew! A novel) shows such an awkward blend of liberal and philosemitic impulses that I cannot resist a few comments. An Austrian, Ferch (1859–1947) authored *Konfessionen eines Freimaurer* (Confessions of a Freemason) and a series of less popular works. Ferch develops the intermarriage theme on a tack different from Felden, taking it as an ideal issue on which to hang a polemic against organized religion. Ferch imagines two fictional Freemasons (Rechberg, a Jew, and Klinger, a Christian) championing the love of Max Weinberg and Albina Strasser against the objections of their parents. This didactic novel, predictable from the first page, endlessly inveighs against religion as outmoded, externalized, formal, and ritualistic. (It should be noted that these are the traditional Christian complaints lodged against Judaism. The fuel of the Jewish polemic—that Christianity is irrational, pagan, and imperialistic—does not fire Ferch's imagination. His freethinking critique of religion thus owes far more to the Christian polemical tradition than he realizes.) Ferch lauds love as capable of uniting people above and beyond confession, though any sexual passion Max and Albina might have displayed is jettisoned in favor of their long-winded dialogues about the nature of Jewish-Christian relations. Ferch takes several opportunities to deny antisemitic claims, especially racialist ones.[83] He makes passing attempts at philosemitism by having the Christian Freemason Klinger praise the Jews: "'I not only defend you, I appreciate you highly.'" Klinger's voice rises warmly to the defense: "'Jews are more active than we are, their lives show more dramatic movement.'" This double-edged philosemitism recedes in the face of Ferch's interest in arguing that intolerance and fanaticism animate all confessions.[84] Whatever contact Ferch had with Jews, a possibility given his Masonic activism, his novel shows no evidence of interest in Jewish life, thought, or tradition.

Although the Christian Klinger (a clear stand-in for Ferch himself) gets the best lines, the Jew Rechberg embodies the ideal pronounced in the title: *Mensch, nicht Jude*. It seems indicative of the situation of would-be defenders of Jews that the imaginary title *Man, Not Christian* would certainly have sounded odd to the ears of the German reading public. It could be argued that Ferch's very title contains a dichotomy more naturally antisemitic than philosemitic; only Ferch's insistence that denominational differences do not really matter "saves" the book from this antisemitic potential, but with no room for any sort of diversity. *Mensch* may be rendered "human" or "man," and though Ferch clearly intends the former translation, the assimilationist challenge here seems to be issued at Jewish males. Rechberg avers that while he remains a Jew his children can depart the community without objection: "'All in all I am a man, nothing more.'"[85] Rechberg regards intermarriage as the proof that a new humanity is emerging and keeps an accurate count of every new occurrence.[86] Max Weinberg adds several similar speeches to the account, chastising his intolerant family and touting the benefits of intermarriage for both sides.[87] Ferch champions the breakdown of all difference; his vision of the future epitomizes what one scholar has called "brutally assimilationist."[88] In the perspective of contemporary multiculturalism this book would hardly qualify as philosemitic, but all is relative. With his two Jewish heroes (Weinberg and Rechberg), his anti-antisemitic diatribes, and his strident advocacy for assimilation through intermarriage, I have little doubt where Ferch's readers would place him in the debate over the Jewish question.

What can we conclude about this ambiguous evidence? Contrary to the common perception, Lessing's *Nathan* was not the last work by a non-Jewish author to attempt to portray Jews or Judaism sympathetically.[89] Although antisemitic hostility peeks through some of these efforts (for example, those of Scholz and Jaques), on the whole the authors considered here created admirable and occasionally believable protagonists. Contrary to the assumption that no Christian authors in Germany knew or cared to know about Jews and Judaism when they sat down to fictionalize them, I have presented at least two examples (Hans Siemer and Emil Felden) that confute this characterization. The novels of Siemer and Felden, both socialists, further suggest that if the official position of the Socialist Party on the Jewish question was limited to anti-antisemitism, some activists complemented that stance with active philosemitism. To a lesser degree, the same could be said for traditional liberals such as Knobloch. Contrary to the assumption that in the eyes of Christian fiction writers Jewish emancipation, embourgeoisement, and *Bildung* remained either objectionable or incomplete, the authors here resolved these issues only to open up more subtle problems in the Jewish-Christian encounter: belonging (*Heimat*), intimacy, and power. The unhappy endings of these literary efforts offer eloquent testimony that the goodwill of these authors outpaced their ability to imagine a successful resolution of the problematical German-Jewish encounter.[90]

The glamorizing of Jewish distinctiveness that took place in certain quarters of German Jewry in the Weimar period presumably had a limited appeal to these authors' target audience. While the Jewish protagonists discussed here were, on the whole, not plucked from Berlin's Scheunenviertel (a Jewish neighborhood or quarter where the least assimilated Jews lived), they offer a spectrum of commitment to the Jewish tradition. Liberal authors inclined toward an assimilationist solution to the Jewish question. But if this assimilationist solution appears brutal and ham-handed in the case of Ferch and Pueschel, then Knobloch, Felden, and Siemer champion a German-Jewish symbiosis as highly desirable. Fictional characters such as Benno Kahn, Michael Eli Lesser, and Moritz Goldstein who embodied the highest standards of Deutschtum and Judentum were significant literary creations, at least as realistic as George Eliot's *Daniel Deronda*. For scholars of German Judenbilder the image of Freytag's Veitel Itzigs casts an indelible shadow over our picture of the range of Jewish representation. How much of that evaluation has been filtered through the lens of subsequent disaster merits further investigation.[91]

4. Missionary Protestants and the Defense of Judaism

Thus far we have examined defenses generated from the German Left. We turn now to the religious Right, specifically, to Franz Delitzsch and Hermann Strack, who combined a missionary agenda with a determined defense of Judaism. Considering the notorious legacy Luther bequeathed German Protestantism on the Jewish question, this development may seem surprising. But it must be recalled that Luther's initial views on the Jews were quite sympathetic, that a wave of Christian Hebraism had stirred up great interest in the texts of Judaism, and that the hair-raising proposals contained in Luther's vicious *Über die Juden und ihre Lugen* (On the Jews and their lies, 1543) were ignored. The development of a Pietist strain of Protestantism, moreover, placed conversion of the Jews prominently on the agenda.[1] Nevertheless, Delitzsch and Strack present a problematic chapter in the history of both anti-antisemitism and Jewish-Christian relations in modern Germany. Studies that have examined the responses to antisemitism have generally neglected their efforts.[2] Studies of the relationship between Christianity and Judaism have focused largely on the emergence of anti-Judaic movements (such as those of Adolf Stoecker, Auguste Rohling, the German Christians) that prepared the way for the Shoah.[3] In either narrative, missionary Protestantism occupies at best a marginal position. Biographies of Delitzsch and Strack, on the other hand, have neither integrated their activities into the history of the responses to antisemitism nor acknowledged the anti-Jewish elements of their thought.[4]

This chapter places Delitzsch and Strack within the history of Jewish-Christian relations and anti-antisemitism in two steps. First, I evaluate their dual role as contributors to the world of Jewish scholarship and as Christian polemicists. Second, I assess the anti-antisemitic activities of Delitzsch and Strack within the context of the missionary movement in general. Throughout, I argue that despite a theological starting point inimical to Judaism, their Judaica scholarship, their contacts with Jewish scholars, and their opposition to prevailing trends in German Christianity consistently led them in pro-Jewish directions. The resulting tension between antisemitic and philosemitic tendencies led to a treatment of Judaism that was highly compartmentalized in a way that left both their philosemitism and their Christian triumphalism intact.[5]

Biographical sketches of Delitzsch and Strack shed some light on their unusual affinities to Judaism. Delitzsch came from a German Pietist background, the son of a Leipzig used goods dealer (Johann Gottfried) who died at age fifty-three and a mother (Johanna Rosina) with whom Delitzsch enjoyed a very close relationship. Delitzsch's background would have been a poor predictor of his career path, as he was neither middle class nor the son of a minister. His affinity for Jews and Jewish topics can be traced to his friendship with Hirsch Levy, a boarder and family friend who served as a surrogate father to Delitzsch and supported his education financially. Their relationship remained a close one until the end of Levy's life, which was preceded by Levy's conversion to Christianity, mediated by Delitzsch. Delitzsch began his Hebraic studies in the Nikolaigymnasium. He received his doctoral promotion at the University of Leipzig in 1842 in philology and theology. In his brief career as a missionary Delitzsch took a proactive stance. He met Jews at trade fairs (*Messe*), acquainted himself with the Jewish community, and sought work and lodging for impoverished converts. Under Leopold Zunz's direction, Delitzsch inventoried the Hebrew manuscripts at the Leipzig city library. From Julius Fürst, one of the first Jewish Orientalists, Delitzsch acquired an understanding of rabbinic literature. Delitzsch collaborated with Fürst in the production of a Bible concordance and with Leopold Zunz in the editing and publication of *Atz hayim* (The tree of life) by the Karaite Aaron ben Eliyahu.

Delitzsch enjoyed popular success as a teacher, preacher, and lecturer, and he advanced successfully in the academic world. Named extraordinary professor in 1844, Delitzsch held positions in Rostock and Erlangen before returning to his hometown of Leipzig in 1867. He maintained his Jewish contacts in Leipzig, working with Rabbi Issacher Ber on a translation of the Psalms and with the brilliant apostate Arnold Bogumil Ehrlich on a translation of the New Testament into Hebrew. To what extent these friendships inclined Delitzsch toward a favorable handling of Jewish subjects necessarily remains a subjective judgment. Although some sociological studies support the claim that exposure to a minority group reduces prejudice, the historian can think of too many exceptions to believe that knowing Jews necessarily meant loving them.[6] Delitzsch certainly had many Jewish collaborators and by the outbreak of the Berlin antisemitic controversy (1879–81) had produced some strikingly pro-Jewish works, discussed below. All in all, it seems probable that his early contacts and scholarship helped Delitzsch resist a more negative appraisal of Judaism later on when both polemical considerations and the spirit of the times (*Zeitgeist*) inclined in that direction.

Hermann Strack's parents, Max and Emilie, were respectable members of the educated middle class (*Bildungsbürgertum*). Max Strack served as the rector of a modern secondary school. Hermann Strack received his promotion in theology and philology from Berlin University in 1872. He studied Judaica with Delitzsch and Johann Heinrich Biesenthal (1800–1886), a Jewish convert to Christianity who worked for the mission. Strack spent the mid-1870s working in the Imperial Library in St. Petersburg, supported by the Prussian government. During this period he learned how to read handwritten Hebrew manuscripts assembled by the Karaite scholar Abraham Firkowitsch (1785–1875). Together with Abraham Harkavy (1835–1919), Strack published a catalog of Hebrew manuscripts in the St. Petersburg library. He received his professor title in 1876 and his license in theology in 1877 but failed to convince the Berlin university authorities to make him a full professor (*Ordinarius*) in the field of postbiblical Jewish studies. Technically, Strack held a position in Old Testament studies. In practice, his most important scholarly work was in rabbinics. Strack enjoyed an even wider circle of Jewish colleagues than Delitzsch. In Strack's obituary, Josef Wohlgemuth pointed to a special relationship between Strack and the Orthodox Berlin rabbinic seminary, Hildesheimers Rabbiner Seminar. "How thankful he [Strack] was for the encouragement that he received from Barth, Berliner, and Hoffmann and how bravely he stood by Hirsch Hildesheimer in his defensive war against antisemitism. But there probably was no Jewish scholar of significance with whom he did not have a relationship."[7]

Allosemitism: The Theological Orientation of Strack and Delitzsch

How can we come to grips with the apparent contradiction that the most determined defenders of Judaism publicly and its most sympathetic interpreters theologically were the same people who actively strove for the Jews' disappearance? What could the term philosemitism mean when describing the views of two men who wished to see Jews and Judaism disappear into "the utopian realization of a Christian paradise?"[8] Three fundamental conceptions of philosemitism have prevailed. First, philosemitism constitutes an authentic tradition—quantitatively and qualitatively—that can be defined and examined in the same manner as antisemitism. On the whole, this conception has been formulated by social scientists and runs afoul of careful historical scrutiny.[9] Second, philosemitism is simply a false category; as one scholar puts it, "a philosemite is an antisemite who loves Jews."[10] But this viewpoint fails to distinguish real from potential antisemitism—a significant difference—and has no language to explain why some non-Jews championed Jews because of their Jewishness rather than in spite of it. The third perspective, articulated by the sociologist Zygmunt Bauman, emphasizes the allocation of a special vocabulary to address the radical otherness of the Jews (allosemitism). Discussions of Jews, at least in the Christian West, have been supercharged before a particular valence, either positive or negative, is assigned. For Bauman, allosemitism may manifest itself as hatred or love of Jews, but it tends to be intense and extremely malleable.[11] My position approximates Bauman's with one modification. Not only is there such a phenomenon as allosemitism, but the examples of Delitzsch and Strack demonstrate that there is such a creature as the allosemite, an individual who assigns both intensely positive and intensely negative judgments to different aspects of Jewry-Judaism.

The Best of Late Judaism (Spätjudentum)

In his seminal *Christians and Jews in Germany*, Uriel Tal argued that liberal Protestants, who appeared to be the natural allies of German Jewry's intellectual leadership, actually generated the ideology most resistant to envisioning a Jewish role.[12] Kulturprotestantismus, or "cultural Protestantism," called for the infusion of the spirit of "primitive Christianity" without traditional dogma, clericalism, and denominational differences. While distinctly liberal in tone, Kulturprotestantismus in principle opposed religious pluralism and in practice left little room for principled dissent. Susannah Heschel's *Abraham Geiger and the Jewish Jesus* demonstrates that in the Christian treatment of the historical Jesus, the liberal Protestant theologians took the lead in severing Jesus from his Jewish background.[13] Since liberal Protestants increasingly rejected the supernatural and dogmatic aspects of Jesus' life, death, and resurrection, his moral teachings and character increasingly became the paradigm of modern Christian life. The more the focus on Jesus the individual, however, the more blatant was the need to explain him in historical context. This involved the Protestant Left, argues Heschel, in a flight from the historical Jesus. Somehow, Jesus had to be made to stand wholly apart from his Jewish background, the New Testament apart from the Old Testament. Liberal Protestant scholars, in Heschel's reading, suppressed their gnawing awareness that Christianity was in many respects beholden to Judaism and akin to Judaism—an alarming prospect.

The intellectual sleight of hand that argued for a historical Jesus but against a Jewish Jesus is epitomized in another Germanic construct, Late Judaism (Spätjudentum). Spätjudentum, itself an unavoidably negative term blatantly reflecting a Christian supersessionist viewpoint, portrayed Judaism since the nearly synchronous end of prophecy (Malachi) and the return of Ezra (both mid-fifth century BCE) as a religion mired in legalities and priestcraft, devoid of spirit, moribund, played out. In this presentation, Judaism was absolutely ripe for a revolutionary figure like Jesus to knock down the already crumbling walls. Christianity breathed new life into a dying religion, while rabbinic Judaism carried on and even exaggerated the casuistic, mechanical, legalistic religion initiated by Ezra.[14]

Generations of Christians had caricatured Second Temple Judaism using prophetic denunciations of Israel's waywardness, New Testament polemical material, selective readings of Josephus and of Philo, and occasionally a smattering of the most inimical rabbinic statements. Adequate materials existed for a negative portrayal of Second Temple Judaism. This view, it hardly needs saying, is patently incompatible with the religious creativity of the Second Temple period, the tannaim, and even early Christianity (such a creative force could not really be generated in a wholly sterile environment). Altogether wrong, this view of a decadent Judaism nevertheless dominated the scholarly field until very recently and can still be found in Emil Schürer's *Geschichte des jüdischen Volkes im Zeitalter Jesu Christi* (History of the Jewish people in the time of Christ) and in the works of Strack's successor at the Berlin Institutum Judaicum, Joachim Jeremias.[15]

Conservative Protestants, who affirmed miracles and traditional dogmas, were less threatened by the specter of a Jewish Jesus than liberals. For conservatives such as Delitzsch and Strack, the Old Testament played the traditional (and critical) role of preparing the way for the New Testament.[16] Conservative Protestants of the nineteenth century looked at Jesus as the very fulfillment of Old Testament prophecy, in this respect not much differently than the unknown authors of the Gospels eighteen centuries earlier. Since conservative Protestants took the New Testament portrayal of Jesus—its tensions and inconsistencies notwithstanding—as a historical given, few of them had any inclination to examine this Jewish background more closely and made only minimal scholarly contributions. Missionary Protestants, however, were interested in this Jewish background, and if this marginalized them among mainstream conservative Protestants, they could investigate without the anxiety that dogged the more historico-critically inclined liberals.

Sandwiched between liberalism and literalism, Delitzsch and Strack developed an appreciably less hostile evaluation of Second Temple Judaism. Paradoxically, this was due precisely to the missionary insistence on embracing Israel if only, in the end, to strangle it. Several factors prompted this tendency. The Pietist tradition, from Callenberg to Delitzsch, had led to a better-than-average estimation of Judaism. The missionaries shared a conviction that only carnal Israel was destined to produce Jesus. They insisted on affirming Jesus' ethnic lineage (physical parentage) and his divine inception. For the liberals, who rejected the incarnation, Jesus' Jewish ancestry was a mere historical accident. Delitzsch and Strack, moreover, were extremely hostile toward neo-Marcions like Adolf von Harnack who wished to sever the Old and New Testaments. All this freed them to present both a more favorable and a more realistic picture of Spätjudentum than that which prevailed in the German academy.

Delitzsch as Judaic Scholar

A cardinal feature of the Spätjudentum school was its denial or dismissal of Jewish creativity in the period of Jesus. This "scholarly" judgment represented little more than a secularized counterpart to traditional Christian supersessionism. From this perspective Delitzsch's scholarly debut, *Zur Geschichte der jüdischen Poësie* (1836), represents a striking dissent.[17] Published at a time when the founders of the Wissenschaft des Judentums were just beginning their labors, *Zur Geschichte der jüdischen Poësie* was an important scholarly contribution.[18] It stressed the unbroken chain of Jewish creativity from the Bible to the present day. Delitzsch lavished special praise on the nonlegal materials in the Talmud and described the haggadic method: "Scriptural verses form the golden border, which are filled by the colorful pictures of popular history."[19] David Kaufmann concisely summarized the stir occasioned by this work: "A Christian, of barely 24 years, stepped before his contemporaries to tell them of the sleeping beauty he had discovered among the thickets of the primeval forest, in the world-forgotten Jewish writings, through which he had made his way with ardent zeal and resolute strength. . . . With wonder the non-Jewish world learned from this book that the Hebrew language had never died, but continuing in undying youthful vigor had developed a richness of poetical styles and forms, . . . that it has served, unchangeable through all times [*sic!*], as the pliant and plastic expression of sacred and secular subjects of every kind."[20]

Franz Delitzsch's *Jüdisches Handwerkleben zur Zeit Jesu* (published in London as *Jewish Artisan Life in the Time of Jesus*) originated as a lecture series delivered to the German youth guild in the winter of 1867–68. In this work, Delitzsch praised the Jews of Jesus' time as hardworking craftsmen, implicitly holding them up as models for contemporary German youth.[21] Delitzsch portrayed Jewish society in the time of Jesus in fairly glowing colors, and, it goes without saying, Jesus is located wholly in a Jewish context. To be sure, in Delitzsch's asides to contemporary realities, we occasionally catch a hint of ambivalence: "The Jewish people have always been laborious, and second to none in the energy, power and inventiveness which go to make up a restless activity."[22] The Jews' "restless activity" notwithstanding, Delitzsch noted that the 1849 Austrian law that permitted landownership to Jews led to "hundreds [of Jews] shut[ting] up their shops and [throwing] aside their peddler's packs to become peasants."[23] Political liberals also rejected the antisemitic canard that Jews were averse to manual labor. But tacitly, Delitzsch made the followers of Jesus typical Jews, at least in respect to their daily trades. The devotees of the mission consistently preferred handwork to the free professions; indeed, this was one area in which missionary journals tended to criticize the Jewish role in contemporary life. Therefore, Delitzsch took aim here not only at a common antisemitic complaint but also at one found in his own ranks. Delitzsch's successor at the University of Leipzig, Gustaf Dalman, extended Delitzsch's interest in the Palestinian economy of the Second Temple period but had little sympathy for the one contemporary Jewish movement—Zionism, dedicated to restoring Jews to their original land and labors.

Delitzsch's reconstruction of one day in Jesus' ministry, *Ein Tag in Capernaum* (A day in Capernaeum, 1871), written during the Franco-Prussian War, cannot be called a very good novella. But as a specimen of advocacy for Jesus' Jewishness it deserves notice. The morning, afternoon, and evening services (shaharith, minhah, and maarib) form the outline of the novella. The book contains dozens of Hebrew words and terms used in Jewish prayer. The endnotes draw mainly from rabbinic literature. Jesus, once again, is placed in an entirely Jewish setting. The confrontation of Jesus with Judaism is limited to two Jerusalemite Jews who look askance at a Galilean they take to be a wonder-worker and a heretic.[24] These Jerusalemites are characterized by Pharisaic attitudes, presumably suspiciousness, skepticism, and superstition, but otherwise there is no hint of demonization in the novel. Quite the contrary—Delitzsch pictured Jesus' Galilean contemporaries going about their daily business, behaving like a bunch of good Samaritans, and expressing a nearly uniform piety. The picture of Jesus at the afternoon worship service differs so dramatically from the Spätjudentum school that it deserves citation in full:

> *The prayer leader (shaliah tzibbor) stood praying before the pulpit of the holy ark with extraordinary reverence. A power of special consecration, emerging from one person, permeated the entire service. Just now, the preliminary Psalms began. Does he join in the prayers? Almost everyone was asking. Rigid, with penetrating and unchanging focus toward the Torah stand, he sat there, but his lips moved, and the voice of the community through the deep emotions of the prayer-community ascended mightily. As the* Shmone Esre *(Eighteen Benedictions) began with the benediction of the father, and the words sounded out, "May the prayers of the father give grace and bring a redeemer to the children of their children, of those who take your name in love," the look of the assembled turned toward him, for if he was not considered by all this redeemer, so all knew that he considered himself as this redeemer. As the* tehinna *(penitential prayer) began, the prayer leader came to the steps of the holy shrine and fell on his face, so he also lowered his face, covered it, like the entire community, with his left arm. As the concluding* kaddish *was intoned, he raised his head, and his countenance gleamed, so that one of his believers whispered to his neighbor, "See the King in his beauty!" With the words of the Psalms: "Fear not for sudden terror and from the storms of the godless, for He will come." With this, the* mincha *liturgy came to its conclusion.*[25]

From the point of view of critical historiography, this scene is a disaster area. That the audience would have any doubt about Jesus' participation in the service seems unlikely. That Jesus would so clearly consider himself the *go'el* (redeemer) and that the audience would also know that this was his self-conception flies in the face of most scholarship in Delitzsch's day as well as our own. That Jesus' mere presence in a synagogue in the Galilee would occasion messianic speculation may be dismissed. But what remains is an undeniably tallith-clad Jesus, praying with other Jews during an ordinary afternoon service. Add to this picture the specific mention of the Shmone Esre, a perennial target of antisemitic hostility, and the result is striking. (Note also the absence of any characterizations of the prayer as spirit deadening or devoid of feeling. This Judaism is vibrant and not simply waiting around for Jesus to revivify much less condemn it.) Taken together, these three books (*Zur Geschichte der jüdischen Poësie, Jüdisches Handwerkleben zur Zeit Jesu,* and *Ein Tag in Capernaum*) present a very favorable picture of Jews and Judaism in the time of Jesus intellectually (creative through the ages), economically (productive, not parasitic), and spiritually (alive, not dead).

Delitzsch as Christian Polemicist

Ironically, Delitzsch's *Jüdisches Handwerkleben zur Zeit Jesu* and *Ein Tag in Capernaum* appeared at roughly the same he began his protracted controversy with Abraham Geiger over the respective roles of Jesus and Hillel. As Susannah Heschel observes, Delitzsch's main quarrel with Geiger was the latter's claim that Jesus took from Hillel but neither said nor did anything to substantively improve upon Hillel's words or deeds. Hillel, to Delitzsch, was not a reformer of Judaism, as were Samuel and Ezra, but rather left everything as it was. This revealing objection indicates that for Delitzsch, Jesus was, to some extent, a reformer of Judaism, though a very radical one and one whose source of teaching was not the chain of tradition (shalshelet ha-kabbalah) but rather direct communication from God. Given Delitzsch's positive view of contemporary Reform Judaism, a theme to which we will return, this is a potentially Jewish appraisal of Jesus' legacy.[26]

Delitzsch's association of Jesus with fellow reformers Samuel and Ezra, however, was neither accidental nor typical. As Delitzsch rhetorically asked in his 1882 pamphlet, *Christentum und jüdische Presse* (Christianity and Jewish press), "Are not Moses, Samuel, and Ezra also heroes for the Christian salvation history [*Heilsgeschichte*]?"[27] For Delitzsch, there were more or less "Christian" tendencies in the Old Testament, but the whole Bible belonged to Christianity. Delitzsch saw no gap between the two testaments. In fact, in an extraordinary image, Delitzsch portrayed the old covenant and the new covenant standing side by side in the three days between Jesus' crucifixion and his resurrection. Unlike the Spätjudentum school, which had Judaism dying since the days of Ezra if not since the destruction of 587–586 BCE, Delitzsch stressed the continuous history of redemption.[28]

To present Jesus, the originator of Christianity, as a Jewish reformer must have set off alarm bells for Delitzsch—after all, this was the essence of Geiger's position. Could not two reformers of Judaism lead the biblical legacy in two different directions? Logically, this line of argument would legitimize Hillel and Jesus as engaging in similar tasks. That degree of similarity, especially given Hillel's chronological priority, was unacceptable to Delitzsch. I suspect that Delitzsch sensed the radical implication; what else could account for Delitzsch's extreme rejection of Hillel as a reformer of Judaism? Delitzsch moved to neutralize the threat. He placed Hillel as one in a long line of Pharisaic teachers, with the usual contrast between the Pharisees as "juristic, casuistic, and nationalistic" and Jesus as "universal, religious, moral, and humane."[29] The equally typical contrast between "spirit" and "letter" shows Delitzsch's willingness to affirm the "findings" of the scholarly world when they could be pressed into the service of Lutheran orthodoxy. These words served as comforting shibboleths of Christianity, absolutely unsupported by Delitzsch's own scholarly investigations of the past twenty years.

Having insisted on placing Jesus in historical context, Delitzsch retreated to remind the reader that Jesus, after all, was divine. To claim that Hillel was a greater jurist than Jesus, for Delitzsch, was like claiming that Alexander the Great was a greater general than Plato.[30] Actual comparison between the two men was inconceivable: "Here is more than Hillel," pronounced Delitzsch confidently. Who Jesus was rather than what he taught set him apart. (Indeed, Delitzsch presents the truly great teaching innovation of Jesus as the ability to grasp both Leviticus 19:18, "You shall love thy neighbor as thyself," and Deuteronomy 6:4, "And you shall love the Lord thy God," in their fullness. This could hardly be called a major innovation, despite Delitzsch's presenting it as such.) Delitzsch agreed with the traditional Jewish praise of Hillel found in the Talmud as "a Hasid and a student of Ezra." Apparently, Delitzsch felt free to elaborate Hillel's merits without fear of conceding anything critical. He had reduced Geiger's presentation of Jesus from threatening to merely offensive.

Geiger's readiness to sever the life and teaching of Jesus from the subsequent history of Christianity was hardly novel. The quest for the historical Jesus, the Holy Grail of nineteenth-century New Testament scholarship, rested exactly on that distinction. By comparison, Delitzsch seems positively simplistic in his reading of Christian history as the inevitable unfolding of a plan of salvation. Most critical contemporaries found little favor in Delitzsch's eyes. He aims his remarks in *Jesus und Hillel* at David Friedrich Strauss and Ernst Renan as well as at Geiger. But there can be little doubt that the fact that Geiger was a Jew made his claims particularly obnoxious. Delitzsch returned to this theme in *Christentum und jüdische Presse*, a book that links his unique view of Spätjudentum and his contemporary evaluation of Jews and antisemites: "If the Jew cannot be convinced that Jesus is the fulfillment of the Law and the Prophets, so he must recognize, that from him [Jesus] a new era commenced, whose blessings have brought benefits even to himself [the Jew]. Are not the Christian people the bearers of culture and civilization? And what were these people before Christianity began to exert its transforming influence? That we know quite well! It is then with [the advent of] Christianity that a new, enduring, spiritually revolutionary, sanctifying principle enters into the world."[31]

In this paragraph, Delitzsch adduced the well-worn Christian argument that an objective look at Jesus' legacy precluded the view that he failed to offer something new and creative. Jesus revolutionized world history for the benefit of the Jews as well as the heathens. Even from the point of view of liberal Protestant scholarship that argument hardly sufficed. As noted, the actual intent of Jesus' life and teaching was disputable, and the route taken by the early Church in its first few centuries struck Harnack and his contemporaries as a descent into institutionalization and Catholicism. From the Jewish point of view, the fallacy of equating worldly success with theological truth had been clear at least since the time of Yehuda Halevy. Considering the oppression suffered at Christian hands for centuries, Delitzsch's reading of Jesus' legacy tasted like sugarcoated history to Jewish tongues. His reviewers were right to be unimpressed.[32]

Strack as Judaic Scholar: The Einleitung

The conflicting sentiments found in Delitzsch's treatment of Judaism are evident at a more scholarly but equally entrenched level in Delitzsch's student, Hermann Strack. Strack, in contrast to his mentor, conceived two works that enjoyed generations of influence: *Einleitung in Talmud und Midrasch* (Introduction to the Talmud and Midrash, hereafter cited as *Einleitung*) and *Kommentar zum neuen Testament* (Commentary to the New Testament, hereafter cited as *Kommentar*). Taken together, as Strack intended they should be, they reveal the strongly competing tendencies toward a highly positive presentation of Judaism and the indisputable superiority of Christianity.[33] (Strack's rejection of antisemitic libels on Judaism also assumed a high-level mastery of Jewish sources. These efforts, which will be discussed below, cannot be termed creative scholarship.) Strack's preface to the first edition of the *Einleitung* claimed to have offered "the first attempt at an objective and scholarly overview of the Talmud." Strack continues: "I have striven honestly to let myself be influenced neither by polemical nor by apologetic interest, but by the truth alone. I shall consider myself amply rewarded for my laborious work if I shall succeed to remove many a prejudice, whether with those who are *unconditionally hostile* to the Talmud or with its *over-zealous admirers*, and to pave the way for a more just and calm appraisal" (emphasis added).[34]

Strack stressed here his freedom from both apologetic and polemical interests. Scholarly evenhandedness may be the keynote of this preface. Nevertheless, we may safely claim that in Strack's day there were more enemies whose prejudices needed correcting than there were enthusiasts whose ardor needed dampening. Even had Strack succeeded in presenting an entirely objective picture of the Talmud, a scholarly chimera, the political significance would have, in effect, been pro-Judaic.

The preface to the fourth edition expressed an accelerated philosemitic (or, at any rate, accelerated anti-antisemitic) momentum. Strack focused on the antisemitic fiction that the Talmud contains secret teachings. He contended that for both Jews and Christians unable to read Hebrew the Talmud is a secret book (*Geheimbuch*), but only in the sense that Julius Caesar's *Commentaries on the Gallic War* is a closed text to those who cannot read Latin. Strack insisted that the rabbinic materials were accessible to all those Christians, like himself, who could dispense with the concept of an eight-hour workday.

The last edition of the *Einleitung* published during Strack's lifetime completed his desire to more fully incorporate the haggadic literature (early editions were titled simply *Einleitung in Talmud*). Certainly, the incorporation of this material offered a counterexample to rabbinic literature as dry and legalistic. Strack also took the opportunity in the 1920 edition to thank some of his advisors, including Jewish eminents such as Ismar Elbogen, J. N. Epstein, Alexander Marx, Saul Horovitz, and Eduard Baneth.[35] From the first edition onward, Strack included opinions from S. R. Hirsch, Ludwig Stern, Leopold Stein, Isaac Wise, and Ludwig Philippson on the question of whether—and to what extent—the Talmud bound contemporary Jewry. Strack thus acknowledged the multiplicity of Jewish outlooks and conceded that it was up to Jews, not Christians, to define the Talmud's role in contemporary Jewish life. Did Strack's *Einleitung* achieve his goal of a "just and calm appraisal"? Certainly, the work contains nothing grossly unfair, inaccurate, or hostile. Whether the *Einleitung* reaches the level of "appraisal" at all may be questioned, since Strack mainly translated and assembled selected talmudic material along genre lines. Jacob Neusner describes Strack's work "as interesting as a telephone book . . . there is no real introduction in an intellectual sense."[36] Strack's contemporary Jewish reviewers were consistently more enthusiastic than Neusner, and it is not difficult to see why.[37] Despite the clinical tone typical of many works of nineteenth-century German *Wissenschaft*, an occasional flash of partisanship bursts forth from the author, surely more likely to have pleased the "over-zealous admirers" more than the "unconditionally hostile": "The Torah, moreover, meant to the Jews the sum and substance of all that is good and beautiful, of all that is worth knowing. Hence it ought to be possible to apply to it all conditions of life, it should comfort, exhort and edify, and it must be shown further that it contained everything even though germinal."[38]

Strack as Christian Polemicist: The Kommentar

Translated into English and Hebrew, revamped by Gunther Stemberger, and republished as recently as 1991, Strack's *Einleitung* remains a useful resource. More influential still is the collaborative work by Hermann Strack and Paul Billerbeck,

Kommentar zum Neuen Testament aus Talmud und Midrasch Erlautet (Commentary to the New Testament as explained by the Talmud and Midrash). In some ways, the *Kommentar* presented itself as a companion to Strack's *Einleitung* but also culminated similar efforts to compare Gospel and rabbinic texts, including the work of John Lightfoot and Franz Delitzsch. As a prolegomenon to his Hebrew translation of the New Testament, Delitzsch had published a Hebrew translation of Paul's Letter to the Romans. In this work, Delitzsch bemoaned the lack of interest in and love for Jewish literature that had flourished during the Reformation. Delitzsch hoped that Jewish readers would be pleased to see Jewish literature discussed in a "non-Eisenmengerish spirit" and that they could relate to New Testament material as part of their national legacy. Delitzsch put the matter baldly: "The emergence of Christianity belongs to the history of Judaism." As usual, Delitzsch's pro-Jewish stance went hand in hand with a missionary agenda. Putting the New Testament into the universally respected Jewish language and into a historically Jewish context seemed to Delitzsch objectively true and subjectively effective. In this book, Delitzsch used the rabbinic materials as the primary background for understanding Paul.[39]

The ambitious Strack-Billerbeck *Kommentar* sought to provide the entire New Testament with a verse-by-verse pony linking the Gospels with rabbinic parallels. The work itself was carried out by Paul Billerbeck (1853–1952). At the time of Strack's death only the Gospel of Matthew had been published, but the book remains Strack's brainchild. What first strikes the reader of any one of the five volumes of the *Kommentar* is the intense amount of labor, the seemingly exhaustive nature of the research into rabbinic materials. It is no surprise that several generations of German Protestants and many American New Testament scholars as well found Strack-Billerbeck a completely satisfactory source for their knowledge of rabbinic Judaism, with disastrous results.[40] In a brilliant address to the Society of Biblical Literature, Samuel Sandmel located four conceptual flaws at the core of Strack-Billerbeck's *Kommentar*, all critical.[41] First, Strack's desire to show the kinship between Judaism and Christianity led him to overstate the importance of Jewish influence. Sandmel wrote, "[T]he impression thereupon exists that the unfolding Christian literature, even after Christendom became gentile . . . still owes some immediate debt to the rabbinic literature, even in passages emerging from Babylonia in the 5th century."[42] Second, Sandmel scored the inability of excerpts to convey "the tone, texture and import of a literature." Strack-Billerbeck thus instilled far too much confidence in Christians who believed that they had mastered rabbinic literature when they had in fact mastered only Strack-Billerbeck. Third, Sandmel considered the "piling up of rabbinic passages" itself problematic in its appearance of authority and its acceptance of the New Testament as adequate to sift the rabbinic material. Fourth, Sandmel noted the central paradox in their missionary attitude toward Judaism: "[Strack-Billerbeck] quote the [Jewish] literature endlessly to clarify the NT. Yet even where the rabbis seem to say identically the same thing, Strack-Billerbeck manage to demonstrate that what Jesus said was finer and better."[43]

To be sure, the *Kommentar* emphasized the historical connections of primitive Christianity and rabbinic Judaism. The very first sentence reads, "The Lord belonged to the Jewish people according to his physical lineage and was a descendant of David. Likewise Mark, Matthew, John, Paul, and Peter and the other authors of New Testament writings (except Luke) were Jews. For a right understanding of their utterances it is necessary to be acquainted with the life and thought of Judaism in that period." The very first footnote of *Kommentar* rejected out of hand the attempt to make Jesus an Aryan.[44] It speaks volumes about the overall animosity toward Judaism found in most German Protestant scholarship that Eduard Lamparter, arguably the most dogged anti-antisemitic pastor in Weimar Germany, regarded Strack-Billerbeck as a text basically sympathetic to Judaism, simply because it acknowledged the relationship between the two faiths.[45] This particular relationship, however, was not one between equals.

The difference in tone and structure between the *Einleitung* and the *Kommentar* points to the fundamental approach of Delitzsch and Strack when dealing with Judaism and Christianity as historical phenomena. Delitzsch expressed great resentment when he felt that the person of Jesus or Christianity was under assault. Where that was not an issue, Delitzsch argued for a suspension of disbelief regarding the supposed evils of Judaism. Throughout his writings, Delitzsch's view of Judaism as an inferior but still biblically based religion comes through consistently. The moment the issue of comparison with Christianity emerges, the intellectual light switch clicks to "off," and the tone recalls the days of medieval religious polemic. Strack portrayed the Talmud and Midrash about as successfully as one could hope, given his Christian upbringing and the secondary scholarship available to him.[46] Rabbinic Judaism represents a legitimate continuation, not a severance, subversion, or perversion, of the religion of the Old Testament. But placed cheek to jowl, Strack cannot help but take sides, and Judaism always comes out the loser.

One could go so far as to say that the only thing wrong with Judaism is that it is not Christianity. But that is not an inconsequential failing. When Gospel and Talmud, Christianity and Judaism are juxtaposed, the former defines the categories, the standards, and the conclusions. Paradoxically, Delitzsch and Strack upheld the affinity of Judaism and Christianity in theory but presented Judaism most favorably when they bracketed out Christianity and discussed Judaism on its own terms. Paradoxical again, despite their collegial relations with Jewish scholars, Delitzsch and Strack usually make their best case for the worth of Judaism when they present Judaism to other Christians, urging them to love the Jewish Jesus, Jewry as the nation that gave the world Jesus, and even contemporary Jews as prospective Christians. The Delitzsch who lambasted the falsities of Auguste Rohling and who called Christians to account for their anti-Jewish prejudices possessed real moral stature. The Delitzsch whose *Ernste Fragen* (Earnest questions, 1888) attempted to convince Jews that Christianity cohered with the Old Testament and their own best religious instincts seemed woefully outmoded even in his own day. Strack's *Einleitung* evidenced a sincere veneration of rabbinic literature. The Strack-Billerbeck *Kommentar* has been judged anti-Judaic by scholars from Samuel Sandmel to E. P. Sanders. Theologically, Delitzsch and Strack were both philosemitic and antisemitic, or, to use Bauman's term, they were allosemites. They were ambivalent in the literal sense (assigning competing values to the same phenomenon) but without the doubt and tentativeness that ambivalence usually implies. They compartmentalized their theological philosemitism and antisemitism, allowing each full play. Was this also the case in their anti-antisemitic efforts? The following section attempts to answer this question.

The Missionary Movement and Antisemitism

Before turning to the specific positions taken by Delitzsch and Strack on antisemitism, it must be noted that they represented a distinctly pro-Jewish standpoint within the missionary movement. The recent studies by Christopher Clark and Wolfgang Heinrichs demonstrate that in their journals the missionaries often portrayed German Jewry as important bearers of a modern, secular, capitalistic culture inimical to their vision of a Christian society.[47] On the one hand, missionaries believed that Jews contributed to the dangerous secularizing of German society. On the other hand, the missionaries were avid detractors of a racial definition of Christianity. They therefore regarded antisemitism as the surest means for dissuading Jews from becoming believing Christians. Johann de Le Roi, the semiofficial historian of the movement, was one of the earliest to recognize and condemn antisemitism as a threat to the Church and to the physical safety of Jews. Yet de Le Roi objected to the prominent role played by Jews in German life and found the warm defense of the Jews by the apostate Selig (Paulus) Cassel deeply offensive, dismissing him as animated by a "purely partisan spirit."[48] Gustaf Dalman, an important missionary figure in both Leipzig and Palestine, defended the Talmud as generally indifferent to Christianity and free of sustained anti-Christian bias. His rejection of English missionary philosemitism, however, leaves little doubt about his personal feelings: "It is unfortunately true, where one does not know Jews [England] there now and then emerges a kind of overwrought enthusiasm, of which it is very questionable whether it could withstand closer contact with the Jews. And unfortunately it is also so, that if we in Germany cannot love them [the Jews], that is because we know them."[49]

Although the preceding paragraph warns against evaluating the missionary outlook as "pro-Jewish," it should not be inferred that Delitzsch and Strack were marginal figures within the movement. Each edited one of the more important missionary journals (*Saat auf Hoffnung* [Sowing in hope] and *Nathanael*, respectively). After his return to Leipzig, Delitzsch became the teacher to an entire generation of missionaries, including Gustaf Dalman, cited above. Strack headed the Institutum Judaicum in Berlin, certainly the intellectual center for the German mission, and taught on the Old Testament faculty at the University of Berlin from 1877 to 1922. Both men appeared frequently and prominently at German missionary congresses and enjoyed enormous respect overseas. Strack's activities as an anti-antisemite made him the best-known missionary in Germany. Considering that the missionary movement as a whole occupied an increasingly marginal position within German Protestantism, the range of views on the Jewish question was substantial, although all missionaries, by definition, saw sincere religious conversion as the key to the solution. Unlike de Le Roi and Dalman, the fierce opposition to anti-semitism on the part of Strack and Delitzsch cannot be attributed to tactics alone. Even though the desire to make more Christians undoubtedly guided the majority of German missionaries in their consideration of antisemitism, they opposed the new movement more stridently than any other group in Germany in the 1880s.

The Jewish question reemerged as a national debate with the Berlin antisemitic controversy of 1879–81. Although resentment of Jewish political equality and economic success had been building since the 1870s, the emergence of Heinrich von Treitschke, Adolf Stoecker, and Wilhelm Marr signaled a new chapter in the history of Jew hatred. The public responses of non-Jewish detractors of antisemitism were generally muted, with one exception. The first observation I would like to make on the nexus between anti-antisemitism and missionary Protestantism is that in terms of sheer quantity, the non-Jewish response to the emergence of the Berlin antisemitic movement in 1879–81 came overwhelmingly from a Christian religious perspective. Theodor Mommsen, motivated by liberal political principles to oppose antisemitism, was better known than any single missionary figure, but he was also a rarity in the 1880s.[50] Not until the second wave of antisemitism in the 1890s and the founding of the Abwehrverein did liberals come to see the fight against antisemitism as an inevitable part of their program. The anti-antisemitic literature of the 1880s came from a Christian perspective, inevitably from champions of the Old Testament,[51] and often from those who sympathized with the missionary per-spective.[52] The polemical response to Stoecker and Rohling, precisely because they decked their antisemitism in the clothes of the Church (Protestant and Catholic, respectively), came almost exclusively from committed Christians.

Second, in terms of expertise and interest, only the missionary Christians were competent and eager to defend Judaism as a religion and the Talmud as a religious classic. For political liberals, the defense of Jews proceeded from a purely secular premise: they were entitled to equality as citizens of a modern state (*Rechtsstaat*). Political liberals formally adopted a policy of noninterference in private religious beliefs. But whereas so much of the antisemitic assault centered on the supposed monstrosities of Judaism (for example, the blood libel, Judaism's supposed misanthropy, the untrustworthiness of Jewish oaths, etc.), the defense of rabbinic Judaism necessarily became a desideratum. Figures like Delitzsch and Strack played a unique role. Strack argued that Christians must defend Judaism precisely because even if the most honorable Jew were to write about the blood libel or the Talmud, he would be suspected of whitewashing.[53] Strack was correct: the German public devalued Jewish testimony about Judaism as untrustworthy. (Even a missionary *opponent* of antisemitism like de Le Roi tended to discount the defenses of Jews and ex-Jews as tainted with "philosemitism.") Political liberals, for their part, possessed neither the desire nor the competence to engage antisemites in this critical arena. The very few liberal Protestants who spoke out against Stoecker and his confreres, most notably Michael Baumgarten of Rostock University, were content to criticize the history of Christian oppression of the Jew and failed to confront the defamation of Judaism in any but the most general terms.

Third, and a completely overlooked factor, only the missionary journals offered non-Jews a sympathetic presentation of Jewish life, unobtainable, on the whole, from non-Jewish pens.[54] Antisemitic arguments and caricatures also made their way into the pages of the missionary journals; the picture is ambiguous, not positive.[55] Nevertheless, looking through journals such as *Saat auf Hoffnung* and *Nathanael*, one finds the following: (1) sympathetic portraits of Jewish religious figures such as David Zvi Hoffmann and Samson Raphael Hirsch, complete with necrologies quoted at length from the Jewish press; (2) serious descriptions of Jewish religious documents (for example, the Shulchan Aruch, the Zohar) and religious doctrines (for example, Jewish views on non-Jew); (3) lengthy book reviews on Jewish books and Jewish authors, fairer and more positive than found elsewhere; and (4) accurate characterizations of the existing religious differences within Judaism. Had Germans read Strack's *Nathanael* and nothing else, an aggressive missionary orientation nationwide would have been possible but not a rise in racial thinking, or support for the revocation of *Emanzipation,* or an attempt to sever and eliminate the Judaic roots of Christianity, three critical components of the antisemitic *Weltanschauung.*

Fourth, intellectual interaction between Jews and Christians on religious matters was relatively infrequent, at least before the Weimar period. Delitzsch and Strack had Jewish colleagues they respected, learned from, and collaborated with in the development of a discipline. To take two examples analyzed above, Delitzsch's *Zur Geschichte der jüdischen Poësie* and Strack's *Einleitung* were both landmark events in the history of the Wissenschaft des Judentums. As Professor David Kaufmann wrote in his searching obituary of Delitzsch, the latter was really the first to impose a periodic structure on the development of Hebrew poetry. Strack's

Einleitung offered the first overall characterization of the Talmud from a non-Jew and the first breakdown of the varieties of rabbinic literature embedded in the Talmud and Midrash. The scholarly contributions of Delitzsch and Strack have long since been superseded, as have those of Leopold Zunz, Abraham Geiger, Moritz Steinschneider, and Heinrich Graetz. Delitzsch and Strack set a higher standard for the presentation of Judaism than that which had previously prevailed. It seems undeniable that their views were colored by their collaboration with an impressive list of Jewish Judaicists.[56]

Fifth, some missionaries considered social contact with Jews desirable and important. In theory, this was motivated largely by a desire to convert Jews, hardly a philosemitic goal. In practice, Delitzsch and Strack had many colleagues whom they surely realized were not about to walk to the baptismal font. In his brief career as an active missionary, Delitzsch was indefatigable in his desire to acquaint himself with Jews. He cultivated relationships at merchant fairs, in the commercial areas of Leipzig, and even in Russia, where he enthusiastically supported a group of Jewish Christians led by the enigmatic Joseph Rabinovitch.[57] To be sure, the cultivation of better Jewish-Christian social relations formed part of the "cultural code" of other discrete groups in German society too. The socialist parties, the peace movement, free fraternities at the university, the early Freemasons, and some technical-scientific institutions created settings where Jews and Christians met, worked, and occasionally fell in love and married. Even the profoundly antisemitic Wilhelm II had his Jewish circle, and in Weimar the interaction of Jews and Gentiles became much broader still. Still, I find it significant that missionary Christians explicitly considered friendly social relations with Jews (even if as would-be Christians) to be an integral part of solving the Jewish question.

In light of these observations, it is worth reflecting why so little was done to forge a tactical alliance between Jews and missionaries against antisemitism. The question becomes sharper when one considers the fundamentally illiberal nature of German liberalism, which also opposed the perpetuation of a distinct Jewish identity.[58] In the 1880s and 1890s Jewish leaders such as Moritz Lazarus who saw the benefits of the missionary defense supported their efforts cautiously.[59] Clearly, Jews could not have been strategic allies with missionary Protestants: their agendas conflicted deeply in every possible respect save one: both groups regarded antisemitism as a serious threat to the health of German society that ought to be combated.[60] But even putting the matter this way imagines a pragmatic evaluation of the missionary world that never took place. Given the long history of Christian attempts to convert Jews forcibly, the overwhelming Jewish commitment to a religiously neutral state, and the growing fears of defection from the ranks through apostasy, most German Jews could only regard missionaries as foes, not friends. Even today, Evangelical Christianity evokes concern and hostility, though

American Jews and some Evangelical Christians have occasionally allied in support of the state of Israel. What deserves notice is that historians of German Jewry, sharing the same liberal proclivities and the caution of their subjects, have passed over the defense of Judaism by missionary Protestants rather cursorily in favor of the defense of Jews by the political Left.[61]

Delitzsch as Philosemite and Antisemite

Theological and personal considerations rather than political commitment drove Delitzsch's opposition to antisemitism. Delitzsch never engaged deeply in the political questions of the day, including Jewish emancipation. In *Wissenschaft, Kunst, und Judentum* (Scholarship, art, and Judaism, 1837), Delitzsch went out of his way to argue that a fair appraisal of Judaism was "absolutely unconnected to the question of the civil equality of Jews."[62] Delitzsch attacked antisemitism most stridently in the course of his polemic with Canon Auguste Rohling. In a letter to Lazarus, Delitzsch maintained, "Judaism has probably never had a worse enemy than Rohling. . . . This pamphlet [*Esther Solymosi oder der jüdisch-rituelle Jungfrauen mord in Tisza-Eszlár* (Esther Solymosi, or the Jewish ritual murder of a virgin in Tisza-Eszlár)] represents to everyone who loves Israel a terrible alternative." Delitzsch chose activism, and he devoted much time and effort to disseminating his exposé of Rohling, even against the wishes of some intimates who thought that he could be using his time more wisely.[63] In *Rohlings Talmudjude beleuchtet* (Rohling's Talmud-Jew exposed, 1881), Delitzsch condemned the embittering of converts' lives by the new antisemitism, although he agreed with Rohling that the Jews had overstepped the bounds of propriety.[64] Against Rohling and other modern Marcions, Delitzsch insisted that the Old Testament was as much a product of divine revelation as the New Testament. He reminded his readers that the founder of Christianity "was indeed a Jew and had there been no Jewish Christians, that is, Messiah-believers, then there would be absolutely no Christianity."[65] Delitzsch portrayed the Talmud as being built on an Old Testament basis and, in effect, as a natural construction of ancient Israel in postantiquity *if* one were to be deprived of the New Testament revelation. Delitzsch rejected the demonic portrayal found in Rohling (and Johann Andreas Eisenmenger before him). The Talmud text contained both gems and detritus, but most of all it constituted

> "an auditorium" in which the voices from five hundred years interpenetrate each other, for next to sense is also nonsense, next to wit also witlessness, next to the love of humanity also terrible intolerance, next to true belief also laughable superstition. One is permitted to think, at least when we bring the character of the times into estimation, whose product

> it [the Talmud] is. Rohling, however, has espied the worst bluebottles and dungflies, which he could find in Eisenmenger—of the butterflies that fly in the Talmud, he knows nothing and wants to know nothing.[66]

Delitzsch's *Rohlings Talmudjude* also appealed to Christian readers that understanding the Jewish rejection of Christianity, at least as an intellectual prerequisite for a fair appraisal of the talmudic material, was warranted: "We are convinced from a Christian standpoint that these proscriptions have served their purpose, and the national principle of religion has no more right to exist. The Jew, however, denies Christianity, even the recognition of it as the religion of fulfilled wisdom and essential salvation. We deplore that, but in order to judge him [the Jew] properly, we must recognize that this is his standpoint. In Rohling's *Talmudjude* there is not a hint [of this recognition] to be found."[67]

The attack on Rohling marked the highpoint in Delitzsch's anti-antisemitic activities. As he returned during his last years to the gap between Church and synagogue, Delitzsch's polemical tendencies reemerged even as he tried to distance himself from antisemites.[68] In his most hostile work, *Christentum und jüdische Presse. Selbsterlebtes* (Christianity and Jewish press as I have experienced it, 1882) Delitzsch opened up with this pronouncement: "From the depths of my soul I am deeply unsympathetic to any antisemitism that keeps its eyes open only to the defects of the Jewish people and not to its virtues."[69] Delitzsch judged the contemporary Jewish press harshly but avoided the usual antisemitic libels. In as simple a matter as defining the Jewish press, Delitzsch insisted that the general press is neither Jewish nor Christian, that its malignant "free spirit" (*Freigeisterei*) was ultimately the product of English Deists and French Encyclopedists. Delitzsch relayed a story about a complainant to a respected journal about the Jewish presence only to be told that there were no Jews on the staff. When Delitzsch discussed the Jewish press, he meant the *Allgemeine Zeitschrift des Judentums*, the *Israelit*, and the *Israelitische Wochenschrift*, in other words, the Jewish press as defined by non-antisemites. Delitzsch further called his readers' attention to the title of his pamphlet: "Jewish press," not "*the* Jewish press"—he did not pretend to give a complete survey of the literature but only some representative examples.

Delitzsch did not conceal his hostility toward those who libeled Jesus. The Jewish press offended Christian sensibilities with tactless statements about Jesus and Christian holidays. More damaging still, the Jewish press pandered to the egotistical instincts of Judaism, fanning the distinction between Jews and Christians and impeding their social and religious rapprochement: "The Jewish press functions to separate Jewry and Christendom instead of bringing them together."[70] Delitzsch was certainly blind to the discrepancy between what he considered legitimate criticism of rabbinic Judaism and unjustifiable derogation of Christianity.

Any derogatory statement regarding Jesus or Christianity struck both Delitzsch and Strack as highly offensive.[71] Nevertheless, Delitzsch took pains to avoid giving the antisemitic camp either ammunition or encouragement, insistently warned against unjust generalizations, and frequently lauded figures such as Leopold Kompert, Moritz Lazarus, and Berthold Auerbach as Jews who managed to be fully Jewish and German simultaneously.[72]

However much antisemites and philosemites (that is, Jewish apologists and Jewish activists) encumbered the great rapprochement, Delitzsch saw signs of hope on the horizon, including Reform Judaism. Delitzsch harked back to a missionary tendency in the first half of the nineteenth century that viewed Jewish religious reform as positive, which contrasted with the turn-of-the-century missionary appraisal of Reform Jewry as the embodiment of modernity.[73] For Delitzsch, Reform Judaism represented an abandonment of talmudic Judaism for prophetic Judaism. Since prophetic Judaism, for Delitzsch, culminated in Christ, Reform Judaism represented an indirect pathway to Christianity. Not that Reform Judaism merited indefinite existence on its own terms, for it failed to recognize Jesus, its own animating spirit. "Reform Judaism is what it essentially is only through the reception of Christian elements but with the rejection of Christ."[74] Delitzsch insisted that the flow of creative influence after the advent of Jesus was one way—from Christianity to Judaism. As Delitzsch put it in *Ernste Fragen*, only the reality of Christianity enabled Reformers to present the traditional commandments (mitzvot) as changeable.[75] Even when Reform Jews supported rationalism, materialism, moral relativism, and religious indifference, Reform Judaism gave unwitting evidence to the influence of Christianity as a bearer of culture and values.[76]

Delitzsch tirelessly emphasized the common features of Judaism and Christianity. Even in his abrasive *Christentum und jüdische Presse*, Delitzsch minimized the gap between the two faiths. "Everything that divides Judaism and Christianity is rooted and culminates in the fact that Judaism condemns the trinitarian God-idea as heathen and, to be sure, as we [Christians] assert, without biblical justification."[77] Six years later, in *Ernste Fragen*, Delitzsch extended this claim to show that Christianity was founded on Jewish roots (the Bible), was consistent with, though superior, to Jewish values found in rabbinic literature, and was responsible for Jewish religious progress since the emergence of Christianity.[78] No doubt Delitzsch and Strack anticipated the messianic disappearance of Judaism no less avidly than their colleagues. Their *Gegenswartarbeit* (work for the present day), to borrow a Zionist phrase, tended to carve out a more significant place for Jews than the more liberal defenders of the political Left.

Mass conversion would have to wait for the return of the Messiah. Delitzsch labored against missionary frustration at the national level, reminding his auditors, "Not nations are saved but individuals!"[79] His sharpest words in "Welche Anforderungen stellt die Gegenwart an die Missions-Arbeit unter den Juden?" (What contemporary demands present to missionary work among the Jews?), a lecture to the German missionary societies in 1870, were directed to those who failed to give support to Jews who had converted, financially, professionally, and spiritually: "For in the poor Jew who comes to us in the name of Jesus, Jesus himself stands before us in the most immediate sense."[80] Delitzsch tied love of Jesus to love of the Jews and especially of Jews born again into Christ. For Delitzsch, every convert offered evidence to doubting Christians and stiff-necked Jews alike that the bridge to the true religion was not an insuperable one. The final solution to the Jewish question would be the Jews' abandonment of a national religion in favor of the one true international faith.

Strack as Philosemite and Antisemite

Unlike Delitzsch, Strack engaged in the hurly-burly of combating antisemitism in court, in the university, and in the mission. From 1880 to 1922 no voice in Germany spoke out against the defamation of Judaism so consistently or with such authority. Despite admitting initial sympathy with the court preacher, Adolf Stoecker, Strack became his most serious detractor, publishing a damning exchange of letters and an analysis of the former's rabble-rousing. In 1893 Strack appealed to the Berlin public prosecutor to stop the dissemination of antisemitic libels. When this effort failed, Strack published the court proceedings under the title *Die Juden, dürfen sie "verbrecher von Religions wegen" genannt werden?* (May Jews be called "criminals on account of their religion"?). His 1891 court testimony in the Esther Solymosi trial served as the kernel for *Der Blutaberglaube in der Menschheit, Blutmorde und Blutritus* (The Jews and human sacrifice), a major apologetic for traditional Judaism. Strack, more sophisticated and scholarly than Delitzsch, was also not entirely free from antisemitic sentiments.[81] In 1897 Strack criticized the Jewish presentation of the mission as a crude business transaction dealing in souls for money (*Seelenschacher*). Jewish opposition to the mission, Strack admitted, was understandable, but the stigmatization of Christian converts was not, nor the conflation of German missionaries with their English counterparts, whom Strack conceded sometimes relied on economic need rather than religious conviction. But Strack insisted that the 2,088 Jews who became Protestant from 1890 to 1894 in Germany did so mainly out of sincere conviction in the truth of Christianity. Strack did not consider how strongly the recrudescence of antisemitism in those years prodded the Jews to leave their religion of birth; he blamed Judaism's failure to display "true religiosity" (*ernste Religiosität*).

    Looking back on thirty years of incitement in his "Geschichte und Wesen des Antisemitismus" (History and essence of antisemitism), Strack made the obvious but often overlooked point that antisemitism was aimed exclusively at Jews.[82] Strack feared the spread of antisemitism and considered it a phenomenon that required constant engagement. In short, "Geschichte und Wesen des Antisemitismus" typified Strack's sense of urgency in the anti-antisemitic campaign.[83] Strack distinguished the causes of antisemitism from the means of spreading it. The "causes" Strack correctly identified with a wide variety of social, economic, and cultural factors, but he did not penetrate more deeply to the underlying motives of Jew hatred. The "means" of propagating antisemitism revealed Strack's excessive focus on religious issues. Specifically, Strack listed the blood libel, kosher slaughtering, the Talmud, the Shulchan Aruch, secret laws and sects within Judaism, the Kol Nidre vow, the sale of soiled meat, and Jewish cowardice as the staples of antisemitic propaganda. Strack devoted several works to refuting these "means," to which we will turn presently. Strack paid little attention to how antisemites galvanized their followers or what antisemitic meant in the antisemites' overall ideology. If there is something of the ivory tower in Strack's response, it does not detract from its moral thrust. Christians must defend Jews because their own self-defense labors under unfair prejudice. Christians must show Jews brotherly love at every opportunity. Christianity must prove itself the universal religion not through force but by word and deed. Finally, to those readers of *Nathanael* who agreed with antisemites that the Jews exerted too much influence, Strack advised: Be better subjects of your state, be better citizens of your cities. This piece of advice not only put the burden of toleration on the majority but did so in a way that looked forward rather than backward—challenging contemporary Christian behavior rather than lamenting past misdeeds.

Eliminating the blood libel as an effective weapon in the antisemitic arsenal ranks was perhaps the only victory scored by the Jews' defenders in the years before World War I. Strack played the decisive role in German-speaking lands. As early as 1882, during the Tisza-Eszlár trial, Strack had given witness in court to the effect that the blood libel was groundless. By 1891 Strack's denial had become a scholarly monograph, and by 1909, the date of the first English translation, *The Jews and Human Sacrifice* had evolved into a major work on human superstitions regarding the use of blood. Strack's foray into religious anthropology demonstrated his grasp of the universal taboos regarding blood, the biblical equation of blood as the essence of life (and therefore God's special property), and his knowledge of rabbinic kashrut laws regarding the consumption of blood. Strack forcefully tied *The Jews and Human Sacrifice*, at first glance a sober piece of scholarship, "to the fight against untruthfulness and superstition" out of his "sacred duty as Christian theologian."[84] The successive forewords to *The Jews and Human Sacrifice* indicate no small amount of scholarly pride in the political defeat of those who tried to stir up demonophobia through these means. However much Strack declared his scholarly objectivity, in the political context of late Imperial Germany it is difficult to avoid construing this work as pro-Jewish. Closely akin in spirit to the founding fathers of the Wissenschaft des Judentums, Strack considered apologetics a legitimate part of Judaica scholarship.[85]

Strack had made extreme efforts to master Jewish texts, and he resented those who had not, namely, antisemites.[86] As Strack often commented, the Talmud was no more a secret text than Caesar's *Commentaries on the Gallic War*. Strack insisted that the Jews neither desired nor would have been able to hide rabbinic texts. Strack's boast that his library possessed the basic talmudic manuscripts and that he was wholly in command of the scholarship betrays a forgivable measure of scholarly hauteur and anger at antisemitic intellectual laziness. Surprisingly, the missionary circle stressed that Judaism was no exotic cult. Gustaf Dalman, sometimes coeditor of *Nathanael* with Strack, asked, "Do you wish to know what contemporary Jewry teaches?" In that case, Dalman continued, examine contemporary books on Jewish religious instruction for children.[87] Another article in *Nathanael* by Heinrich Laible condemned the Papist plans to suppress derogatory notice of Jesus and Christianity in the Talmud as an idea foiled by God's intervention.[88] Delitzsch complained, "The most cultivated [*gebildetesten*] contemporary Christians know far more about the religious books of the Indians, the Persians, and the Chinese than of the Talmud and Midrash."[89] From Delitzsch to Strack, this stream of missionary thought had become more insistent: the mastery of Jewish texts was possible, desirable, and critical for contemporary Christians. The missionary circle's emphasis on religious texts cohered with their overemphasis on Judaism the religion as the source of Jewish identity and encouraged overconfident assertions about "the spirit of rabbinic Judaism." But their confrontation with the texts of the Judaic tradition at least anchored them to assessments based on reality instead of paranoid fantasy.

Strack's attitude toward Yiddish displays distinct philosemitic tendencies. As any student of German Jewry knows, Yiddish, the Jewish language of the Pale of Settlement, offered a perpetual target of hostility. Stigmatized as a corrupt German, generally called either "jargon" or the far more hostile *mauscheln*, Yiddish symbolized the failure of Jews to achieve Germanness.[90] Strack's familiarity with Yiddish, which he customarily referred to as *mame-loschen* (mother-tongue), first occurred during his three year sojourn in Russia (1873–76). Prompted by the impact of World War I and the influx of Ostjuden, Strack determined to write a book on Yiddish grammar and usage entitled *Jüdischen Wörterbuch*. As usual, Strack stressed the scholarly importance of the project for understanding Jewish culture but just as clearly emphasized that his was a work done for the benefit of the Protestant Church and the German people. Heinrich Laible expressed this pro-Jewish orientation in his review of Strack's *Jüdischen Wörterbuch*:

All too little have blind Jew haters in Germany heeded the truth of the universally known, indeed, the famous quotation of Ernst Moritz Arndt, "So far as the German tongue sounds." Far beyond the actual borders of Germany extends the German speech zone and, with it, Germany itself. All over the extra-German earth, where "Jewish" is spoken, there are German oases. While the Jews have other characteristics in customs and religion aplenty, the German tongue, which they speak, is an inextricable characteristic that stamps them as Germans. This fact, unhappily for those who hate the German tongue, makes the Jews over the world dear and valuable to us.[91]

Laible, whose writing is tinged with nationalistic and imperialistic coloration (not surprising for 1916), nevertheless considers Yiddish a legitimate and inseparable part of the German language. He aligns Yiddish-speaking Ostjuden with the national interest over against antisemites who are blind to Arndt's definition of German culture as existing everywhere the "German tongue" is heard.

In *Das Wesen des Judentums* (The essence of Judaism) Strack conjured up a strange animal with a philosemitic body and an antisemitic tail. His title signaled that the book, originally delivered as a lecture at the international missionary conference in Amsterdam, intended to contribute to the debate sparked by Adolf Harnack's *Das Wesen des Christentums* (The essence of Christianity). For Strack, Judaism possessed great strength, bound together as it was by ancestry, memory, and hope (*Verwandschaft, Erinnerungen,* and *Hoffnungen*). Strack emphasized the consciousness of God's positive deeds as opposed to the usual lachrymose presentation of past suffering. He noted the high degree of Jewish agreement on the sanctity of the Pentateuch, undercutting the claim that, riven by denominational strife, Judaism did not stand for any viewpoint. He observed the overall confidence in messianic fulfillment, whether personal or not, negating the presentation of Judaism as a religion only of the past and Jewish loyalties to it as based mainly on nostalgia. Strack drew on his decades of observing Jewish life to infuse the work with a verisimilitude rarely present in Christian descriptions of Judaism. So goes the body of Strack's text, presenting strength after strength, until we arrive at the tail, for all these strengths instilled a lofty self-consciousness (*Selbstgerechtigkeit*) that blinded Jews to the need of an extraordinary God to redeem the depravity of mankind. Judaism thus blinded Jews to the fallen state of humanity, keeping true salvation at arm's length.[92] It hardly needs saying that this judgment proceeded from Christian theology, not from empirical evidence—the conclusion of Strack's work is a pure non sequitur. Philosemitic and antisemitic to the end, Strack's *Wesen des Judentums* presented Jewish life as more vital and Jewish theology as more flawed than liberal Protestants realized.

Allosemitic Trajectories: The Legacy of Delitzsch and Strack

Allosemitism proves to be a helpful concept that eluded contemporaries of Delitzsch and Strack and subsequent scholarship alike. Certainly, Delitzsch's self-conception was avowedly philosemitic; as his daughter recalled in a published obituary, he wore the older crown of Judenfreund with pride. His anti-antisemitism resulted from a philosemitism born of personal contacts, study, and a rejection of Christian theological tendencies that marginalized the Old Testament. Nevertheless, his Lutheran orthodoxy made room for more traditional Christian feelings of superiority, supersessionism, and an annihilating chiliasm.[93] Delitzsch, whose anti-Judaic and pro-Judaic tendencies were compartmentalized and displayed variously according to the setting, must be described as antisemitic, philosemitic, and anti-antisemitic. Strack's self-perception was more complex than Delitzsch's. While Strack too had had at least one Jewish apostate as a teacher and enjoyed close ties with many Jews, he repeatedly declared himself neither antisemite nor philosemite: "I am not a 'Philo-semite' in the now generally accepted sense of the word."[94] In his book *Herr Adolf Stoecker, christliche Liebe und Wahrhaftigkeit* (Mr. Adolf Stoecker, Christian love and truthfulness), Strack attacked as superficial the division of all contributors to the Jewish question as either "antisemitic" or "philosemitic," although he himself employed these terms.[95] Philosemitism, for Strack, meant the uncritical championing of everything Jewish. He therefore denied the moniker philosemite adamantly but eagerly engaged in the defense of Judaism.[96] Every one of Strack's works, even the *Kommentar*, aimed at improving the evaluation of Jews and Judaism in Germany. Despite this, Strack's advocacy of Jews and Judaism coexisted comfortably with anti-Judaic prejudice.

Allosemitism may manifest itself either philosemitically or antisemitically or both. If we examine the trajectory of some of the successors to Delitzsch and Strack, we are drawn to the conclusion that only their unusually high level of involvement with matters Jewish permitted Delitzsch and Strack to compartmentalize these competing tendencies successfully. Deprived of these encounters, their successors reverted to traditional anti-Judaism. The following cursory survey (which would require further investigation) hints at this negative trajectory.

On the positive side of the balance, we have the encouraging example of Strack's successor in Berlin, Hugo Gressmann (1877–1927). Gressmann took Delitzsch's suggestion for creating a chair for a professor of Jewish studies a giant step forward by supporting a Jew for the position. Gressmann invited Jewish scholars to speak at the Institutum Judaicum, granted that they would be better able to represent Judaism than Christians, and supposed that Jews also considered that they possessed the "absolute religion." As an Old Testament scholar, Gressmann rejected a slew of typical appraisals inimical to Judaism. He mocked the standard caricature of an Old Testament "God of Wrath" and rejected the caesura between pre- and postexilic Judaism put forward by Wellhausen and others. To Gressmann, Judaism remained a coherent religion from first revelation to the present. Ulrich Kusche justly calls his discussion of Gressmann "Toward a Religion of Equal Rights."[97] August Wünsche (1839–1913), a student of Delitzsch, became an important translator of rabbinic materials into German. Wünsche continued Delitzsch's willingness to present contemporary Jewish scholarship to the Christian academy as well as the latter's spirit of collaboration. Wünsche joined Rabbi Joseph Winter in publishing the anthology *Jewish Literature since the Close of the Canon*, praised as "a model for later selections from Jewish literature."[98] Johannes Müller (1864–1949), another Delitzsch student, rejected missionary work altogether if it functioned to uproot Jews from their *Volk*. Jesus needed to be seen as "the fulfillment of a nationally and religiously true remaining Judaism." Müller thus rejected the old-style missionary activity as "against the essence and path of the Kingdom of God."[99] Thus it could be argued that the thorough de-demonization of Judaism found in Delitzsch and Strack contained the seeds of regarding Judaism as a legitimate religious path.

But a more ominous trajectory can also be found in the ranks of the succeeding generation. Johannes Hempel, who directed the Institutum Judaicum in Berlin from 1937 to 1945, found it possible to toe the Nazi line. Hempel, Alfred Bertholet, and Joachim Jeremias never challenged the basic dichotomies of primitive Christianity and rabbinic Judaism enshrined in the Strack-Billerbeck *Kommentar*. Ferdinand Weber's *System der altsynagogalen palästinischen Theologie* (System of old synagogue theology), identified by Christian critics from Moore to Sanders as a principal culprit in keeping unfair dichotomies of Christianity and Judaism alive, won the plaudits of his old teacher—Franz Delitzsch.[100] Delitzsch's youngest son, Friedrich, stirred up a huge controversy with his book *Bibel und Babel*, regarded by most Jewish scholars as an assault on their claim to spiritual-intellectual creativity. Even Johannes Müller, who believed Jews had a right to remain within their *Volk*, joined the German Christians.

These speculations regarding the allosemitic legacy of Delitzsch and Strack should not obscure the basic conclusions reached in this essay. From the emergence of political antisemitism from 1879 to 1881, missionary Protestants spoke out against antisemitism even as they continued to harbor anti-Jewish sentiments. Delitzsch and Strack mounted the most aggressive defense of Judaism in Germany before World War I, a reality that has been glossed over in the historiography.[101] We find in Delitzsch and Strack a view of Second Temple and early rabbinic Judaism least colored by the regnant Spätjudentum approach. While affirming the inevitable conversion of the Jews, they envisaged a greater role for Judaism in Germany's religious landscape than did liberal Protestants. Delitzsch and Strack did not approach the first tentative steps toward religious dialogue that occurred in the Weimar Era, and they do not approximate a late-twentieth-century notion of religious pluralism. To judge by the obituaries in the Jewish press, however, German Jews would have risked the threat of a few more apostates for a few more defenders of the caliber of Delitzsch and Strack, and that says a great deal.[102] German Jews needed all the friends they could get, even if these friends were mainly "enemies of my enemy."

Part 2. Philosemitic Tendencies and Individuals

5. The Gentile Reception
of Herzlian Zionism

The Limits of Autoemancipation

Beginning with Leon (Lev) Pinsker's *Selbstemanzipation* (autoemancipation, 1882), Zionists have insisted that Jews control their own fate, leaving it neither to God nor to others. But in reality, the distinction between emancipation and autoemancipation could not be as absolute as Pinsker suggested. Even Pinsker, a Russian physician, wrote his tract in German and directed it to Western Jewry. Theodor Herzl understood the limits of this dichotomy: his Zionism was too dependent on international diplomacy to ignore the non-Jewish world. From the First Zionist Congress in 1897 until the outbreak of World War I, Zionism attained world prominence due in large measure to Herzl's theatrical and journalistic sense of how to project mass support and cultivate public opinion. Congresses and committees, Jewish student groups, publications in the European vernaculars, organizations dedicated to land purchases all served to promote (and Westernize) a movement that had begun as clandestine cells in the Pale of Settlement. The Balfour Declaration, granting international recognition to the Jewish desire for a homeland in Palestine, must be understood in the context of a brutal war. But had Zionism not achieved a measure of prominence before 1917, the Balfour Declaration would not have been issued in the first place. How Zionism made it onto the map of world consciousness, where it has remained, is surely a topic that deserves consideration.

Early histories of Zionism, written before Israel's independence, took great pains to mention Gentile precursors and to document Gentile support.[1] Historiography since 1948 has paid less attention to the reception Gentiles accorded early Zionism. Except for Norman Rose's important book on British philo-Zionists and Michael Praeger's sketch of pro-Zionist sentiment in the modern era, scholarly attention has focused on idiosyncratic figures such as the Reverend William Henry Hechler and Friedrich, the grand duke of Baden.[2] Rose himself distinguishes between the deeds of Gentile Zionists and their "roots" and "motivations."[3] Rose's attitude reflects a post-1949 verdict that what really matters about Zionism is its political success. But Zionism began as a revolution in Jewish consciousness, with profound implications for Jewish and Gentile interaction.[4] Perhaps the time has come to revisit the Gentile reactions to Zionism in the German *Kulturbereich*—Herzl's native language and the "official" language of early Zionism.[5]

This chapter makes two claims. First, it claims that the early movement consciously promoted its Gentile ties and advertised its Gentile support. During the critical first decade of 1896–1906, this "foreign policy" was really an attempt to stir up Gentile sympathy and knowledge—it could be termed a policy of cultivating philosemitism, though of a different variety that interested Jewish apologists of the liberal-emancipationist outlook.[6] An analysis of the Zionist journal *Die Welt* validates a perceptive remark of the late Salo Baron: "In the case of Jews, we must remember, anti-Semitism or philo-Semitism has always played the role of the people's foreign relations, parallel to those affecting states in their relations with one another."[7] To paraphrase Gershom Scholem, early Zionism "returned Jews to history." By World War I there were Zionist interests and projects ready to be spotlighted. Philosemitism prepared the groundwork for practical endeavors.[8]

My second claim has to do with Herzl's message and with Gentile "readings" of things Jewish; namely, Herzl understood that a variety of Christians with a variety of mutually exclusive worldviews found something attractive in his brand of Zionism. That the solutions these non-Jews offered to the Jewish question reflected their own presuppositions comes as no surprise. Yet this variety helps us to grasp how three figures as varied as the missionary Protestant Carl Friedrich Heman, the literary radical Hermann Bahr, and the liberal Bertha von Suttner all found a way to write and lobby in favor of Herzlian Zionism. Herzl's own character, his open-ended approach to potential supporters, his sincere belief that he possessed the key to the Jewish question all provided well-intentioned non-Jews with a way to support him, despite their disagreement with certain Zionist fundamentals and with each other. The parallels between the antisemitic assault on Jewry and the Zionist critique of Jewish life in the Diaspora have been frequently noted. As Jacob Katz observed, several antisemites regarded themselves as saying something very akin to Zionists.[9] Non-Jewish "misreadings" of Zionism existed among the ill intentioned and the well intentioned.[10]

Projecting Christian Support: Die Welt

Since Amos Elon's biography, Herzl's theatrical staging of Zionism has been acknowledged. Research published in *Kesher* has further documented the press coverage accorded early Zionism.[11] Notwithstanding the opposition of Western Jewry, the foreign press reported favorably and widely on the First Zionist Congress, attended by several prominent non-Jews. Herzl had reason to hope for support from beyond the pale of Jewish life. He was determined to cultivate and publicize that support, partly through his brainchild, *Die Welt*.[12] *The Encyclopedia of Zionism and Israel* describes *Die Welt* (1897–1914) as "a new force in Jewish life. Its columns carried accounts of developments in Jewish affairs. . . . In addition, the paper stressed Zionist activities, Hebrew culture (particularly literature), and Jewish history and art."[13] Grandiose and internationalist, a glance at *Die Welt* tells us still more about the movement: it was political, modern, straightforward, and polemical. The provocative front page of the first issue bore, in yellow, a globe inside the Star of David and proudly proclaimed itself to be a Judenblatt (Jew paper).[14]

The number of articles and notices dealing with the Christian reception of Zionism or the Christian perspective on world Jewry or Christian attitudes toward the Jewish question in *Die Welt* is striking. At least a dozen major articles appeared in both 1897 and 1898 and half a dozen in 1899. Birthday greetings and obituaries dedicated to figures like the grand duke of Baden and the Reverend Hechler could not have been more appropriate, given their services to the cause. *Die Welt* praised Kaiser Wilhelm II's world politics and overlooked his antisemitism, attempting to give the impression of imperial favor. Minibiographies of friendly non-Jews graced the pages. Two long articles by Hutchins Hapgood, the American Protestant muckraker on Yiddish theater, appeared as well. Literary efforts—prose and poetry—punctuated many issues. Although a self-described Judenblatt, the very first issue of *Die Welt* announced a circular (*Rundfrage*) that posed the following four questions (an allusion to the Passover Haggadah?) to Christian "authors and politicians." These questions and the responses they generated serve as our point of departure:

- What do you think about Zionism?
- Don't you believe that Zionism can improve the lot of the Jewish masses and solve the Jewish question?
- Don't you think it is in Turkey's interest to settle hard-working, tax-paying Jewish farmers?
- Don't you believe that the European states can solve the Jewish question through a legal recognition of the Jewish people?[15]

The respondents formed a varied group: Hechler, Herzl's personal prophet; Baroness Bertha von Suttner and Hermann Bahr, whose relationships to Herzl will be discussed below; the Rumanian minister Pres. Demeter Stourdza; Father Ignatius, a Welsh monk; the Polish statesman Stanislaus von Kozmian; and the British prime minister William Gladstone. By the end of the year several more Christian witnesses had been called, including the archbishop of Westminster; the journalists Arnold White and Jaques Behar; the novelist Friedrich Fürst Wrede; Jean Henri Dunant, the founder of the Red Cross; and Johann Graf Badeni, a Jesuit and nephew of Poland's president.[16] Most of these responses were long on sympathy and short on knowledge. (After all, the First Zionist Congress did not meet until late August of that year.) Few respondents were in a position to offer any tangible aid to the movement. The prominence of this series, "Christen über die Judenfrage," tells us more about what the editors of *Die Welt* wished to project to their readers than about the depth of Christian support.[17]

Die Welt, despite its Germanic orientation, regarded itself as the organ of world Zionism—indeed, of world Jewry. French testimony dealt principally with the Dreyfus affair. On 4 February 1898 *Die Welt* reproduced a long article by Emile Zola from *Le Figaro*.[18] "Für die Juden" (For the Jews) offered a standard rejection of antisemitism, indistinguishable from the defensive tone of German liberals: "Above all, what reproaches are raised against the Jews, with what are they charged? If the Jews had centuries to learn to love money and how to earn it, their concentration in this area only follows; you must follow them in this area, and you must develop your abilities in order to battle them with their own weapons."[19]

Zola's article would have been more accurately titled "Against the Antisemites." Zola chided the Christian world for the Jewish deficiencies that he accepted as real and mocked the paranoid fear that "hardly 5 million Jews" would impose their will on 200 million Catholics. Zola returned several times to the theme of a dwindling Jewish minority, a fact that should have shamed antisemites and encouraged assimilationists. Zola called on French society to facilitate complete assimilation. "If there are still Jews, that is your fault. They would have long disappeared and melted away had you not forced them to defend themselves, to stick together, and to pass on their race."[20] Zola and Herzl agreed that Western Jews were willing to assimilate, but their conclusions contradict this assertion. Zola demands intermarriage, abjuration of race hatred, and "the work of unity, humanity, and liberation [*Befreiung*]." Since Zola claimed that antisemitism had no deep roots in France and was soon to be defeated, this demand must be read as endorsing assimilation. Why, then, did the editors publish this diatribe in the nationalist *Die Welt*?

Whatever the answer, this article was no fluke. On 27 May 1898 *Die Welt* carried another article by another prominent Dreyfusard, Georges Clemenceau.[21] Although Clemenceau had come to the same conclusion about Dreyfus's innocence, he displays animosity toward French Jews; his rhetorical flourish that he would have similarly defended a Christian against the fanaticism of the Talmud projected a wholly unnecessary, not to mention unreal, image of Jewish power. Clemenceau took pains to avoid giving the impression that French Jewry possessed the moral upper hand in this scandal. Indeed, most of the article derides Jews who refused to support the Dreyfusard cause. Clemenceau attributed hyperpatriotic asseverations to a sycophantic desire to prove French Jewry "more royalist than the king."[22] He was angered at the radical democrat L. L. Klotz, a deputy from Montidier who opposed revision. Clemenceau attributed this hyperpatriotism not to the affair (the very name Klotz, like Dreyfus, suggested a German background) but rather to an innate Jewish quality. He wrote, "Above all he [the Jew] respects power, for he is induced by his Oriental viewpoint regarding the inevitability of the history of suppression that submission to outside power will in the end work to his advantage."[23] Clemenceau implied that Jews do not make good citizens because their Jewish qualities compromised their objectivity. As Clemenceau said nothing about Jewish nationalism as a remedy, *Die Welt* seems to have willed him into agreement with Zionism *ex silentio*.

Lord Salisbury's "Living and Extinct Nations" linked suffering and nobility in a typically lachrymose presentation—his reading of Jewish history as "suffering and oppression" matched Herzl's closely.[24] Salisbury's optimism regarding the Jewish future must have resonated well in the ears of Zionist leaders constantly being mocked for utopianism. Salisbury wrote, "It hangs entirely on the Jews themselves whether or not this idea [Zionism] can be realized. If only 40 percent from their ranks engage themselves energetically for the matter, its success would be certain."[25] Zionism never came close to achieving 40 percent support from the Jewish world (at least not before Hitler), but here was a prominent English figure insisting, in agreement with Herzl's *Altneuland* (Oldnewland), that Zionism was no fairy tale. The concluding sentence of Salisbury's address must have made readers proud: "The Jewish nation, which could successfully survive a stormy 2,500 years, possesses enough patience and fortitude to successfully follow through an undertaking such as Zionism."[26] For the editors of *Die Welt*, Britain was special. British philosemites were more forthcoming than their Continental counterparts, and Herzl himself was an Anglophile. Most important, Britain in 1903 supported the ill-fated East Africa project to find a temporary asylum for Jews suffering from pogroms, a project that Herzl championed. *Die Welt* was extremely eager to demonstrate that it enjoyed Gentile support, even when this was somewhat debatable. The author of "Minister Chamberlain über die Judenfrage" (Minister Chamberlain on the Jewish question) rejoiced in Chamberlain's use of the term the "Jewish people," even while the article ignored his non-Zionist conclusion that "their national properties and religious steadfastness make Jews the most loyal citizens of the states to which they belong."[27] A stream of reports on prominent British statesmen, scientists, and adventurers filled the pages of *Die Welt* before World War I.[28] These expressions of sympathy and practical suggestions fall into the category of pre–foreign policy as well as philosemitism, dealing with emerging realities in East Africa and Palestine and projecting a sentiment that Zionism could tap.

The depredations of the Pale of Settlement provided plenty of raw material for a negative appraisal of the Jewish condition at the fin de siècle. *Die Welt* covered the terrorization of Pale Jewry unflinchingly but contained better news as well. Sympathetic figures from Eastern Europe were quoted after each new wave of pogroms.[29] Since Herzl and other Zionists had come to the conclusion that the situation of Jews in the Pale was intolerable, why did *Die Welt* bother to record the views of the benevolent minority?[30] Why devote numerous articles showing that even in Eastern Europe the Jews had their champions? It was the inherent liberalism of Herzlian Zionism, emphasized by Arthur Hertzberg, Steven Beller, Jacques Kornberg, and others. However much Zionists desired to show that antisemitism rendered Jewish life in the Diaspora unbearable, they also wished to show that antisemitism contained its own remedy. This innate optimism of Herzl, as Hertzberg argued in *The Zionist Idea: A Historical Analysis and Reader*, enabled him to confront the reality of antisemitism without the despair of a Pinsker.[31] To apply Hertzberg's point, *Die Welt* wanted its readers to know that even in the Pale there were righteous Gentiles who sympathized with the Jewish plight—and who could lobby for its rational solution.

Since German was the first language of the journal's founder, editor, and much of its staff, the prominence of German-speaking Christian contributors was predictable. Nearly half (seven sixteenths) of the contributors to the Christians on the Jewish question series were Germanophones. The vast literature produced in German on the *Judenfrage* enabled the editors to demonstrate virtually any proposition: that most Germans were antisemites; that there were dozens of German philosemites; that Germans believed in emancipation; that Germans did not believe in emancipation. Like hesitant students in a multiple-choice exam, the editors of *Die Welt* chose all of the above. Christian enthusiasts for Zion won a special place in the journal's pages. Jean Henri Dunant had been engaged for decades in trying (unsuccessfully) to stir up support for the idea of restoring the Jews to Palestine. Writing from nearby Geneva after the conclusion of the First Zionist Congress, Dunant assured newcomers: "Believe me, there are Protestants who are as Zionistic as the most convinced orthodox Zionists of the Basel Congress, and they are such through the ideal itself, through an ideal feeling without political, religious, social, or personal interest."[32] Friedrich Fuerst Wrede, who traveled in the same literary circle as Herzl, did not believe that antisemitism could overturn emancipation. Wrede conceded to world Jewry the right to decide whether it was a religious confession or a people (*Volk*). He insisted that if the Jews "really desired it," the force of nationalism would guarantee their success and the support of the right-minded, even if the host countries would be impoverished by the Jews' departure. Similarly philosemitic if more romantic than rational was Paula Winkler's effusive "Betrachtungen einer Philozionistin" (Confessions of a philo-Zionist).[33] Paula Winkler, later Paula Buber, was a Catholic-born avant-garde author who encountered Zionism while a university student in Vienna. Dunant's example demonstrated lineage and depth of support; Wrede's, the sympathies of the secular intelligentsia; Winkler's, a passionate love for the Jewish people and the Zionist cause. Baron Maxim Manteuffel, supporter of agricultural training farms for Jews, testified to the sheer excitement of the Zionist enterprise, calling his "three indescribable days at Basle" and his trip to Palestine the most profound moments in his life.[34] More than ever, wrote Manteuffel, he believed in Zionism's success.

These views qualified as pro-Zionist and pro-Jewish. Other views from prominent Germans were less transparent. Werner Sombart, the economist who attributed modern capitalism to the Jews, was a perennial Zionist favorite, lauded by a variety of Zionist journals and student fraternities.[35] Sombart, a *völkisch* nationalist who later endorsed the Nazis, supported a segregationist solution to the Jewish question—as, arguably, did Zionism. But Sombart was not the only antisemite featured in the pages of *Die Welt*. Heinrich Driesman's article, deriding Jewish racial pride, clashed with the views of some Zionists that Jews should be defined as a race.[36] While publishing views like Sombart's and Driesman's, in retrospect, could be considered playing with fire, they were pro-Zionist. A number of pamphlets combined antisemitism and Zionism. One of these, by the Austrian Camilla Theimer, *Antisemitismus und Nationaljudentum* (Antisemitism and national Judaism), conceded that the Jews "are only that which we, the Aryans, have made of them."[37] Nevertheless, this "full-blooded Aryan" considered the Jewish desire to assimilate futile, while Zionism offered "to restore to the Jews their lost human dignity." A Herzl enthusiast, "long before I knew his Zionist writings," Theimer had no doubt about Jewish abilities but wished to see them deployed elsewhere. Herzlian Zionism offered Theimer a morally palatable way to forward a segregationist solution to the Jewish question.

More baffling was the publication of views of anti-Zionists (or non-Zionists) who happened to be philosemitic. Arthur von Suttner, president of the Austrian branch of the Abwehrverein, defended his organization against Herzl's claim that it demonstrated Gentile nobility but also Jewish impotence. Herzl wrote: "Jews [without backbone] should not be protected by the Verein zur Abwehr, its members are too good for that. But Jews who are upright want to defend themselves and must do so, and even this will raise them but a little in the esteem of their adversaries. The Verein zur Abwehr can do us one more favor: It should disband."[38] Suttner replied that as an Austrian and as a humanist, he had no choice but to oppose a campaign of vilification—had it been initiated against Protestants or Muslims, wrote Suttner, he would have reacted no differently.[39] Bertha von Suttner, an Austrian peace activist whose close collaboration with Herzl will be discussed below, contributed several articles to *Die Welt*. Eventually a regular contributor, her initial words in *Die Welt* expressed a very guarded view regarding Zionism's desirability: "I ask whether assimilation is not preferable to the formation of a new state and nation. I desire all reasonable people to assimilate to the higher type of European or cultivated human [*Kulturmensch*], an idea that is now in the process of becoming and that is beyond national, religious, and social conceit and fanaticism."[40]

At times, explaining the motivations of the editorial board stymies logic. How to explain the inclusion of a lengthy obituary of Mathias Jakob Schleiden (1804–81), a botanist who became an impassioned critic of Christianity's abuse of Judaism?[41] *Die Welt* related the Norwegian writer Björnstjerne Björnson's story about buying a winter coat in Chicago from a Jewish furrier who was distraught to have his fears about Russian pogroms confirmed. Björnson wrote to express his disgust at antisemitism and his admiration for a nation that cultivated such deep feelings in its fellow members.[42] Articles such as these presumably functioned to reassure readers that there were Christians who cared and took notice of Jewish suffering—the loose thread tying together a wide range of non-Zionist Christians who appeared in *Die Welt*.

During its first decade, Zionism attracted the attention of some important figures in German life. The first major figure to appear in *Die Welt* was Pastor Friedrich Naumann, whose article in the Berlin weekly *Die Zeit* was reproduced with praise.[43] Naumann understood very well that Zionism opposed the project of assimilation. He grasped that Zionism was meant above all for Ostjuden, whose misery demanded a solution and whose emotional connection to Zion was still strong. He intuited the importance of a legal charter and the role of the Zionist congresses as parliaments-in-exile and as morale boosters for the movement. Raising the question of Zionism's feasibility, Naumann noted the colonial aspirations of other European nations but believed that the German-cultural orientation of European Jewry (including the preservation of the Germanic language Yiddish by 5 million Jews) promised an alliance with the Christian German colonists of Palestine. Were 5 million Jews to settle in Palestine, a figure that seemed feasible given that even ancient Israel had a population of 2 million, Naumann felt sure the Jewish entity would be viable—and valuable for German colonial interests. Naumann had no doubt too that the diminution of Europe's Jewish population would ease the intensity of the Jewish question. His conclusion dovetailed with Zionism's determination to prove technocratic feasibility, a factor that held little interest for enthusiasts such as Hechler.

"Karl Kautsky über Judentum und jüdisches Proletariat" (Karl Kautsky on Judaism and the Jewish proletariat) reproduced an interview given to the London Jewish-socialist journal *New Times*.[44] At the time, Kautsky was one of Germany's leading socialist theoreticians, an opponent of both antisemitism and Jewish nationalism. Predictably, Kautsky dealt with the particular natures of Jewish and English socialism. He praised the intellectual contributions of Jews to Western civilization, in particular economics, which he attributed to their particular psychic construction and social circumstances. Kautsky held that Jews had a special gift for abstract and critical thinking. Kautsky, acting as a shadchan for the Jewish and non-Jewish proletariat of London, presented these gifts as the perfect complement to the English working man's natural love of freedom. Together, these forces could be expected to effect a revolution in the English socialist movement. Kautsky did not mention Zionism—he believed in the orthodox Marxist solution to the Jewish question. But the editors seized on Kautsky's willingness to talk about the Jewish nation, noting that only a few years earlier Kautsky had not even conceded that the Jews constituted a nation. That, apparently to the editors of *Die Welt*, offered sufficient justification for declaring victory.

Die Welt, Herzlian Zionism's first sounding board, set a low threshold for determining Christian support.[45] One did not have to favor Zionism or even be aware of its existence. One did not have to like Jews personally, and disliking Jewish assimilators was an advantage. One did not have to have any practical orientation to the Jewish question. In time, the bar was raised as Zionism became better known and won some actual (as opposed to theoretical) supporters. Despite this shift, *Die Welt* continued to publish a wide range of Gentile opinion, cultivating a sense that some non-Jews understood and cared about Jewish problems. Contrary to Pinsker's supposition, "What will the goyim say" continued to matter to the party of autoemancipation.

Three Gentile Supporters of Herzl

Carl Friedrich Heman (1839–1922), an Orientalist at the University of Basle, belonged to the German Protestant millenary tradition of men such as Carl Zimpel, Johannes Lepsius, Herman Maas, Gustaf Dalman, and, of course, the Reverend Hechler. These men wrote tracts, established organizations in the Holy Land, visited the Zionist congresses, and gave material support to the movement. Hechler, by virtue of his friendship with Friedrich, the grand duke of Baden, appeared at one point to be a pivotal figure in winning imperial support. These figures have been consigned to historical footnotes, but they shed light on how Zionism so quickly caught the world's attention. This examination also illuminates how Herzl deftly encouraged the perception of a congruity of aims between Christians and Jews while underplaying the discordant elements.

Heman presented his credentials as an expert on the Jewish question fifteen years before the emergence of Zionism. In *Die historische Weltstellung der Juden und der moderne Judenfrage* (The historical situation of the Jews and the modern Jewish question, 1882), Heman advanced the thesis that the Jews' nationality and religion were inseparable. Unlike the Wends, who accepted their amalgamation to the German nation, and unlike the French and Polish minorities, who had no expectations of playing a role in German culture or in wielding power, German Jewry demanded the best of both worlds. But in a Christian state, reasoned Heman, this expectation could not be realized. For Heman, the Jews faced a clear choice.

They could opt for amalgamation, which would include a voluntary abandonment of their religion, without which their national sentiment would wither away. Alternatively, German Jews could accept their national distinctness and surrender all positions of influence. At this stage, Heman regarded either an assimilationist or a segregationist solution as acceptable. He raised the possibility of the Jews returning to their homeland but without any accompanying proposals.[46] Heman's subsequent claim that he had been advocating a return to the Jewish homeland for fifteen years was considerably exaggerated. Nonetheless, with the advent of Herzl in 1896–97, Heman became a convinced Zionist, defending Zionism before a missionary movement that saw secularism as the very embodiment of the Antichrist.[47]

Hechler and Heman were not the only Christian messianists energized by the advent of Herzl. Edward Browne, an American Baptist, barraged Herzl with letters, prophetically suggesting that Florida might be suitable for Jewish settlement should Palestine prove unavailable.[48] Ernst Rohmer, an Alsatian writing under the pseudonym "Zionicus," praised Herzl's *Der Judenstaat* and clearly regarded Herzl in a messianic light.[49] The Englishman H. d. Ablaing affirmed his belief in the Jews' messianic role, offered financial support for Russian Jewry, and promised Herzl diplomatic aid. Ablaing, who had previously told Herzl that he looked forward to the day when Jesus would rule over both Christians and Jews, wondered "whether you [Herzl] have ever asked Him His blessing and help, which He is so ready to give when asked."[50] The messianic aura surrounding Herzl extended beyond Jewish circles.[51] As Heman wrote: "The name of the man who has been allotted the role of calling the Jewish national movement to life will remain unforgettable in the annals of the Jewish people [*Volk*], because with his appearance a new epoch of Jewish history has begun, an epoch that, when it reaches its goal, promises to lag behind none of the glorious ages of ancient Jewish history. [The name of the man] is Dr. Herzl."[52]

What Heman found appealing in Herzl's person and message is clear. Both men shared a view that Zionism was the solution to an otherwise unsolvable European Jewish question, that Zionism could effect a fundamental improvement of Jewish character, and that Zionism could forge a bridge between West and East in the Holy Land.[53] Heman was a genuine enthusiast, but a closer look at his interpretation of Herzlian Zionism on these points indicates that philosemitic goals were deeply embedded in antisemitic premises.

Herzl believed that antisemitism was a problem for both Jews and national governments, and he interpreted Jew hatred mainly along economic lines, namely, as the natural product of middle-class economic competition. Heman conceded that the love of assimilated Jews for Germany could not be doubted but considered this a political love only. Culturally, assimilated Jews wished to be cosmopolitans; religiously, they wished to be Jews, keeping distinct customs and demanding to be buried in separate cemeteries. Whereas Zionists argued that the striving for assimilation exacerbated anti-Semitism, Heman went an important step further: "The Zionists have also recognized that this assimilation striving [*Assimilationssucht*] is actually the cause for contemporary antisemitism."[54] On another occasion, Heman described the popular antipathy for Jews on racial and national lines as grounded in human nature—should Mongolians or blacks move to Germany and claim brotherhood, they would call into existence an antiblack or anti-Mongolian movement.

Judging from his pre-Zionist ruminations about mass conversion and the possibility of assimilation, one can assume that Herzl expected a withering away of the Diaspora. Heman again took a Herzlian premise in an uncomfortable direction. Although he assured the readers of *Die Welt* that the emergence of Zionism would not encourage antisemites, *Das Erwachen der jüdischen Nation* (The awakening of the Jewish nation, 1897) clearly saw no future for European Jewry once Zionism succeeded. Since an alternative to minority Jewish status would soon exist, European governments would be justified in pressuring the remaining European Jews to convert or to have Jews voluntarily abandon their recently won equality. Heman wrote, "The only [answer to this question], the only way out of this confused, uncomfortable situation, is the free-willed resignation by the Jews of German nationality."[55] Heman used Herzlian Zionism to reconcile an eschatological vision with profound hostility to pluralism.

Herzl's underestimation of the national aspirations of indigenous Arabs was a great failing (as Ahad Ha'Am recognized), but it was not born of malice. Heman, on the contrary, took umbrage at the current political situation in the Middle East, writing, "In whose hands the Holy Land belongs cannot be a matter of indifference to Christians."[56] Heman's defamation of Islam and vision of Jews as surrogates for Christian imperialism departs from Herzl's naïveté. Contemptuously dismissing the Reform Jewish pretensions to a universal mission, Heman boasted that Christian missionaries were bringing monotheism to the Third World.[57] As to Judaism's role as the mother religion to Islam, Heman writes, "Here, also, it would be better for the rabbis to keep silent. Judaism certainly has no reason to be proud of the daughterhood [*Tochterschaft*] of Islam." Judaism was morally inferior to Christianity, but Islam stood "far below both" and fit poorly into Heman's eschatological framework. While contemporary scholars may contend over whether the colonialist elements within Zionism are latent or blatant, the possibility of a twentieth-century Crusade carried out by Jewish soldiers was music to Heman's ears.[58]

How did Herzl and Heman, who met once, briefly, after the end of the Second Zionist Congress, react to each other? The few letters they exchanged permit only tentative conclusions. Heman seemed at pains to demonstrate to Herzl that his status as secretary for the missionary Basel Friends of Israel did not mean that he wished to convert Jews into Christians. Heman insisted that turning Jews into

Goyimchristen would be a calamity for both sides. Heman expected a state that only Jews could build. "*Der Israelit* [a German Orthodox Jewish journal] has called me a missionary. Oh! If I could be called a missionary I would rather be called a missionary for Zionism! That is the idea to which the future belongs."[59] Like Jewish predecessors such as Nathan Birnbaum and Ahad Ha'Am, Heman combined admiration for Herzl's practical accomplishment with a touch of jealousy. Heman reminded Herzl that he had been agitating for Zionism for fifteen years. Heman was not above lecturing Herzl as to the true nature of the movement. At the end of the Sixth Zionist Congress Heman expressed his hope that the East Africa project had been definitively abandoned, calling it the "ruin and the suicide of Zionism," without any acknowledgment that Herzl had supported the scheme and put his leadership on the line.[60] Responding with thanks to a letter from Herzl, Heman noted that the name given to the newly established Culture Commission was ill chosen. Expressing a view much closer to Martin Buber's Zionism than Herzl's, he wrote, "It [the commission] does not deal with culture but rather with a moral-religious renaissance of the Jewish people."[61]

We can guess at Herzl's response to these missives, which included a request for an honorarium. But Herzl had a soft spot for religious fanatics—as long as they were Christians. Turning down a second article from Heman, Herzl explained that the analysis would furnish too much material for Zionism's enemies, even though he agreed with every word. Admitting in his charming manner that he always felt a bit chauvinistic that Jesus was a Jew, Herzl closed with the excuse that while opportunism was disgraceful, pragmatism in the service of a cause was necessary. A few days later, Herzl begged forgiveness for failing to answer Heman's most recent letter. Herzl again stressed his agreement with Heman's expectation for spiritual greatness from Zion but insisted that the tree had to be planted before it would bear blooms.[62] Heman continued to support Zionism after Herzl's death.[63] Like other enthusiasts, however, the apex of his activity coincided with the appearance of Herzl and was fueled by his relationship with Herzl.

Hermann Bahr (1863–1934), a pioneer of modernist literature, met Herzl at the University of Vienna in the 1880s.[64] Bahr was instrumental in the pro-Wagnerian student demonstrations, which came close to having him expelled and which led directly to Herzl's resignation from Albia, the student fraternity, when it adopted antisemitic membership restrictions. Bahr admired the Austrian antisemite Georg Schoenerer, but by the 1890s his attitude toward Jews and Judaism had changed dramatically, typical of Bahr's many oscillations throughout his career. During an extended stay in Berlin, Bahr formulated the idea of conducting an international interview on the theme of antisemitism. The resulting book, published in 1894, offers exactly what Bahr hoped it would at the time of publication: frank assessments of the Jewish question in the early 1890s.[65] *Der Antisemitismus. Ein International Interview* did not have a clear anti-antisemitic agenda, as did some of the other *Rundfrage* circulated in the same period. Efforts to combat antisemitism, Bahr held, were futile, for antisemitism was an end in itself, "the morphine of little people."[66] Despite this depressing prognosis, his introductory comments leave no doubt that Bahr had turned his back on antisemitism. In 1895 Bahr married a Jewish actress (Rosa Jokl), with whom he would remain until 1909. His father, Alois, opposed the marriage and, for a time, forbade the young couple to visit the parental home. The next year Bahr fought a duel in a Jewish student's stead, Jews being unable at the time to claim "satisfaction" against antisemitic slanders. By this time Bahr had become a leading member of the writers and artists known as the Jung-Wien circle, many of whom were Jewish. It is clear from his diaries and letters that Bahr traveled in a mixed Jewish-Christian circle that included, on its periphery, his erstwhile fraternity brother, Theodor Herzl.[67] Although Bahr turned toward Catholicism and conservatism in his later years, he remained opposed to antisemitism, undermining racial determinism in his novel *Die Rotte Korahs* (Korah's rabble).[68]

Herzl stood at the center of Bahr's Zionist sympathies, although Bahr initially described *Der Judenstaat* as "Don Quixoterie."[69] Herzl soon won Bahr over, although, as we shall see, Bahr's take on Zionism remained idiosyncratic. During their walks in the Austrian capital Herzl confided in Bahr his struggles to get the movement on its feet. Bahr's diary entries indicate how deeply he and his friends were moved by Herzl's death—and his impressive funeral: "It was only at Herzl's funeral that I began to understand fully just what he meant. The procession lasted for hours. I went with it. And I realized that I was in an alien world. This dark mass murmuring words incomprehensible to my ear was moving through Vienna toward the Promised Land. And Herzl's achievement is this: He restored to his people the feeling of their home [*Gefühl einer Heimat*]."[70] Elsewhere, in a similar vein, Bahr wrote: "Those who only knew Herzl from the editorial desk or from premiers, or the feuilletonist, the gentle charming mocker, Herzl the man of the world, would probably poke fun at the Herzl who carried the Polish Jew in his heart. I, however, have known Herzl the Jewish person."[71]

Bahr had keen insight into the prominent role that honor played in Herzl's worldview, and, like Herzl, Bahr also favored a "Great German" (Grossdeutsch) solution while at the same time idolizing Otto von Bismarck. In other words, Bahr knew very well the nationalist ethos and the Viennese world that nurtured Herzl. Nevertheless, placing Herzl correctly in a Zionist context eluded him. For Bahr, Herzl represented the authentic Jew with deep feelings toward his nation. Recalling Martin Buber's famous distinction between the leader (Herzl) and the teacher (Ahad Ha'Am) as well as the position Herzl took on the East Africa proposal, Bahr's verdict seems hilariously wrong. If anything, the congresses restored Herzl's sentiment of a homeland, not the other way around. To credit Herzl with having the Polish Jews ever in his heart is also a strange judgment considering his contempt for his "army of schnorrers" and the fact that Herzl went to the Jewish masses only after the Jewish plutocrats had shown him the door. Yet Bahr was in good company in his estimation of Herzl as Europe's noblest Jew—not since Moses Mendelssohn had one man become the lightning rod for expectations of an improved Jewish individual and corporate future.

Bahr's idiosyncratic view of Zionism knew no limits. Bahr said that he became a supporter of Zionism on "aesthetic" grounds. Not only would Zionism allow Jews to lead nobler lives, undisturbed by poverty and filth, the ideal itself would prove inspirational to Jews whatever its actual prospects of success.[72] Although he admitted to initially opposing Zionism as a Jewish chauvinism, Bahr had come to the view that "Zionism is good for the Jews and good for our culture."[73] He declared himself "swept away" by the archbishop of Canterbury's image of the world as a quilt and individual nations its composite colors. The solution to the Jewish question, which the rationalist Herzl described as a mathematical formula or as an engineering feat, Bahr had transformed into romantic poetry.

Even after fifteen years of Zionist sympathy Bahr remained unique. In an address given to the Jewish circle in Prague in 1911, Bahr "confessed" that he had married a Jewish woman and had many Jewish friends yet was not a Jew—notwithstanding reports in the antisemitic press.[74] Bahr described the manifold ways in which European society still refused full admittance to the Jews, a theme he had also raised in his review of Herzl's play Das neue Ghetto (The new ghetto).[75] Bahr then revealed that his greatest insights into the Jewish question came not from his marriage, his various friendships, or his studies but from his close acquaintance since youth with the greatest Jew of his era: Theodor Herzl. The latter's passage from German nationalist to cosmopolitan to Zionist impressed the chameleon-like Bahr deeply, who helped elevate the drama of the Dreyfus affair into what became the myth of Herzl's Zionist conversion. Rather than dwelling on Herzl's view of the Jewish future, amply spelled out in Der Judenstaat and Altneuland, Bahr emphasized Herzl's recognition of "the psychological error of assimilation." Bahr admitted he understood the efforts of Jewish colonial enterprise too little to pass judgment, "and in any case they [the colonizing efforts] seem not essential."[76] Bahr concluded that Zionists needed to arrive at an awareness of their own nationality—they could then become good, brave citizens of their individual states. When the Jews felt themselves to be a nation, they would invariably stand on the side of humanity, freedom, and the people.[77] But Herzl, it must be emphasized, wanted practical results. What riveted Bahr's attention was the personal salvific role Zionism could play for the Jewish individual. To put it another way, Bahr understood Herzl much better than he understood Herzlian Zionism.

I have already discussed Bertha von Suttner's role as a pivotal figure in founding the modern peace movement and the Austrian branch of the Abwehrverein. Both of these affiliations stemmed naturally from her liberal milieu. The same, however, cannot be said of her sympathies with Jewish nationalism.

Bertha's support for Zionism, an unusual stance for someone associated with the liberal Abwehrverein, emerged from her personal and professional relationship with Herzl. Like many of Herzl's admirers, Bertha found him strikingly handsome.[78] The Suttners also found Herzl a witty and gracious guest, and the baroness's diaries have nothing but praise for Herzl's wife and children.[79] Social compatibility made for a good working relationship. In 1899 Herzl arranged for a subsidy that enabled her attendance at the first International Peace Congress. Herzl had unsuccessfully lobbied the *Neue freie Presse* for this support and was forced to put her on the payroll of *Die Welt*, to which she submitted a couple of articles on the events that took place in The Hague. Herzl saw the peace conference as a place to cultivate allies and to bring Zionism to the attention of assembled Europe, but mainly he was repaying a political debt.[80] Several months earlier, Bertha von Suttner had written Czar Nicholas II, an ardent admirer, on Herzl's behalf. Typically, Herzl had not only asked Bertha to use her connections with the czar but also instructed her to stress the particular contributions that Zionism could make to a workable solution of Russia's Jewish question.

Beyond social and political collaboration, the two undoubtedly shared a willingness to imagine a future others derided as utopian. Herzl's *Altneuland* and Suttner's *Lay Down Your Arms!* both drew inspiration from Edward Bellamy's 1887 utopian classic *Looking Backward*. As Steven Beller argued in his biography of Herzl, the latter imagined a land where Jews could realize emancipation (a liberal goal) in a postliberal setting.[81] Similarly, Suttner wished to realize the promise of nineteenth-century liberalism purified of its militaristic coloration. Despite the futuristic orientation of these novels, they also pay homage to the older *Bildungsroman* tradition. The main characters, Martha von Trilling and Friedrich Lowenberg, are thinly disguised stand-ins for their authors. Both protagonists undergo a private as well as a political journey in which surface cynicism (*Altneuland*) and naïveté (*Lay Down Your Arms!*) are ultimately overcome by self-realization and devotion to a greater goal. The creators of these novels recognized this affinity. The Suttners loved *Altneuland*; it was the last book that Bertha read to Arthur on his deathbed.[82] If Herzl was dubious about the success of the peace movement, he praised Bertha von Suttner as "noble," a supremely positive buzzword in his vocabulary. After Herzl's death, Bertha wrote Albert Fried, "Herzl's last wish, that his remains be transported to Palestine, pleased me greatly. It is a proud Zionist word. I would imitate this and direct my urn to remain in Gotha only until the construction of the first Peace Temple."[83] Fried, who remained Jewish only out of loyalty to an oppressed minority, was the closest of Bertha's many Jewish collaborators. The impact these non-Jewish Jews had on her understanding of the Jewish question is not clear. No doubt these friendships helped inoculate her against antisemitic sentiment and provided her with examples of Jewish idealism. But only Herzl was essential in fostering her pro-Jewish activism.

Bertha von Suttner and Herzl, authors of utopian novels, champions of un-popular causes, were kindred spirits. Herzl's particular brand of Zionism (liberal, modern, and culturally European rather than specifically Jewish) helps to explain Bertha's affinity. The goals of European Jewry, whether liberal or nationalist, could be reconciled to her vision of a league of nations guided by progressive principles. This end-goal made it possible for her to fight for Jewish equality within Europe and also support Herzl's liberal, modern concept of a Jewish state. But it was her personal relationship with Herzl that engendered Suttner's unusual passage from liberalism to philo-Zionism. In two articles written for *Die Welt*, Bertha von Suttner defended Zionism as a tool for the restoration of Jewish self-esteem, as a practical defiance of antisemitism, and as necessary for the creation of a safe harbor from persecution. [84] Viewed as a means of making Jews into good Europeans, of achieving emancipation by other means, Zionism could be reconciled with her international-ist ideals. Herzl's own cultivation and urbanity, along with his liberal vision, helped Bertha von Suttner defend Zionism against detractors in the peace movement and in the Abwehrverein. Had Suttner equated Zionism with Ahad Ha'Am's call for a "complete national life," with the militarism of a Vladimir Jabotinsky, or even with the anti-assimilationism of some German Zionists, not even Herzl could have aroused her sympathies. Her Zionism, unlike that of Heman and Bahr, was not a "misreading." It was, however, selective.

Conclusion

The opening contrast between Pinsker and Herzl was deliberately exaggerated. Pinsker wrote his tract in German, not Russian or Yiddish, and his own subtitle, *Mahnruf an seine Stammesgenossen von einem russischen Juden* (An appeal to my nation by a Russian Jew), recognized that the Jews of Eastern Europe would require substantial aid from beyond their own circle in alleviating their misery. Herzl, despite his numerous Christian contacts and his desire to solve the Jewish dilemma through international diplomacy, remained within the party of autoemancipation. His advice to the Austrian Abwehrverein to disband leaves no doubt that the restoration of Jewish character needed to be a Jewish task. Still, Herzl devoted considerable time and energy to cultivating Gentile support. He lavished attention not only on kaisers and kings but also on Christians of lesser rank, even when their material contribution to the movement was insignificant.

Die Welt, Herzl's creation intellectually and financially, sought to convince its readership that Gentiles, too, considered the Jewish question significant and solvable. Christians who supported Zionism, whatever their motives, were allies, just as assimilationist Jews were opponents. To his allies Herzl selectively confided his trials and tribulations, including his sometimes rather severe judgment on world Jewry.[85] Herzl's personal magnetism played a large role in "converting" Heman, Bahr, and Suttner as well as Hechler, Maxim Manteuffel, and Börries von Münchhausen, to list only those who knew him personally. No doubt these figures (like many Jewish Zionists) misconstrued parts of Herzl's program and overly equated Herzl with the entire movement. Nevertheless, these Christians saw a Herzl—as a messianic figure, as an artist re-creating himself, and as a liberal impatient with liberalism's failure of imagination—to which they could respond enthusiastically. Ironically, a movement that formally rejected philosemitism as unnecessary did much to cultivate it and succeeded by emphasizing a Jewish agenda that was neither a by-product of emancipation nor a resolution of class conflict. The customary reticence—Jewish and Christian—to place specifically Jewish needs in the foreground did not guarantee success. Its opposite, so it seems, did not guarantee failure.

6. Christian Author, Jewish Book?

In the introduction to this book I took Thomas Mann (1875–1955) as an example of why preponderance of evidence and biographical trajectory deserve consideration when assessing the relative antisemitism and philosemitism of a given figure. While there can be no doubt that Mann continued to harbor residual anti-Jewish sentiments until the end of his life, they were gradually eclipsed by pro-Jewish ones. His own political gravitation leftward played an important role in this progression, as did his ever-growing circle of Jewish friends and supporters. Mann's admiration for Chaim Weizmann and Judah Magnes as well as the Nazi persecution of the Jews made him a progressively stronger supporter of an independent Jewish state. Mann's fictional characters display both negative and positive traits associated with their Jewishness. (Being a subtle portrayer of personalities, Mann included very few characters in his works who lack shadings of good and bad.) The following chapter began as a polemic against scholars of German literature who neglected the Jewish dimension in Mann's *Joseph und seine Brüder* and as an exploration of the particular sort of midrashic technique he employed in penning what I consider a philosemitic classic. I remain convinced that this tetralogy, composed over twenty years and by far the longest of Mann's works, has not received its due when scholars evaluate Mann's position on the Jewish question.

Thomas Mann's *Joseph und seine Brüder* has been evaluated from many perspectives: as a *Bildungsroman*, as an historical novel, as a clever manipulation of tradition and myth, as an antifascist parable, even as an obsessive exercise in homoeroticism.[1] But Joseph has been analyzed only episodically as an example of Bible commentary.[2] This fact owes more to the academic division of labor than to the content of the work, which, while vastly expanding the Genesis tale, follows it with surprising fidelity.[3] In the first place, Mann was taught by Germanists interested in the recognized genres of European literature, not by Bible scholars. Second, before the "comeback" of the Bible as a recognized artistic masterpiece, deserving of the same analysis bestowed on other literary classics, Bible commentary meant the atomizing techniques of "higher criticism," with which Mann indeed has little in common.[4] But there are other forms of Bible commentary typically neglected by Mann scholars of an earlier generation. The following verdict on Mann's treatment of the concluding verses of Genesis 37 encapsulates the problems generated by this neglect: "He [Mann] devotes whole pages to the question—not raised in the Bible but obviously interesting to a Realist—why Joseph, when he was sold, did not get in touch with his father or tell the Midianites about him."[5] I am not a Germanist by training and do not know whether or not Mann should be classified as a "Realist." But I am certain that rabbinic midrash also devoted "whole pages" to this issue and that that supplies an important impetus for Mann's treatment. To be sure, the affinity of Joseph to rabbinic commentary had already been noted in the mid-1950s when Ludwig Lewisohn referred to the *Joseph* cycle as a "super-midrash," but that evaluation found little echo in subsequent scholarship.[6] With the exception of a single, stellar doctoral dissertation, Mann's use of midrash has never received thorough analysis.[7] A measure of the neglect of the Mann-midrash connection may be found in Eckhard Heftrich's massive and magisterial *Geträumte Taten: Joseph und seine Brüder*. Heftrich relegates the connection to a footnote even where the connection begs mention, as in the discussion of Serach, a trivial figure in the Bible but an important one to both Mann and to Jewish legend.[8] Heftrich nowhere alerts the reader to Mann's fascination with a woman described by midrash scholar Marc Bregman as a "product of the collective Jewish imagination."[9]

Whether Lewisohn meant the "super" in "super-midrash" as a qualitative (very good) or quantitative (very big) judgment, he points to an obvious problem of categorization. Midrash, a word whose root meaning is to seek out, inquire, demand, was a genre of Bible commentary that flourished from the early rabbinic period until the end of the first millennium, and its practitioners, as far as we know, were all educated Jewish males. On the one hand, therefore, Mann's *Joseph* cannot be any more of a midrash than other modern works that also employ other genres. The Isaac poems of Amir Gilboa and Hayim Gouri, Cynthia Ozick's celebrated "Ruth" essay, Margaret Atwood's *The Handmaid's Tale*, and Anita Diamant's blockbuster *The Red Tent* are clearly not midrashim the same way the classical rabbinic midrashim are. The neglect of Mann's utilization of biblical and rabbinic sources by Germanists, however regrettable, demonstrates that the book can be read on its own. Simply put, *Joseph und seine Brüder* is a novel.[10]

On the other hand, if the salient features of midrash include verse-centeredness, problem-oriented commentary, imaginative rather than logically systematic exegesis, and, above all, an endless expanding of the biblical text, then Mann's *Joseph* passes muster easily.[11] Even more than the rabbinic material he so often cites, the very method Mann employs draws on rabbinic techniques. Deliberately anachronistic speech, a naming obsession born of an abhorrence of anonymity, the setting of (unrelated) events on Jewish holidays, frequent citation and allusion to other parts of Scripture (or rabbinic traditions), lengthy and imaginative etymological speculation, meticulous yet fanciful calculation of elapsed time from one event to another, enumeration of reasons for a specific act or nonact, an untiring interrogative voice: these are some of the implements in Mann's tool kit that turn 13 chapters in Genesis into a 1,207-page novel in translation. The answer to the question, Is it midrash? turns out to be as obvious as it is uninteresting: yes and no.

But more interesting questions can be broached, beginning with this one: How did Mann, who grew up in a Protestant household reading the Luther Bible, have access to rabbinic techniques of interpretation? One of the few scholars to pay attention to Mann's biblical sources, Clayton Koelb, writes about the *ketonet passim* (translated either as "coat of many colors" or "long-sleeved garment") as follows: "It is almost as if Mann had used a Hebrew concordance to search out every occurrence of this special term." Strike "almost as if," and Koelb is absolutely correct.[12] Mann did not know Hebrew, a potential prerequisite for the title midrashist, but this lack would disqualify most non-Israelis—Jewish or Christian. Nevertheless, Mann assiduously researched the spellings, meanings, and etymologies of biblical words. Most importantly, he seems to have nearly memorized the relevant sections of *Die Sagen der Juden* (The legends of the Jews), one of Yosef Bin Gurion's important collections of midrashic folklore.[13] Anyone acquainted with the Bible and Midrash will find these quotations artfully strewn throughout the novel. Rabbi Jakob Horovitz's work *Die Josephserzählung* (The Joseph story) supplied many additional rabbinic insights into the lacunae of the biblical narrative.[14] To sum it up, through correspondence with Horovitz and his own studies, Mann made himself as familiar with biblical and rabbinic traditions as any non-Hebraist could be from the 1920s to the 1940s.[15]

The midrashic method is unmistakable; still, one would like to think that Mann acknowledged this influence. He did. The following letter from Mann explicitly acknowledges his borrowing from the rabbis and partly explains why midrashic techniques in *Joseph* have not received the attention they deserve. Mann himself deliberately submerged them: "One might be inclined to see in *Joseph und seine Brüder* a Jewish novel only for Jews. Well, the choice of Old Testament material was certainly no accident. . . . To write a novel with Jewish spirit was certainly timely, especially because it seems untimely. And it is true, my story holds fast with half-joking earnestness about the dates of Genesis and often reads like a Torah-exegesis and Torah-expansion, like a rabbinic Midrash. And yet the Jewish is overall in the work only the foreground, only one style among others, only one layer."[16] Whether or not *Joseph und seine Brüder* should be classified as midrash, the largest novel by the greatest twentieth-century Germany writer, penned on two continents, certainly deserves to be addressed from the perspective of Bible commentary. I would like to argue that, midrash or not, Mann's *Joseph* is in some ways a distinctly Jewish commentary on the Bible. I make this claim despite the work's Christological elements and despite the fact that Mann's relationships to the Jewish world and to Jews remained ambivalent.[17] Before noting the specifically Jewish components of Mann's *Joseph* as a Bible commentary, some evaluation of

Joseph's success as a Bible commentary in general seems called for. As a point of departure, I will take issue with a few points in Gabriel Josipovici's *The Book of God* with its respectful but ultimately negative estimation of Mann's *Joseph* as Bible commentary.[18]

Mann as Bible Commentator: Gabriel Josipovici and the Sages

Josipovici objects that Mann's characters have access to knowledge that the Scriptures intend only for the reader and, in the case of Job, not even for the reader but for God alone. Citing the example of Tamar, whom I will also discuss at length, Josipovici finds her knowledge of her future role conducive to a superiority she ought to lack. Similarly, Joseph expresses too much self-knowledge. Mann's Joseph, who recognizes that he was "cast" as the hero and his brothers as the villains, tells his brothers at the very end of the work, "'You have missed the meaning of the whole story we are in.'"[19] To Josipovici, this statement indicates a knowledge that falsifies the distinction between personal struggle and historical fortunes so emblematic of Genesis.

Josipovici's chapter "The Man in the Field" analyzes the stray encounter in Genesis 37:15 between Joseph and a mysterious, anonymous figure, described in the Bible only as *ha-ish* (the man). As Josipovici correctly notes, this encounter causes lots of trouble for modern commentators who try to reconcile the patently transitional nature of the passage with Joseph's seemingly extraneous encounter with ha-ish. (Why couldn't Joseph have simply found the brothers without any help?) For the rabbis, who regarded everything in the Book as necessary and noncoincidental, the encounter becomes an opportunity for commentary. Typically, the medieval exegetes offer varied reading of this figure. Rashi (1040–1105) identified *ha-ish* as the angel Gabriel; Ibn Ezra (b. 1092) calls the figure a human wanderer; Nachmanides (1194–1270), combining the two, made ha-ish the personification of divine intent. Mann has the stranger (1) interrogate Joseph and send him to Dothan dressed in the ketonet passim; (2) return to taunt Reuven at the pit; and (3) return again to converse with Joseph on his passage down to Egyptian bondage.[20] For Mann, *ha-ish* plays a variety of roles, and, like the rabbis, he strenuously weds him to various parts of the story. For Josipovici, Mann's feverish activity signals an inability to speak with Scripture's commanding voice, an apologetic approach altogether at odds with the narrative mood of Scripture.[21] "This then, finally is what distinguishes the biblical narrative from that of Thomas Mann. Mann cannot allow a figure to appear in a work who seems merely arbitrary."[22]

Josipovici implies that in the end Mann surrenders to the traditional Christian preference for fulfillment narratives, in other words, tidy endings.[23] From Josipovici's vantage point, Mann's reading of Genesis may well be preferred to traditional Christian readings that make all narratives point to theologoumena and all the prophets point to Jesus. Mann's use of myth avoids the reductionism so often found in the fulfillment approach. But both approaches are flawed. To Josipovici, "the man in the field," like the man in Mark 14:51–52 who flees the scene of Jesus' arrest naked, represents "the primacy of narrative over interpretation. How they came to be there will never be known. That they are there cannot be gainsaid. To interpret them away, to provide explanations as to why they are there, is to do away with the Joseph story."[24]

For Josipovici, the proper response to the Bible or, at any rate, the reader response that the Bible demands is acceptance with or without understanding. Abiding mystery rather than a rush toward fulfillment characterizes the Book of God. Josipovici may well be right about the literary character of Tanakh, but then it must be conceded that the rabbis also "do away" with the Bible. As Josipovici's own examples indicate, the rabbis, like Mann, found unexplained mystery, anonymity, and unexplained coincidence unsatisfactory. The midrashim are continually tying discrete scenes and characters together to form a seamless whole. Biblical characters in midrashim frequently act anachronistically (consider the kashering of the meal Abraham serves the three guests) and frequently display prophetic foresight in detail (consider Miriam's words to Amram persuading him not to divorce Jocheved). Characters like Pharaoh's daughter, seemingly a mere vehicle in the biblical narrative, are provided in the midrash with a lineage, a motivation, a theology—and a name. Without gainsaying Mann's ironic sense, both Mann and the rabbis appear to be "horrified at the briefness and curtness of the original account" (*Joseph*, 667). This desire to complete the tale rather than any specifically Christian fulfillment fixation more plausibly characterizes Mann's artistry.

Although he has much harsher words of rebuke for traditional Christian misreadings of the Bible, when push comes to shove Josipovici concedes that rabbinic culture also fails "to read [biblical] books as they demand to be read."[25] Citing Rashi's conclusion that to avoid redundancy Genesis 37:24 ("The pit was empty, there was no water in it") must imply that the pit contained snakes and scorpions, Josipovici rhetorically asks: "Is Rashi being particularly acute here? I think not. I think we feel him to be wrong because he is explaining what does not need explaining." Rashi is engaging in "bad reading" or "reading but not listening." Why? Because, Josipovici informs us, in the Bible words count as they do in any well-told story and not as they do in crossword puzzles.[26] In other words, Rashi should accept that parallelism, in which the second half of a verse often repeats the thought contained in the first half, typifies biblical discourse. Rashi should not make such a big deal of an empty, waterless pit.[27]

As a judgment from the field of comparative literature Josipovici's claim that Rashi is misreading may be right, but I see no reason to privilege that perspective.

To argue that a literature such as rabbinic midrash, which hung on every word, verbal hint, and scribal affectation, somehow "does away" with the Bible by foisting "interpretation" over against "narrative" seems counterintuitive, if not perverse. Josipovici himself observes that the Bible does not mean itself to be read as "mere literature." In reality, it is exactly the fact that the Bible demands real-life application that has powered the Jewish-Christian-Islamic interpretative traditions. I agree that both certainty and uncertainty regarding the biblical message are essential components of a true reading.[28] But familiarity with the midrashic formula introducing mutually exclusive understandings of a single verse "and another thing" or a glance at the rabbinic Bible with its numerous conflicting voices indicates that rabbinic culture knew how to keep the unresolved alive. It merely shifted the uncertainty from the realm of narrative to the realm of interpretation. Mann's playful awareness of what the Bible permits seems closer to midrash than to the grimly earnest Josipovici: "But since when, may I ask, does a commentator set himself up in competition with his text? And besides, is there not as much dignity and importance attached to the discussion of the 'how' as to the transmission of the 'what'? Yes, does not life first fulfill itself in the 'how'? Let us remind ourselves once again that before the story was first told, it had to tell itself—with an exactitude of which life alone is master, and to attain which a narrator has no hope or prospect at all" (*Joseph*, 667). Thus Josipovici's central claim, that Mann's interpretative method violates the primacy of narrative, fails. Nevertheless, Josipovici deserves our thanks for focusing our attention on how traditional Christian and Jewish commentaries differ both in their conclusions and in their interpretative styles. He also convincingly shows us that every commentator on the Bible adopts a posture on how that text ought to be read. The question becomes not whether Mann is a midrashist but how Mann's interpretation works and where we place Joseph in the context of Jewish and Christian exegesis. I would like to answer that question by focusing mainly on one chapter from the last of the four novels: the story of Judah and Tamar.

Christian Author, Jewish Book? Mann's Rereading of Genesis 38

Mann's prologue to Helen Lowe-Porter's English translation acknowledges *Joseph the Provider* as the one volume conceived, executed, and completed on American soil. One can easily speculate on the role Mann's own exilic status played in this novel. Joseph, after all, lived most of his adult life in exile. That Mann gradually warmed to the central character of Joseph, originally conceived as an Ancient Middle Eastern confidence man, is well known. The author and the creation were both exiled in Paradise, as Anthony Heilbut's book title nicely expresses it. The Jews, it goes without saying, represent the exilic people par excellence. No doubt Mann recognized that he shared a certain fate with a largely Jewish émigré community. There are many patently philosemitic touches in the book, probably even more than in the first three novels. But I would not push this point far. By 1940 Mann's external circumstances were quite comfortable. He and Katya had built a house in the Pacific Palisades, Thomas had become the semiofficial voice of Germany in exile, and he had been invited, more than once, for cocktails at the White House. Still, Mann faced a serious narrative problem, possibly exacerbated by living near Hollywood: the lack of a leading lady. His rediscovery of Genesis 38 solved this problem: "I had no female character in stock to balance Rachel of the first and second novels, the Mut-em-enet of the third[,] and it took a long time before I became aware that I had one after all. It was Tamar, the daughter-in-law and seductress of Judah, whom I made into Jacob's pupil, an Astarte-like figure, endowed, at the same time, with features from the Book of Ruth; and in a half-humorous style I developed her into the prototype of human ambition" (*Joseph*, xi–xii). Ruth Klüger has called *Joseph* both the most Christian and most philosemitic of Mann's literary efforts. Klüger's judgment is correct, but the selection of Tamar as a heroine argues more for the philosemitic than for the Christian dimension.[29] Tamar has long been one of those biblical characters who attract both supporters and detractors; the line of division in her case often runs between Jewish and Christian commentators. Even before Robert Alter's *The Art of Biblical Narrative* called scholarly attention to the literary integrity of the received text and to the many verbal and thematic ties that bound the intervening chapter to both Genesis 37 and Genesis 39, modern Jewish exegetes had broken a few lances for Judah's Canaanite daughter-in-law.[30] Neither Jewish nor Christian Bible commentary is monolithic, and on Genesis 38 a number of contrasts can be found within each tradition.[31] But in the case of Tamar, Jewish commentators consistently champion her actions, while Christian commentators tend to condemn her.

The Dortmund rabbi Benno Jacob noted: "Tamar has been described as a woman who wants a child at any price, disregards law and custom and risks life and honor for her purpose. Actually, the story, often regarded as objectionable, is the crown of the book of Genesis and Tamar one of its most admirable women." Benno Jacob continues, describing Tamar as Canaan's *Gastgeschenk* (departing gift) to Israel and a symbol of the "triumph of spirit over blood." For Benno Jacob, Tamar served as a moving rebuke to the racial legislation enacted by the Nazi regime.[32] Close in spirit to that of Jacob, here is Mann's own explicitly antiracist aside: "Blood kinship is always possible to demonstrate if one takes in enough of the picture" (*Joseph*, 1018). Quite a different mood emerges from the Protestant Gerhard von Rad's verdict: "It is certain that she [Tamar] did something quite unusual and even repulsive for the ideas of her times."[33] Rad's moral disdain for Tamar seems little more than a secularized restatement of Martin Luther's provocative gloss on

Genesis 38: "Since this chapter embraces nothing except the account of Judah's production of children and his departure from his brothers, and besides this, the account of the most disgraceful incest with his daughter-in-law Tamar, a familiar question recurs: Why did God and the Holy Spirit want to have these shameful and abominable matters written and preserved and read in Church?"[34] Although the Luther Bible was Mann's primary text, he did not share Luther's attitude toward Genesis 38, expressed in the derogatory subchapter heading "Judahs Blutschande mit dem Thamar" (Judah's incest with Tamar). In the Jewish-Christian dichotomy over Tamar, Mann stands firmly in the "Jewish" camp: "She might be called the most amazing figure in this whole story—few will be found to deny it" (*Joseph*, xii, 1036).[35] Tamar is not perfect. Mann draws her as the model of vaulting ambition, and he acknowledges, like the rabbis, that the greater the man or woman, the greater the warring impulses within:[36] "There she stands, tall and almost sinister, on the slope of her native hills; one hand on her body, the other shading her eyes, she looks out upon the fruitful plains where the light breaks from towering clouds to radiate waves of glory across the land" (*Joseph*, 1042). Tamar, like all of Mann's major characters, including Jacob and Joseph, is a complex blend of strengths and shortcomings. This mode of characterization also seems to place Mann more in the tradition of midrash than in the tradition of Christian prefiguration, which tended to divide biblical characters into black (pre-Jews) and white (pre-Christians).[37]

Mann recognized the improbable casting of Tamar as a major character. In a letter to his confidante, Agnes Mayer, Mann noted: "[I]t is remarkable how in a book the unanticipated, improvised things often succeed best. I decided only very late to insert the episode."[38] In the novel Mann introduces Tamar with a tone that mixes gentle chiding and ingratiating irony: "Her name was Tamar. We look around at the faces of our hearers and see on but few, only here and there, the light of knowledge. Clearly the great majority of those who are here to learn the precise circumstances of the story do not recall, perhaps do not even know, the bare facts. We might be disposed to censure, did not the common ignorance jump with the advantage of the story-teller, by adding to the importance of his task. So you really no longer know, or to your knowledge have never known, who Tamar was?" (*Joseph*, 1015). For Mann, Tamar exemplifies the self-made woman. We know her through her own resolute efforts, and explaining this resolve becomes the linchpin of Mann's reading. Scripture's portrayal of why Tamar insists on bearing the seed of Judah's family seems inadequate. Women in the Ancient Near East wanted children, but why does Tamar continue to insist on this family? Unlike the situation of Ruth, a figure with whom Tamar must be compared (see below), one can hardly presume close familial relationships. Scripture gives no hint that the nameless "daughter of Shua" enjoyed an intimacy with Tamar comparable to that of Ruth or Naomi. Nor are Tamar's marriages with the creepy Er and Onan a likely source of identification with the Israelite people. The biblical narrative goes out of its way to emphasize Judah's indifference to Tamar's plight, culminating in the brutal sentence (only two words in the Hebrew), "Take her out and burn her." From a narrative point of view, Tamar ought to have found a luckier family for her third attempt at marriage and children. In short, she lacks motive. Exactly here, Mann steps in: "What is not known, since the chronicle passes it over, is Tamar's connection with Jacob, which after all is the indispensable premise of the whole episode and a remarkable secondary action within our whole history, which we interpolate while at the same time being aware that that history[,] . . . the history of Joseph and his brothers, is itself an interpolation in an epos incomparably vaster in scope" (*Joseph*, 1016). In a few pages, Mann has Jacob relate the story of the family wanderings, beginning with Abraham and culminating in the promise of Shiloh (Genesis 49:10). We will return to the Christological motifs of that long-disputed verse. For now, let it suffice to note that Mann has provided Tamar with ample motive to force her way into the story. Through Jacob's instructions, she realizes that Israel's true line of descent cannot run through either Joseph or the three older brothers: "Not love could guide the course of inheritance, and where love has gone, nothing but justice remains. Justice was the horn out of which the oil of anointing must trickle on the brow of the fourth. Judah, he was the heir" (*Joseph*, 1029).

Having provided Tamar's motive, Mann also provides her with the means of entering the story, for the narrative Tamar inhabits is not impermeable. Playing with the findings of biblical scholarship, Mann noted that if Genesis 38 is inserted into the *Joseph* cycle, then the *Joseph* cycle (Genesis 37–50) itself becomes a piece of wisdom literature inserted into the patriarchal narratives. In a magnificent doubling action, Mann makes Tamar the pivotal actor-redactor of the text. She pushes herself into the story and hence into the history, but at the same time she pushes Genesis 38 into the *Joseph* cycle so that Joseph can push his way into Genesis. Mann brilliantly dissolves the borders between character and reader, author and book: "Tamar, the native girl, daughter of quite simple Baal-farmers, moving within this episode of an episode—had she a notion of the fact? The answer is: quite certainly she had. . . . It is not for nothing that the word I used above, the word 'interpolation,' keeps coming into my mind, as though it had a will of its own. Interpolation, insertion, pushing in: these form the motive of the hour, they were Tamar's watchword and mainspring. She was bent on pushing herself into the great history, and she did it, with amazing strength of purpose" (*Joseph*, 1010). Mann returns to Tamar's staggering accomplishment at the end of the chapter. Having traced the lineage of David back through Boaz and Ruth to Tamar's twins, he notes: "All that lies far hence in the open future and belongs to the great history of which the story of Joseph is only an interlude. But into this history has been interpolated and there for ever remains the story of the woman who would not at any price let herself be put aside, but with astounding tenacity wormed herself into a place in the line of descent" (*Joseph*, 1041–42). Tamar makes people uneasy. She fits roughly, maybe even jaggedly, but the fit is also permanent (as is Genesis 38). This ending also returns us to Mann's opening question: "So you really no longer know, or to your knowledge have never known, who Tamar was?" She did what she could to worm herself into the history and the book. But the Book itself needs to attend to its readership from time to time, and that is precisely Mann's accomplishment: he inveigles us into a fresh reading of a story we think we already know very well. With bold invention, Mann makes Tamar the pupil of Jacob; Mann himself, however, becomes the pupil of Tamar.

Mann relies on the basic biblical literacy of his audience and uses that knowledge, again employing a rabbinic technique, for characterization. Already having described Tamar as "a seeker" who felt dissatisfied with "the nature-worship of her own tradition," Mann places Ruth's most famous words in Tamar's mouth, "'Thy people are my people and thy God my God'" (*Joseph*, 1032). Mann deepens the connection to Ruth in several ways, many of them anticipated in the midrash. Whereas Genesis 38 ends with the birth of Tamar's twins, this genealogy is explicitly extended by Mann to link the boys with Boaz, highlighting the Davidic connection. This connection is made more emphatic when Mann, in a Nietzschean mood, concludes his Shiloh discussion: "Now Tamar was a woman, she was the woman, for every woman is the woman instrument of the Fall and womb of salvation" (*Joseph*, 1029).[39] The passage of Canaanite (or Moabite) to Israelite shows both women as interpolators into Israel's national drama. Mann seemingly had Ruth's status as proselyte in mind when he had Tamar exclaim, "But I as I now am, new-born and thine image, cannot be bride to an uninstructed one and who prays to images of wood and stone" (*Joseph*, 1032). The relationship that Jacob and Tamar enjoy also recalls that of Ruth and Boaz. In the Scroll of Ruth, the text injects ambiguity into whether Naomi or Ruth is responsible for the seduction of Boaz and whether Ruth or Naomi is the true mother of the child Oved. Mann describes Jacob, more than once, as "a little bit in love with her [Tamar]," but he is also her father, teacher, and would-be redeemer (*go'el*).[40] Mann's Tamar oscillates between Judah and his children as possible seed providers, but there can be no doubt that either generation will be only a surrogate for Jacob himself.

The clearest connection between Tamar and Ruth, however, lies in their being dual beneficiaries of a Levirite marriage, a Halachic connection far more important to the rabbis than to the Christian exegetes. If, until now, Mann relies on the rabbinic principle "There is no before or after in Torah" in order to allow Ruth (a character in the Hagiographa) to fashion Tamar (a character in the Torah), he now retraces his steps.[41] Mann makes Tamar the instigator of a Levirite marriage, convincing Jacob that only by the force of law will Judah allow his second son, Onan, to take up where his firstborn son, Er, left off. Jacob, relating this new proviso in the law to Judah, sparks this father-son dialogue:

> "Thou makest, Israel, as though that were the established fact, and it is so only because thou hast but now thyself introduced it—I know well by whose advice."

> "God speakest out of the maid," responded Jacob. "He has brought her to me that I make her acquaint with Him, that He may speak out of her."

> Then Judah rebelled no more, but ordered the wedding. (*Joseph*, 1035)

Tamar is not only a Ruth redivivus (predivivus?), she is also a prophetess and even a lawgiver. In this she recalls not only Devora, who, after all, judges the nation of Israel under a palm tree (*tamar*), but also that other famous prophetess, Miriam. Just as Miriam watches on the banks of the Nile to see the outcome of her prophecy, so Tamar, in Jacob's final "blessing" of the brothers, awaits to see Jacob declare Judah's fate as successor: "They listened amazed. Only one among them all knew it and had waited eagerly to hear it" (*Joseph*, 1092, 1186). Through Tamar, then, runs not only the seed of the Davidic line but also the spirit of proselytes and prophetesses. Only Hulda, of the three women explicitly described in the Hebrew Scriptures as a prophetess, has nothing to contribute to Tamar.[42] In Mann's Joseph, Hulda is the ass who bears Joseph to his fateful encounter at the empty, waterless pit.

There remains one serious objection to treating Mann's *Joseph* unambiguously as a Jewish book: his frank use of Joseph to prefigure Jesus and his various messianic touches. There can be no doubt that Joseph's arrival at the pit on a white ass, his three days in the pit, and his emergence point to Jesus Christ. With clear awareness of the subsequent role Genesis 49:10 played in Jewish-Christian polemics, Mann has Jacob culminate his instructions to Tamar on this theme. "The assumption would be entirely wrong that it was only upon his death-bed . . . that Jacob spoke of Shiloh the hero" (*Joseph*, 1028). On her own, Tamar concludes that Shiloh was "star of the son of man, the son of the election, who was promised to the seed of the woman, that he should tread the serpent underfoot" (*Joseph*, 1029). This is frank Christian prefiguration. Ruth Klüger comments: "It [*Joseph*] is also Mann's most Christian book, for Joseph is a precursor of Jesus and has many characteristics of Christ, which are yet to come. Joseph is not the Salvation, however, without him there is no Redemption. That is likely the most positive mental attitude toward Judaism that can be expected from a believing Christian."[43] Yet even here, I think Klüger underrates Mann's ability to be Christian in as philosemitic a way as possible.

Note the attention placed on family and procreation as the key to the story and to the deliverance. The subtitle is *The Fourth*, meaning Judah, not *The Tenth*, meaning David or however many generations the New Testament figures out to Jesus' birth. Note also the absence of any explicit reference to Jesus Christ, by no means ruled out by Mann's ironic use of deliberate anachronism. If this is meant to be Christian kerygma, it is suspiciously tentative. Here Josipovici's distinction between the ultimate purpose of Jewish versus Christian commentary can be cited against reading Mann too Christologically: "Here the injunction is not to study the Scriptures in order to find grace and be made a new man [Christianity], but to tell a story in order to remind those who were not present of what once happened [Judaism]."[44]

My claim that Mann's *Joseph* reads more convincingly as religious pluralism than Christian supersessionism demands more than the argument from silence presented above. I offer the lengthy, self-consciously anachronistic discussion of Passover between Jacob and Joseph (*Joseph*, 316–19) as my final piece of evidence.[45] This Passover discussion, turning on the animal sacrifice holiday (hag pesach) before its combination with the holiday of unleavened bread (hag ha-matzot), takes place over a chess game Joseph allows Jacob to win as a means of "conning" him out of his mother's garment, the fateful ketonet passim. Mann ingeniously allows the patriarch and namesake of Israel to play the role of questioner of traditions and his youthful son, soon to be Egyptianized, to play the role of tradition's defender. In their modern discussion of outworn (*überständige*) customs, Joseph adopts the position that it is best not to inquire to closely into tradition's origins: "But doth the blithe tip know overmuch of the dirt-encrusted root. No, for it hath come out beyond it with the Lord, swayeth in the air, and thinketh not thereupon. . . . If we want to have the pious tradition taste well in our mouths, by all means let us leave the underneath things quietly underneath" (*Joseph*, 318).

Whether or not this reflects Mann's artistic contempt for the methods of source criticism then in ascent or his innate Lübeck conservativism, Mann winds up defending a sensible enacting of hoary traditions. Since the tradition here is Passover, the most widely observed holiday in modern Judaism, this tack can only be seen as pro-Jewish, as is the defense of ritual slaughter, a perennial target for antisemitic hostility.[46] Joseph counsels his father to adopt a laissez-faire attitude and "not to let himself to be moved to undue haste and so to destruction" (*Joseph*, 318). Joseph then delivers the clinching argument for continuing the animal sacrifice: "Or else we wait on time, whether God might not for once glorify Himself in us by a great redemption and deliverance; which then we would make the basis of the feast and its legend, and sing songs of rejoicing. Have I, in my folly spoken consolingly?" (*Joseph*, 318). If this is a "fulfillment" reading, it points more naturally to the historical event of Exodus than to Jesus.

Mann and Midrash: Why It Matters

Whether or not Mann spoke "foolishly" in devoting twelve hundred pages to retelling the biblical story of Genesis depends on readers' cultural loyalties. That Mann spoke "consolingly" can be attested by the glowing letters Mann's many Jewish readers sent him and by his gracious replies. Ruth Klüger's view that Mann's *Joseph* offers a rare example of the German Jewish symbiosis from a Christian strikes me as warranted. Mann began his Joseph project in Munich in 1923, prompted, in part, by Goethe's observation that the biblical account of Joseph was "too short, and one feels inclined to put in the detail."[47] By the time Mann finished the Joseph project in 1943 while an émigré in the Pacific Palisades, the German-Jewish symbiosis was over.

The ultimate purpose of Mann's *Joseph* was artistic, not political. Although I have tried to argue that a Jewish sensibility pervades the novel, the very terms "Christian" and "Jewish" are admittedly too broad to apply in a procrustean manner. As in the first century of the Common Era, so also the twentieth showed that the confessional lines between the two religions could be easily overdrawn. Even the contention that the midrashic methods of *Joseph* prove its "Jewish" nature could be disputed on the grounds that midrash constitutes only one genre of Jewish discourse. I wish only to argue the following: first, Mann's *Joseph* can be evaluated meaningfully as a Bible commentary, and this dimension adds to our appreciation of the work; and second, the playful, detail-oriented, speculative, reconciling, holistic narrative of *Joseph* is more consistent with a midrashic approach to the text than to anything found either in traditional Christian exegesis or to the source-critical school of Bible scholarship regnant at mid-twentieth century.[48]

Mann's professed intention was to write a human-book, not a *Judenbuch*; we should take him at his word. Mann's own speculation on his novel's future readership seems a fitting end to this chapter, and his bourgeois-aesthetic notion of quality probably comes closer than "Christian," "Jewish," or "philosemitic" to the categories that meant the most to Mann: "How will posterity regard this work? . . . I do not know and no one can tell me. But as the son of a tradesman I have a fundamental faith in quality. What is it that has helped many a product of human hands through the ages, given it strength to resist the centuries, and restrained mankind in its wildest days from destroying it? Only one thing: quality. The song of *Joseph* is good, solid work, done out of fellow feeling for which mankind has always been sensitively receptive. A measure of durability is I think, inherent in it" (*Joseph*, xiii–xiv).

Nahida Remy began her popular 1891 book *Das jüdische Weib* (*The Jewish Woman*) with two striking and methodologically conflicting observations. Remy stated that "in order to comprehend woman, one must study the history of her slavery."[1] Her readers might have expected from such an opening sentence a striking manifesto for the emancipation of Jewish women, doubly oppressed by gender and by religion, and they would not have been disappointed. Remy passionately defended the "pure," "noble," and "innocent" Eve on the grounds that, having no power to discern good from evil, she had no reason to heed God's command and reject the serpent's tempting offer. In a misreading of the biblical text worthy of the midrash, Remy rendered God's final punishment of Eve, "*v'hu yimshal bach*" (Genesis 3:16), as "and he shall be like thee," departing from a tradition that consistently read in the verse "and he shall rule over thee" a divine mandate for male dominance.[2] With many acerbic asides, Remy lampooned the need of men to control women instead of summoning up the self-control to master their own sexual selves.[3]

Yet Nahida Remy's second sentence, "to correctly judge the Jewish woman, one must compare her with the women of other nations," introduced her prevailing method. In chapters titled "Antiquity," "The Christian Idea about Woman and Marriage," "Jewish Literary Women," and "Jewish Benefactresses," Remy argued the superiority of Jewish tradition over its pagan, Greco-Roman, Christian, and contemporary German counterparts both in portraying women nobly in literature and in assigning women a meaningful role in life. As we shall see, Remy's Jewish apologetic crowds out her feminism, and we are left with an essentially conservative prescription for the modern Jewish woman, to wit, "the only way to an honored and prominent position is the practice of the virtues of their foremothers."[4] This chapter attempts to reconstruct, through a reading of Remy's life and work, the path by which her philosemitism subverted her protofeminism. As these two impulses compete and intertwine, a brief consideration of each term seems appropriate.

Certainly, contemporary standards of feminist consciousness cannot be imposed on the earliest period of the movement, and this is especially true of German feminism. Despite the presence of political liberalism, a growing middle class, and a Protestant majority (the conditions typical of countries that spawned feminist movements in the nineteenth century), German feminists generally enunciated a more conservative agenda than their American or English counterparts.[5] Bismarckian Germany's conservatism and authoritarianism alike checked the radicalism of the organized feminist movements. German women were slow to win rights of property ownership and marriage without parental consent, slow to gain admission into the universities, and slow to overcome occupational discrimination. The battle for suffrage, a sine qua non of feminism elsewhere, was hotly debated among German feminists. The Allgemeiner deutscher Frauenverein (1865) and the Bund deutscher Frauenvereine (1894) fought mainly for better educational and occupational training, usually with the specter of spinsterhood and prostitution in the background. It would simply be erroneous to assume that German feminists aimed at equality between men and women.[6] The bulk of bourgeois feminists agreed with Friedrich Naumann's statement that "all other woman's work makes way for the work of motherhood."[7] Remy's lauding the role of the Jewish woman as wife and mother consequently cannot be offered as evidence of "subverted" feminism. I wish to highlight Remy's consistent subordinating of the interests of women to the "higher" consideration of the interests of Judaism and her privileging of the model of the traditional Jewish woman as a paradigm for the future.[8]

The German feminist movement and modern antisemitism were in their infancy when Nahida Remy came to intellectual maturity. At a time when the prevailing "cultural code" was antisemitic and antifeminist, Remy's case offers an unusual example of negotiating two dissident interests. The ambivalence of German philosemitism has been noted above. A few examples are required to demonstrate how adept the German intelligentsia was in its ability both to praise the Jews and to bury them. On his seventy-fifth birthday, the novelist Theodor Fontane, after poking fun at his enthusiastic Jewish readership, concluded:

> *Abram, Isack, Israel,*
> *Alle Patriarchen sind zur Stell'.*
> *Steffen mich freundlich an ihre Spitze,*
> *Was sollen mir da noch die Itzenplitzel*
> *Jedem bin ich was gewesen,*
> *Alle haben Sie mich gelesen,*
> *Alle kannten mich lange schon*
> *Und das ist die Hauptsache . . ." kommen Sie, Cohn."*[9]

Despite the Jews' avid support, in striking contrast to his preferred Junker audience, Fontane could not overcome his innate prejudices, which were easily kindled into anti-Jewish expressions. Throughout his life and despite a large number of Jewish acquaintances, Fontane oscillated between applauding and detesting his "semitic" audience.[10] The economist Werner Sombart became a sought-after speaker in German-Jewish intellectual circles on the strength of *Die Juden und das*

Wirtschaftsleben (The Jews and modern capitalism). The credit Sombart gave to Jews as innovators of a capitalistic ethic contained a thinly veiled condemnation of German Jewry. Among the many scholarly licenses that he granted himself, Sombart found hidden Jews at every turn of the road toward capitalism. Jews and their baptized descendants "still retained Jewish characteristics"; "again and again men who contribute to the development of capitalism appear as Christians who in reality are Jews." Sombart and his reception in Jewish circles provide another startling example of the ambivalence of German philosemitism. [11]

Even the most ardent philosemites in Wilhelminian Germany unwittingly expressed a patronizing attitude toward Jews and struggled with the intense "otherness" of the Jew. Take the comments of Paula Winkler-Buber, a woman who devoted her energies to the career of modern Judaism's most famous religious thinker, who spoke out publicly in favor of Zionism, who moved to Israel after the Nazi seizure of power, and who converted to Judaism:

> *You ancient people! You wonderful people! Just see how strong your blood is even in the worst of you, and how it will rise up again despite your will . . .*
>
> *How I love you, people of sorrow! How strong your heart is and how young it has remained! No, you shall not go under in the confusion of alien peoples. In being different lies all your beauty, all happiness and joy of earth remain your own! . . .*
>
> *How I love you, you people of people, how I bless you!*[12]

Remy's philosemitism, which led to her conversion to Judaism and her adoption of the name Ruth Lazarus, was remarkably free from the ambivalence, patronizing, and stereotyping characteristic of German philosemitism. While several features of *The Jewish Woman* merit elaboration, the most remarkable feature of this work is the author herself. Nahida Remy, a Catholic by birth, had become a Judaic scholar, had mastered Hebrew, and within a few years after the publication of *The Jewish Woman* had authored three additional studies about Jewish culture: *Das Weib in Bibel und Talmud* (Woman in Bible and Talmud, 1892), *Kulturstudien über das Judentum* (Culture studies on Judaism, 1893), and *Humanität in Judentum* (Humanity in Judaism, 1894). In 1895 Remy married Moritz Lazarus, her second husband and a renowned Berlin University professor and Jewish communal leader, and completed her own spiritual quest by adopting Judaism. Remy related her singular path to Judaism in the autobiographical *Ich suchte dich* (I sought you). This revealing memoir offers the key to understanding *The Jewish Woman*, published seven years earlier. [13]

Desertion formed the central motif of Remy's childhood. She was born Anna Maria Concordia in Berlin in 1849. Her father, a Prussian officer, abandoned her in infancy. Her mother also left her, whether for reasons of health or money is uncertain, with an aristocratic Catholic Pietist in Italy for three or four years. This woman, referred to only as "the Countess," imposed a rigorous and at times physically abusive regimen on the intelligent and sensitive girl. She was removed from her hometown, her mother tongue, and her mother, and so waiting for her mother to rescue her occupied a large part of the girl's fantasy life. In both *The Jewish Woman* and *Ich suchte Dich*, Nahida Remy recalled the boisterous, capable, and good-natured butcher's wife in her hometown of Flatow, West Prussia.[14] Early on, perhaps, this Jewish woman represented a caring female role model and an important counterexample to Remy's own dysfunctional family.

Nahida Remy probably received a more tangible push toward philosemitism after being beaten by the Countess and then comforted by a Jewish servant named Amalie.[15] Once again, the theme of Jewish able pragmatism surfaces: Amalie, who also lives apart from her mother and her family, sends them a portion of her earnings to help with their support. The event that occasioned Remy's beating is also significant. She was not, as the Countess suspected, reading racy Italian and French classics. She was poring over the Hebrew Scriptures, her favorite book. What the young Nahida Remy loved about the Bible—even if she did not articulate it as clearly as the mature writer Nahida Remy–Ruth Lazarus recollected years later—strikes me as believable, namely, the great emphasis placed on family life and the strong role of the mother that typifies the Hebrew Bible generally and the family narratives of Genesis in particular. The intense loyalty of Sarah, Rivka, Joheved, and Hannah to their favored child struck Nahida as a forceful contrast with statements of Jesus such as "Who is my mother? Who are my brothers?" and, to his own mother, "Woman, what have I to do with you?" When Amalie comforted the bleeding girl, she also pronounced a benediction recalled by Remy as follows:

> *What did you speak to me, Amalie?*
> *It was Hebrew.*
> *Hebrew? Yes! The language in which your "God of Love" also spoke. Nahida regarded her closely. She did not understand her, but she felt that Amalie meant well.*
> *And what did it mean? It is simply an exclamation: "God should protect you"* [Gott shaumeir sein].[16]

Nahida Sturmhöffel, an early feminist and our hero's mother, eventually took her when she was about twenty-four back to Flatow, West Prussia, which was then a town of about two thousand inhabitants. In a letter to the editor of *Lexicon der deutschen und österreichen Schriftstellerin der Gegenwart* (Lexicon of German and Austrian authors of the present), Nahidy Remy draws a grim portrait of her mother, who became increasingly poor and reclusive until her death in 1889.[17] Not surprisingly, Nahida Remy's childhood became easier only by degrees. Estranged from her classmates by dint of her nonconformist tendencies and independent thinking, Nahida Remy recalled conversations with her school's Protestant pastor. Confronting Pfarrer Tobold, the first sympathetic Christian figure in *Ich suchte Dich*, with her preference for the Old Testament and her disbelief in the need for an intercessor, Nahida Remy guaranteed his refusal to confirm her in the Evangelical (that is, Protestant) Church. Associating Roman Catholicism with the hated Countess, Remy now shut the doors to Protestantism too. In her own words, "she was to one and the other a stranger."[18]

Whereas Nahida Remy obviously experienced her familial situation as a deprivation, it removed a major encumbrance to her personal autonomy as an artist. Unlike the majority of the thousands of nineteenth-century German female writers, Remy did not use a pseudonym, nor did she need to submit to the control of a male authority. In fact, Remy made her way in the world quite successfully. In 1873 the twenty-four-year-old actress, playwright, and free-lance writer met and married the noted theater critic Max Remy. Details in her autobiography are sparse, but the couple clearly did not live happily ever after.[19] Max Remy became ill shortly after their marriage and died in 1881 as a major debate over the Jewish question raged in the German press.[20]

Once again Nahida Remy had been abandoned. Her successful career—for she was now the celebrated author of *Sizilianische Novellen und Skizzen* (Sicilian short stories and sketches)—apparently did not resolve her spiritual longings. At this point, however, Remy found the path that would put an end to her perpetual otherness. The medium, once again, would be a combination of female bonding and Judaism. Prompted by an interest in the Jewish question, Remy immersed herself in the Jewish histories of Isaac Marcus Jost and Heinrich Graetz; she devoured Moses Mendelssohn's *Jerusalem*. William Herzberg's *Jüdische Familienpapiere* (Jewish family papers) so impressed her that she wrote the author in Jerusalem, where he directed a Jewish orphanage. The decisive push toward claiming a Jewish identity came through when Herzberg put Remy in touch with Frau Zerline Meyer, an intelligent, elderly Jew who lived nearby in Berlin.

Through Zerline Meyer, Nahida's Jewish circle expanded considerably, including, among others, Rabbi Solomon Kohn and Moritz Lazarus. At Lazarus's prompting, a Leipzig publisher approached Remy to write *The Jewish Woman*. With her usual industry, Remy immersed herself in the task. Her emotional fondness for Judaism was bolstered by the sources of tradition, and Remy augmented her storehouse of Jewish experiences by frequent visits to Berlin's Potsdamerbrücke synagogue, the site of Franz Rosenzweig's famous Yom Kippur conversion. Describing her project, as usual, in the third person, Remy wrote, "She learned to know and understand this people, and because she learned to understand them, she had to love them." Would that every investigation into Judaism—then and now—had such results! Naturally, the critical response to *The Jewish Woman* and the ones that followed were uniformly positive from the Jewish side. There can be little doubt, based on Remy's crowded lecture circuit, admiring letters, and requests for copies of her book from Poland to Bombay, that Nahidy Remy had found a receptive audience and that world Jewry had found an ardent defender.

The intellectual colloquy between Nahida Remy and Zerline Meyer developed into a warm emotional bond. Frau Meyer had also been abandoned in a certain sense: as Remy related, alone among her large family, Zerline Meyer had remained true to Judaism. Letters from Nahida Remy to Meyer about her lectures and book reviews read like a daughter proudly confiding to her mother. Shortly before her death Zerline Meyer presented her Judaica library to Nahida Remy. In a moving elegy, Remy commented: "One is only a true, good Jewess who learns, loves, and honors Judaism. One not need be a scholar, but one must cleave to Judaism with one's whole heart."[21] Nahida saw herself as the true inheritor of Zerline Meyer, and the proof of her being a worthy heir and daughter was her loyalty to Judaism. With the search for a mother completed, the erstwhile actress and novelist found a new vocation: "the struggle against Christian prejudice against the Jews and the elevation of a noble self-consciousness among the Jews themselves."[22] Writing *The Jewish Woman* provided Remy with the opportunity to realize that vocation and to confirm her Jewish legitimacy. Her chapter "Jewish Apostates" is highly revealing. While Remy assigns the role of seducer to the Protestant Pietist Friedrich Schleiermacher, she directs her anger at the *salonnières* (salon Jewesses) who succumbed to his wiles.[23] Although it may be fair to focus only on female apostates in a book dedicated to the subject of Jewish women, in her autobiography Remy's shock that some modern Jews were oblivious to their Judaic heritage was directed solely at women. In a series of exclamations, Remy chastises Jewish women: "She saw Jewesses impatient to cut short discussion, when it came to the history of their coreligionists. . . . She saw Jewesses who drew back from her because they 'feared' that the discussion would return to the three great prophets, whose names they had forgotten. . . . She saw Jewesses, who only waited until the death of their mothers or fathers, in order to have themselves baptized."[24] To describe Jewish apostasy as a female practice at a time when more males than females apostatized and to say that it is purely a matter of character, with no reference to the enormous pressures on German Jews to conform to the majority religion or to the weaknesses of the German-Jewish subculture's nurturing of Jewish identity, cannot be considered a balanced treatment.[25] I hazard a psychological guess here that touches on the limits of Remy's feminism and philosemitism alike: her (volitional) redefinition of Jewishness that "one is only a true, good Jewess who learns, loves, and honors Judaism," which allowed Remy into the fold, also required that some Jewesses be read out of the fold. As an avid reader of Genesis, Remy knew that the firstborn was frequently supplanted: inheritance entailed disinheritance.

Although her formal conversion to Judaism came four years after its publication, *The Jewish Woman* represented a psychological breakthrough for Remy. Before discussing the impact that her unique path to Judaism had on her presentation of Jewish women, we must briefly ask, What sources did Nahida Remy have at her disposal? Along with the historical and philosophical works already mentioned and her knowledge of biblical Hebrew, Remy quoted specialized monographs on the role of the Jewish woman and the haggadic sections of the Talmud translated by August Wünsche and Ignaz Goldhizer. It seems likely that Moritz Lazarus's understanding of Judaism as "Sittenlehre als Gottesdient" [ethical teachings as divine service] had a profound impact on Remy.[26] Whereas Lazarus's liberalism imparted his *Ethics of Judaism* with an abstract flavor typical of the "essence of Judaism" approach, his role as a founder of *Völkerpsychologie* (ethnopsychology) as well as his small-town Posen upbringing attuned his ears to the organic life, folkways, and humor of the Jews.[27] Already inclined by Remy's personal encounters to view Judaism as a living, breathing entity rather than an abstraction, the reader of *The Jewish Woman* is struck, to quote Yosef Yerushalmi's description of the ex-Marrano Isaac Cardozo, "not by its erudition per se, but the manner in which it was acquired. For we see here, how largely by means of translations, a man like Cardozo was able to receive not merely the content but the very texture of Jewish tradition."[28] The case of Cardozo, like that of Remy, offers testimony to the degree to which one can identify with a tradition (even one as daunting as Judaism) to which one was born a stranger. The Marrano challenge—to reclaim an identity that has been alienated from the individual—strikes me as apropos for Remy. No wonder that she identified strongly with the Moabite Ruth, the classic "convert" of the Hebrew Scriptures. The many examples of Remy's ability to capture the very texture of Judaic tradition may be summarized in her treatment of prayer in the Hebrew Scriptures. Probably working from the original Hebrew, she focused on confidence, gratitude, and praise—not faith, hope, and charity—as the language of Jewish devotion. In the following quotation, note not only the way in which Remy captures the intimacy that the traditional Jew felt toward the Almighty but also her willingness to turn the woman's experience into the norm: "This ever recurring praising, a calling to the Lord, and this continual thinking of the Eternal, this referring to Him [*sic*] the great and the small, the joyful and the sorrowful events, this is a characteristic trait of Biblical woman nay, of all the Jewish people."[29]

To make a case for Remy as a feminist, consider her unusual ability to convey a world in which female experiences were cognitively central rather than peripheral. The attention given to women in Lazarus's massive *The Ethics of Judaism*, for instance, is minimal. The studies of Gustav Karpeles and Meyer Kayserling, published around the same time as Remy's *The Jewish Woman*, presented little more than a "connect the dots" sequence of famous Jewesses from Deborah to the present.[30] But Remy's works represented not only the rich and famous but also women in the setting of marriage, family, and the workplace. Nor did Remy overlook the venues where women cultivated their personal piety, characterizing visits to the mikveh as providing the "freedom and time to develop the inner religious life."[31] Not surprisingly, Remy's portraits of Jewish women approach idealization. In the chapter titled "The Jewish Mother," after relaying a few stories of children abused by their Christian mothers, Remy wrote, "I can safely assert that no Jewish mother would be guilty of such unnatural conduct. I do not believe that a Jewish mother would even send her into a factory."[32] One wonders what Bertha Pappenheim, who founded the Jüdischer Frauenbund in order to combat Jewish white slavery, would have thought of Remy's depiction![33] Idealization is also a form of stereotyping, yet Amalie's benediction years earlier led Remy to master Hebrew, not to glamorize or to demonize it. As far as her Jewish apologetic allowed, Remy remained committed to presenting the social reality of Jewish women, including the drudgery, labor, and disappointments.

Remy's feminist tendencies evaporate when the subject threatens a positive appraisal of Judaism. On the biblical view of divorce, Remy contended that the Talmud rectified "the incomplete Bible text." As a philosemite and Bible enthusiast, she could not believe that the Deuteronomic law actually says: "When a man finds something shameful in [his wife], he writes her a note of divorce, gives it to her and dismisses her."[34] Remy also defended the test of the bitter waters for the sotah (the woman suspected of adultery) as a psychologically acute way to force an admission of guilt. That men were never forced to drink such waters, despite what Remy said elsewhere about their "tendency" to stray, seems not to deserve mention. Remy joined male apologists in blaming the discrepancy between Jewish ideals and current realities on women: they alone had the task of preserving "a pure and spotless family life." Likewise, Remy's praise of the Talmud for interceding on the part of the "weak and helpless" (women, in the case of divorce) is taken as proof of idealism, not as a situation demanding redress.[35]

During the Imperial period, German women made substantial inroads as wage earners in the burgeoning industrial economy, in the school systems, and even in some of the free professions. New vistas opened for middle-class Jewish women as well, and they soon occupied a notable place in the universities, which were previously an all-male domain. In the 1890s, moreover, German feminism became more assertive in demanding that greater attention be paid to the right of a woman to cultivate her individuality. Who could have been better positioned to create a synthesis of feminism and Judaism than a gifted autodidact with the key to a critical bastion of Jewish male authority: control of the normative texts? Yet for the psychological reasons described earlier, Remy insisted that women must define themselves first and foremost as wives and mothers. Remy warned that the Jewish woman should not imagine that "she acts wisely and well if she imitates in everything the non-Jewess, and obliterates every distinction between the latter and herself."[36] Remy encouraged other Jewish women to study Judaism in order to identify, not to revise. Quite typically, this extraordinary woman with an extraordinary career delimited her feminism sharply. And though her path to Judaism was unique, like many other Jewish women in German society she needed to choose between the competing claims of religion and gender.

Remy's philosemitism developed in tandem with a resolution of her abandonment by her mother, yet it cannot be overlooked that Nahida Remy had been abandoned by her father first. There is insufficient evidence to demonstrate that her marriage to Lazarus closed the circle of abandonment-redemption, yet it seems plausible, given that Lazarus, who was twenty-five years older than Remy, was first introduced to her as a mentor and played a catalytic role in her gravitation toward Judaism. Whatever the psychodynamics behind their marriage, it proved to be happy but brief; after seven years, Moritz Lazarus died in 1902.[37] The bulk of Ruth's efforts from that time until her death in 1928 were devoted to the publication of Lazarus's voluminous writings, little read today by scholars of either cultural anthropology or Judaic thought. Postwar inflation eroded Ruth's savings, and she had to sell their home in Merano. The publicist Julius Brodnitz, in a short obituary titled "Nahida Remy. Ein Wort der Erinnerung und des Dankes" (Nahida Remy: A word of remembrance and thanks), recalled meeting her in a small flat, paid for by the Central Verein deutsche Staatsbürger jüdischen Glaubens (Central Organization of German Citizens of the Jewish Faith, cv). Brodnitz concluded, "If one would honor our great Moritz Lazarus, one must not forget Nahida Remy."[38] I suspect that our hero might have found that eulogy less sexist than we do; I imagine that she would prefer to be remembered not only as Nahida Remy but also as Ruth Lazarus.

Nahida Sturmhöffel Remy Lazarus was an exception to the rule. Her principal historiographic value inheres in what light she can shed on that rule. In Imperial Germany it took courage to say, "Your people shall be my people; and your God my God" (Ruth 1:17). Remy articulated a monolithic agenda for Jewish women that few would endorse today. That she was able to identify with Judaism to such an extent as to articulate a Jewish agenda at all fixes one pole of the continuum of German attitudes about Jews, which ranged from virulent antisemitism on one end to the philosemitism of Nahida Remy on the other.

8. *The Apostate as Philosemite*

The notion of apostate as defender seems even more of an oxymoron than German as philosemite. In Jacob Katz's classic portrayal of the late Middle Ages, European Jewry and Christianity were drawn up in opposing religious camps. Whatever the objective factors leading a medieval Jew to the baptismal font, conversion was generally experienced in religious terms.[1] Typically, the Jewish apostate was hostile to his former faith and often played an important role in the forced disputations of the medieval world. In modern times, another kind of apostasy emerges, namely, those who opted out of Jewish identity for pragmatic reasons.[2] In Western Europe, opportunistic conversions outnumbered religiously motivated ones, though the motivations of an individual cannot always be neatly disentangled.[3] By the start of World War I, the number of German Jews who converted to Christianity probably approached 20,000. The range of attitudes on both sides—toward those who apostatized and toward those who remained Jews—varied according to the times as well as according to national and individual circumstances. Understandably, pragmatic converts in Germany tended not to call attention to their Jewish roots or expend much energy bringing other Jews over to their way of thinking. Yet even in modernity, "sincere" conversion persisted. Contemporary examples such as the Jews for Jesus movement and the case of Oswald Rufeisen (aka Brother Daniel) illustrate the possibilities for dual loyalty that open up when ethnic descent and religious conviction are separated. Jews for Jesus and Brother Daniel represent two instances of retaining pride in Jewish descent while abandoning Jewish religion. In America and Israel, however, positive constructions of Jews and Judaism are either normative or easily achievable. Far from trying to disassociate from their Jewish past, the "messianic congregations" that dot America's religious landscape trumpet their roots. In Imperial and Weimar Germany, quite the opposite was true. The cases of Selig Cassel and Edith Stein, sincere converts who continued to exhibit pride in their descent, are certainly unusual. I hope to demonstrate, nonetheless, that this case study of the "apostate as philosemite" is fraught with the intensity and paradox so typical of the modern German-Jewish experience.

What led Selig Cassel to the baptismal font in 1855 remains unclear. Cassel makes only passing comments in his many writings. His only preconversionary statement that sheds light on this decision, "The Prussian Citizen and Jewish Belief" (1850), analyzes the reversal in the Jewish progress toward emancipation between the edicts of 1812 and 1847. If we consider that Cassel served in the Royal Library in Erfurt and in the Prussian House of Deputies after becoming Paulus Stephanus, we encounter the sort of advancement suggesting pragmatic or opportunistic conversion. With no other evidence we would have assumed that a minimum of religiosity led to his decision, and wrongly so. In the summer of 1867 Cassel was persuaded by the Reverend W. Ayerst of the London Society for the Conversion of the Jews to take up the ministry of Christ Church Koniggratzerstrasse in Berlin.[4] On 5 January 1868 Cassel conducted his first service; for the next twenty-three years he preached, lectured, and wrote. He was a star at German missionary society meetings. He ran a flourishing church and Sunday school. At the Leipzig Messe, Cassel addressed an audience of one thousand. With evident pride, he quoted the Mainz *Israelit*: "How strange that people passing for religious Jews should voluntarily come and listen to a sermon from a man who has turned his back upon the synagogue."[5] A sophisticated student of history who had studied with Leopold Ranke in Berlin and a confident exponent of Judaica, Cassel's oratory was both impassioned and learned. In a letter published in Hermann Strack's missionary journal, *Nathanael*, Cassel claimed to have converted 60 Jews to Evangelical Christianity between 1880 and 1885, a figure he placed at 100 in a letter to the home office in London in 1890.[6] These figures, dwarfed by the growth of Berlin's Jewish community, were impressive by the standards of the notoriously unsuccessful missionary movement. Perhaps as many as 12,500 Jews converted to the dominant Evangelical faith in Imperial Germany, but very few did so at the behest of missionaries. Still, Cassel may have been Germany's most successful missionary.[7]

Cassel's career came to an abrupt end in 1890 when the Berlin police informed Christ Church that it must install an emergency exit. Cassel, as he was bound to do, informed the London office, which wired back a telegram instructing him to close the church at once. Despite his twenty-three years of service, Cassel had been terminated. The official reason given by the society was, of course, financial. Yet the mission was largely self-supporting, and missionary salaries were hardly munificent. In a bitter letter Cassel took the closure as a sign of the times: that the mission simply failed to interest Christians any longer. As England abandoned the conversion of the Jews as a national metaphor and the societies turned their attention to sub-Saharan Africa, many donors probably felt similarly to one of Cassel's allies in London, who told him: "The Jews have money enough to establish a mission for themselves."[8] Cassel never overestimated the commitment of others to the Jewish mission. As he wrote in a detailed report of missionary life: "That they [Christians] are Christian they find natural; that others can become Christians seems to them improbable."[9] Research into the London Society's records might disclose additional motives for his dismissal, but Cassel was well aware that he had irritated German missionaries with his pro-Jewish attitudes. Johann F. A. de

Le Roi, the historian of nineteenth-century missionary efforts, derided Cassel's writings as "carried out absolutely on the Jews' behalf, dictated entirely by a party spirit." Cassel never publicly charged that his vigorous polemics against antisemites contributed to his dismissal. But the possibility remains that Germany's most successful missionary lost his position for being a semitic philosemite.[10]

Cassel earned his credentials as a defender of the Jews during the first great antisemitic debate of 1879–80. Of the dozen or so pamphlets Cassel authored in opposition to antisemitism, the two most developed were responses to Heinrich von Treitschke and Richard Wagner. The latter's 1850 screed "Das Judenthum in der Musik" had been republished by the *Bayreuther Blätter* during the antisemitic debate. Wagner wished "to destroy the old Jewish God who had slipped into a foreign Christian world" and remove the influence of that Judenbuch, the Old Testament, as a means of freeing the creative impulses of German culture.[11] Wagner's Marcionist challenge to Jesus' semitic ancestry and the severing of Old and New Testaments went to the heart of Cassel's faith and elicited a slew of arguments ad hominem and substantive. Accusing Wagner's "Das Judenthum in der Musik" as being inspired by jealousy toward Felix Mendelssohn "because he came from Jewish stock and enjoyed many warm friendships in cultured Jewish circles as everywhere," Cassel exulted at how quickly the Jews had amalgamated the culture of the West and made significant contributions to the arts—especially to music.[12] Cassel rejected Wagner's Renan-inspired conjecture that Jesus the Galilean was a non-Jew. Not only did the evidence of the Gospels lead one to the opposite conclusion, but also theologically Jesus could not be the seed of David without this biological link. The revelation of Jesus, contained in the prophets, preceded the Christian Church. The Judengott of Wagner's essay was none other than the Christengott who came to fulfill, not destroy, the covenant begun with Abraham and legislated with Moses.[13]

Wagner claimed that contemporary German culture was not Christian but a "barbaric-Judaic mix." Cassel objected on two grounds. First, the "civilization of the Nibelungen" was incompatible with Christianity, but the Old Testament was Christianity's necessary preparation. Second, Cassel also found contemporary Germany woefully un-Christian exactly where it betrayed the shared values of the two testaments. How could Wagner, ostensibly a Christian, deny in word and deed the promise of God to Abraham in Genesis 12:3 that "all the families of the earth shall bless themselves by you"? How could a Christian betray Abraham's practice of lobbying for those in need of spiritual rehabilitation as he did for the inhabitants of Sodom and Gomorrah? Even if Wagner's view of German Jewry were just, berating them was no fit Christian response. Cassel combined his biblicist concept of Christianity with his political conservatism in his departing shot at the Bayreuth bully: "Peace and quiet will be an ephemeral delusion without humanity and love toward one's enemy and toward the Jews."[14]

The willingness to praise the Jews' accomplishments and to criticize the un-Christian sentiments of their detractors is equally evident in Cassel's *Wider Heinrich von Treitschke and fur die Juden* (Against Heinrich von Treitschke and for the Jews, 1880). As the rhetorical norm of anti-antisemitic literature was to declare oneself neither an antisemite nor a philosemite, the second part of this title announced Cassel's aggressive approach. Rather than Treitschke's, the prominent Berlin historian's, slogan "Die Juden sind unser Unglück" (The Jews are our misfortune), Cassel contended that the Gospels' "salvation comes from the Jews" (John 4:22) ought to be the guiding principle of the Prussian state's attitude toward the Jews.[15] As a politician in the thick of the 1848 debates, Cassel reminded Treitschke, who was fond of complaining about all that Germany had done for the Jews, that the logic of the liberal program, rather than Christian love, had led to Jewish emancipation. Cassel had no sympathy for Treitschke's xenophobia, terming "pseudonational chauvinism the direst enemy of the Gospels." To Treitschke's objection that the hard German head could not be easily Judaized, Cassel pointed to the French frivolity and English materialism that Germany had imbibed with little difficulty during the previous decade.[16]

With this observation, Cassel believed that he had penetrated to the heart of the antisemitic movement, namely, scapegoating the Jews for the materialism that had overcome Germany since the mid-nineteenth century. What made this analysis unique from a Christian perspective was Cassel's interest in the deleterious effects of modernity on the Jews themselves. He wrote, "The Jews have lost their believing semitic spirit among German heathenism."[17] The Jews, who in prior ages kept the Sabbath, observed the dietary laws, and studied the Talmud, had become legally free through emancipation, but spiritually they had been cut adrift. Whereas antisemites considered emancipation a dangerous unleashing of the Jewish spirit in Germany, Cassel considered emancipation a dangerous unleashing of heathen materialism that claimed for its casualty all religious piety. Small wonder, in Cassel's opinion, that racialism, the real misfortune (*Unglück*) of the era, flourished and was entertained by the putative intellectual leaders of the nation. To be sure, Cassel did not let the Jews entirely off the hook. Since 1848 the Jews had deceived themselves in regarding civil equality as the Messiah, and they had erred in thinking that as these legal barriers fell, so too would prejudice against them. While many Christian voices regard antisemitism as primarily a Christian failing, Cassel's insistence that the Jews had been victimized by modernity in equal measure to Christians appears to be novel. Cassel's millenarian desire to convert Jews was driven by the fear of universal secularism, not by fears of Judaization.

Without dwelling on his own Jewish roots, Cassel never tired of reminding Germans that at Christmas "we approach the crib of the semitic child, whose semitic parents shepherded him while the angels sang semitic songs."[18] Unlike many members of the Leipzig circle (the conversionary movement centered around Franz Delitzsch), Cassel had no fears about the Church becoming Judaized. Repeatedly, Cassel insisted that Christianity merely fulfilled Judaism or, more precisely, the potential inherent in the semitic religion of the Old Testament. Cassel taught a variant of Christian supersessionism that did not turn on an assertion of Christianity's superior ethics but only on its universal applicability. The opposition of the Jews to the truth of Jesus the Christ was the opposition of a national *Volk* to an all-encompassing humanity that knew neither heathen nor Jew.[19] The Jewish collective shared with Wagner and Treitschke the sin of chauvinism. Cassel explained the difference between Friday night kiddush and communion as expressing the difference between "the limited fleshly love of a people for one another and the love of God between all peoples, where not the flesh but the spirit, not the children of a particular people but rather [all] the children of God" participate.[20] To Cassel, the Jews' denial of Christ exhibited the same mistake as did their futile rebellions against Rome: both emerged from the Jewish insistence on being different.

The Jews' lachrymose history testified to the penalties for their insistence on religious dissent. If their reintegration into Western civilization had enabled Jewry to produce a Giacomo Meyerbeer or a Felix Mendelssohn, their denial of Christ had led to the overall passing of the scepter of spiritual accomplishment from the Jews to the Christianized Greco-Roman world. Cassel did not waste his time trying to prove that the rabbinic literature anticipated Jesus as the medieval scholastic Catholic tradition had, nor did he shed much ink defending the Talmud, as did Delitzsch and Strack.[21] The Jewish past offered the most glaring proof that they had cut themselves off from salvation. Cassel accepted the tenets of Christian political triumphalism. He cataloged every offense to Jesus and early Christianity and demonstrated that, tit for tat, Jews received punishment in return. One of these examples suggests the sort of Jewish self-conception that may have led Cassel to apostasy: "The Jews have abused Christ and his followers, and covered them with reproachful names—and their own honorable name Jude, which in the heroic time of the Maccabees deserved its glory, has become a name of reproach. As a term of reproach one who bears this name is himself shamed."[22]

With Cassel, we are able to trace the theological residuum of a Jewish identity, although we are unable to specify the path that led him to baptism. Quite the opposite is the case with Edith Stein, the youngest of eleven children born to a Jewish merchant family in Breslau (now Wroclaw, Poland) in 1891, one year before Cassel's death. Both came to Christianity as mature adults: Cassel as a thirty-four-year-old, Stein as a promising philosopher in her late twenties. Both came to Christianity after years of study and speculation. Both came from Jewish families in Silesia—although Cassel's Grosglogau was a town, Stein's Breslau contained Germany's third largest Jewish population. Neither dwelt on the details of their conversionary experience, although with Stein, we know many of the relevant facts.[23] But the differences between the two cases are striking. Like most German-Jewish converts, Cassel joined the dominant Evangelical faith, while Stein became a Roman Catholic. Cassel's conversion, it seems, led to a severance of ties with his family. Stein continued to enjoy close if strained relations, especially with her mother. Whereas Cassel was a publicist, a battler for souls, and a scrappy polemicist in his missionary endeavors, Stein coaxed friends and relatives into the bosom of the Church through letters and discussions.[24] Her interventions on behalf of Jewry, as we shall see, also tended to be behind the scenes, unlike Cassel's denunciation of Stoecker, Wagner, and Treitschke.

The greatest difference between these two philosemitic apostates, however, is certainly their respective posthumous reputations. Paulus Cassel has earned a few footnotes. Stein, on the contrary, made her mark in a variety of ways: as a noted expositor of Edmund Husserl's phenomenology, as a feminist, and, posthumously, as Saint Teresia Benedicta a Cruce. Indeed, Jewish Catholic controversy over Stein's beatification has focused disproportionate scholarly attention on her death. Rather than tread this well-worn path and without any pretense of offering a comprehensive reading of her life and works, I have focused on Stein's childhood and path to conversion.[25]

Edith grew up during the Imperial period in a distinctly Jewish family. The Steins sought relatives or acquaintances for marriage partners and shunned its one intermarried member—a severe sanction by the standards of the time. Although Auguste Stein's business brought her into contact with Gentiles, Jews predominated in the Stein children's primary social circle. Stein's autobiographical *Aus dem Leben einer jüdischen Familie* (*Life of a Jewish Family*) recalls Pesach and the Days of Awe (she was born on Yom Kippur) as the religious high points of the year. Nevertheless, Stein cannot be called an Orthodox Jew, as her biographers have insisted on doing, as this suggests a much higher level of observance and learning than her autobiography indicates.[26]

Siegfried Stein, Edith's father, died when she was only two, and Auguste Stein's energies were principally devoted to supporting the family's material needs. Auguste Stein's own formal Jewish education had ended when she was a girl, and although her parents had given her lessons in German and French, neither she nor her children learned more than rudimentary Hebrew. Years later, Edith brought a Latin breviary to her mother's synagogue; one should not assume this choice was purely theological. A well-educated, turn-of-the-century German Jew would be very comfortable in Latin; Hebrew was a far rarer acquisition. Like many of her male contemporaries (she was five years younger than the renowned philosopher Franz Rosenzweig), Stein found Judaism very unsatisfactory by the time of her adolescence.[27] Auguste's simple piety has been offered as a reason that we should be surprised that Edith fell away from Judaism and announced her agnosticism while still a teenager. On the contrary, the lack of a sophisticated articulation to the question "Why be Jewish?" demanded by so many German-Jewish youths in the postemancipation era drove many to the baptismal font, albeit after a lengthy journey. Nothing in Edith's autobiography or letters indicates any involvement with Jewish learning.[28]

The one encounter relevant to evaluating Stein's relationship to the teachings of Judaism supports this picture of a young woman well acquainted with a Jewish lifestyle but sharing the general fin-de-siècle disdain for Judaism as a religio-intellectual system. Having asked the journalist Eduard Metis, the only one of her relatives who would truly qualify as Orthodox, whether he believed in a personal God, Stein recalls his answer and her response that God was spirit. Nothing else could be said about it. "To me it was like receiving a stone instead of bread."[29] On another occasion, Edith and Eduard were walking together on a Friday afternoon. When Edith passed her house, she gave him her briefcase to hold while she went inside to fetch something. Realizing that the Sabbath had started, Edith apologized for making Eduard "carry," a violation of Sabbath law. Eduard dismissed her concern by noting that he had a foot in the entryway; "carrying" was only prohibited outside. Stein remembers thinking that this was the sort of talmudic hair splitting (*Spitzfindigkeit*) that repelled her, but she said nothing.[30] To belabor the point, her attitude represents a spiritual alienation from Judaism, not a sympathetic commitment to it.

Stein was hardly alone in being the child of German Jews whose loyalty to the ancestral faith obviated a concerted effort to pass it on to a younger, more secularized, and better educated generation.[31] Under the spell of the Göttingen circle, Stein was drawn to a reappraisal of religion in the midst of several who had recently found their faith. Husserl, the center of this circle, was born Jewish, converted to Protestantism, and later in life toyed with Catholicism. Anna Reinach, also a recent convert from Judaism to Protestantism, impressed Stein with her fortitude after the death of her husband, Adolf Reinach (another philosopher-convert), at the front in 1917. Max Scheler, of partly Jewish descent, moved in and out of the Church. Stein's pivotal moment came in the summer of 1921 while staying with Hedwig Conrad-Martius, yet another Göttingen philosopher. Looking for some bedtime reading, Stein picked up a book about the life of Saint Teresa of Avila, read it through until dawn, and declared herself ready to become a Christian. Conrad-Martius indicates that Stein's conversionary moment—as was so often the case—was the product of a longer process that finally resolved itself. As with many others who took the plunge and others (like Rosenzweig) who did not, Stein's conversion was long in preparation and took place in a social circle likely to be supportive of her choice.[32]

From the day of her baptism, 1 January 1922, onward, Stein balanced her philosophical career, her increasingly intense religious life, and her family responsibilities. For Cassel, Christianity seems to have reconciled biblicism, millenarianism, and antisecularism. For Stein, Christianity represented ground zero from a faith perspective. Catholicism put her back in touch with all the components of her life—her connection to the Jewish people included. Nevertheless, despite her statement to her Jesuit confessor, Father Hirschmann, "You don't know what it means to me to be a daughter of the chosen people, to belong to Christ not only spiritually but according to the flesh." I have been unable to isolate any distinctively Judaic components in Stein's theological and philosophical writings.[33] Stein's self-conception of belonging to Christ's fleshly lineage may have imparted a sense of Jewish belonging that transcended her close family connections, but I see no evidence that it prompted a working-through of religious tensions. Perhaps Stein felt the way another Jewish convert to Christianity put it when he recollected his Hanukkah conversion: "I believe that I was never a better Jew than today."[34]

Stein frequently alluded to her Jewish upbringing and Jewish family in letters to various Church figures. As recounted in the English foreword to her *Life of a Jewish Family*, Stein had been previously approached by a priest to recount her life. While the Church prized these conversionary autobiographies, Stein's dwelt on neither Jewish blindness nor her own spiritual transformation, the usual themes. Rather, she opposed the realities of Jewish existence against the realm of stereotype. Noting that there were many Germans who knew Jews personally and whose "sense of justice is outraged by the condemnation of this people to a pariah's existence," Stein decried the contemporary situation in which a social wall was being built between Christian and Jewish existence and warned against the inevitable results: "[But] many others lack this kind of experience [of Jews]. The opportunity to attain it has been denied primarily to the young who, these days, are being reared in racial hatred from earliest childhood. To all who have been thus deprived, we who grew up in Judaism have an obligation to give our testimony."[35]

Stein did not lack the courage to make a public profession of her Jewish descent. Her philosemitism, however, is best evidenced by the relationships she maintained with her mother and siblings, all but one of whom remained Jewish. Totally confident of the truth of her religious position, she was even less inclined than Cassel to be hostile toward her community of birth. Yet Stein was not free from the convert's typical urge to convert others. Some of her closest friends reported that she had approached them to convert after she had become a nun. Kaufmann and Metis both severed their relationships with Stein for a number of years after her conversion. Stein also played a pivotal role in the conversion of her sister Rosa and a number of other Jewish-born "seekers." Despite her deep desire to see them brought into the Church, Stein respected the loyalties of the rest of her family. Writing to the poet and novelist Gertrud von Le Fort shortly after the Nazi seizure of power, Stein described her relationship with her mother's faith as follows:

> *I have never told my mother about you. It was not possible to give any of your writings to her because she declines anything that is beyond her Jewish faith. For that reason too, it was impossible at that time to say anything to her that might have somewhat explained the step I have taken. She particularly rejects conversions. Everyone ought to live and die in the faith in which they were born. She imagines atrocious things about Catholicism and life in a convent. At the moment it is difficult to know what is causing her more pain: whether it is the separation from her youngest child to whom she has ever been attached with a particular love, or her horror of the completely foreign and inaccessible world into which that child is disappearing, or the qualms of conscience that she herself is at fault because she was not strict enough in raising me as a Jew. The only point at which I believe you might make contact with her is the very strong and genuine love of God that my mother has, and her love for me that nothing can shake.* [36]

The ascent of the Nazis opened a new chapter in the lives of all German Jews. In 1933, to the distress of her family, Stein entered the Carmelite Order. She also appealed to Pope Pius XI to issue an encyclical on the Jews' behalf. She was refused a direct audience, although, according to secondary accounts, she received a benediction for herself and her family. [37] From 1933 to 1942 Stein kept up her academic work and her familial correspondence. With her sister Rosa, a fellow convert to Catholicism, Stein was deported from the Dutch Carmelite convent of Echt in the summer of 1942 and murdered by the Nazis on the morning of 9 August. Her last words upon being deported from the convent were reportedly, "Come Rosa, let us go for our people." [38] In her own mind, Stein died a willing martyr for the Jewish people.

On first glance, these case studies seem very peripheral to the German-Jewish experience. Most German Jews remained loyal to their community; those who did not were motivated by the pragmatic benefits of joining the majority faith. I will conclude, therefore, with two observations aimed at dismissing these cases as marginal and unimportant. First, the modern separation of Jewishness into ethnic and religious components has widened the pathways in which the modern Jew can walk and still feel part of the Jewish experience. In Zionism, Bundism, and Reconstructionism, this is evident in a very positive sense. But the same bifurcation can work the other way too, enabling a sincere claim of Jewish identity while the betrayal of a key component of the Judaic legacy takes place. The apostate as philosemite is thus a case study in Jewish identity in the modern world. Cassel and

Stein offer testimony to the divisibility and permeability as well as the tenacity of Jewish identity in the most unlikely circumstances. Second, Germany was generally hostile toward Judentum, but not uniformly hostile. The missionary movement and the religious-philosophical Göttingen school constituted two (unlikely) magnets for Jewish "seekers." Missionary Protestantism and Göttingen's version of Roman Catholicism both rejected a racialist neopaganism that was growing in Cassel's day and came to fruition in Stein's lifetime. That neopaganism and racialist Christianity proved to be a far greater danger than Judaism was a realization that came too late for the Christian churches and too late for European Jewry. The anti-Judaic traditions of the churches militated against accommodating, either ideologically or personally, the philosemitism represented by the likes of Selig Cassel and Edith Stein, two devout Christians and proud Jews.

Appendix
The Case for Philosemitism

One answers us that philosemitism is no program. Stefan Zweig writes that in the name itself inheres a program that goes too far: "Love is too much to ask; to not hate already suffices." And yet philosemitism is a program if it constitutes the antithesis to antisemitism. Everything that is not destructive, uprooting, thoughtless should find a place here.

M. H. J., "Appell an Hirn und Herz"

Finally, to state the entire issue clearly and sharply: even to speak of "A Jewish Question" verges upon and perpetuates an anti-Semitic element that, while vanquished, remains imminent . . . In those periods [Imperial and Weimar] the kind of philanthropy that sought, in and of itself, to vindicate the Jews was nowhere to be found; it did not fall within the range of acceptable discourse.

Ernst Bloch, "The So-Called Jewish Question"

None of the philosemites of the Kaiserreich considered here had an accurate recognition of Jews as Jews; rather, they all constructed an idealized Jewish cross-section as a fictive partner in conversation. An actual dialogue did not transpire.

Michael Brenner, "Gott schütze uns vor unseren Freunden"

The area delineated and separated by the notion of anti-Semitism (the cutting criteria being hostility to Jews and hostility to the Jews) is too narrow to account fully for the phenomenon the notion intends to grasp; it leaves aside quite a few socio-psychological realities without which the understanding must remain inconclusive if not faulty. I propose that what must be explained first—what indeed must stand in the focus of explanatory effort, is rather the phenomenon of allosemitism, of which anti-Semitism (alongside philosemitism, as it were) is but an offshoot or a variety.

Zygmunt Bauman, "Allosemitism: Premodern, Modern, Postmodern"

1. Philosemitism: Sentiment, Not Segment

What can we conclude about the presence of philosemitic sentiment in Imperial and Weimar Germany? If understood as pro-Jewish tendencies existing in discrete individuals or groups, philosemitism was widespread. Prominent Germans proved willing to reject antisemitism. Prominent Germans proved willing to speak out in favor of positive Jewish qualities, albeit stereotypical ones. There was, however, no philosemitic *tradition* or *movement* in modern Germany. Even the Abwehrverein, though it included many members who had positive feelings for Jews and Judaism, hewed closely to its defensive title. Even the German peace movement stopped short of taking an official stand on a "Jewish" issue. Like other left-wing movements, pacifists included Jews in their ranks without explicit reference to their Jewishness. Some missionary Protestants loved certain aspects of Judaism, but their Christian supersessionism made this a love-hate affair; many missionaries were more hostile than friendly to Jewish interests. Liberal Protestants like Michael Baumgarten of Rostock and Eduard Lamparter of Stuttgart were out of step with their counterparts on this issue. Ignaz Döllinger was the most prominent Catholic theologian to mount a principled ideological attack on antisemitism. (The anti-antisemitic parliamentary positions of Catholic Center politicians such as Windhorst and Leber were mainly the product of pragmatic considerations.) Aristocratic, racialist, and chiliastic supporters of Herzl had no leverage—they were an atomized group without significant impact on political life. The fact that pro-Jewish sentiment never coalesced into "a program," as the editors of the short-lived journal *Der Philosemit* hoped, is powerful testimony to the German desire for an *Einheitskultur*.

2. Philosemites: The Personal Touch

A number of individuals offer us a glimpse into the process by which positive feeling for a minority group gradually eclipsed negative feelings. Nothing suggests that these people were immune to antisemitic feeling. Quite the contrary—many testified that they considered themselves antisemitic by inclination and upbringing. No doubt, certain psychological structures enabled these figures to take a path away from Jew hatred, but in most cases these predispositions are impossible to identify. What may be asserted is that the encounter with a member (or members) of that group was pivotal to the process. Personal relationships often served as the catalyst to a reevaluation of the group as a whole. The "contact hypothesis" regarding racial prejudice finds strong support in this study. Even in cases where the passage away from anti-antisemitism was already under way (Hellmut von Gerlach is one example), personal encounters accelerated the process. Little evidence supports a dramatic conversion to philosemitism, although there were cases of sudden disenchantment with antisemitism. The path to philosemitism was rarely a conversionary experience but rather a gradual process.

3. Philosemitism and Jewish Learning

A striking feature about these philosemites is their determination to acquire information about Jews and Judaism. For missionary Protestants, this development is not surprising and needs little commentary; for Delitzsch and Strack, their learning expressed their philosemitic inclinations. In the novels of Heinrich Siemer and Emil Felden, two socialists, not only do the authors evince a considerable immersion in Jewish studies, they give their Christian characters a similar impulse. *Die jüdische Frau* served Nahida Remy as a vehicle for reading herself into the Jewish tradition. Thomas Mann's use of Jewish sources constitutes an important dimension of his masterwork, *Joseph und seine Brüder*. Friedrich Wilhelm Foerster and Heinrich Coudenhove-Kalergi became impressive, if idiosyncratic, Judaic autodidacts. Gerlach may not have been so studious, but he bothered to acquaint himself with the basic facts of Jewish history. These figures bolstered their sentiments with learning, tacitly equating antisemitism with ignorance and sensing that their positive inclinations toward a despised minority needed intellectual scaffolding. The persistence of this tendency argues against overstating the degree to which Gentile sympathizers did no more than construe fictional Jewish partners with whom to dialogue. (In any event, does honest dialogue necessarily require a scientifically precise evaluation of the Other?)

4. Finding a Social Context

The survival of philosemitism sentiments in a hostile environment required a social circle. Often, this social search corresponded to a political move. Hellmut von Gerlach's autobiographical *Von Rechts nach Links* offers a perfect example. The final positions of right-wing figures such as Walter Bloem, Wilhelm von Scholz, and Werner Sombart, all of whom wound up in the Nazi camp, suggest that without the reinforcement of social support, philosemitic sentiments withered. Franz Delitzsch's complaint to Moritz Lazarus that some Christian friends found his efforts on behalf of Judaism objectionable indicates the former's sense of isolation. Jewish contacts played an important role in fostering otherwise unappreciated efforts. Within the world of leftist liberalism, free student fraternities, *Heimat* clubs, peace societies, and editorial boards, a mixed social circle of Christian and Jew offered the philosemitically inclined confirmation that the antisemites had it wrong and that Jews were worthy colleagues.[1] The cases of Thomas Mann and Nahida Remy–Ruth Lazarus indicate that Jewish contacts could not only dilute hostile attitudes but strengthen positive ones.

5. Philosemitism and Socialist Loyalties

Scholars disagree over German socialism's record on antisemitism.[2] On the one hand, there are those who stress the antisemitism of the founders (especially the Jewish renegade Lasalle and the Jewish-born Marx), the willingness to excuse anti-semitic excesses as misplaced class-consciousness, the refusal of orthodox socialism to allow any special Jewish dimension within the movement, and the occasional outbursts by the intellectual leadership condemning Jews as bourgeois.[3] On the other hand, there are those who stress the successful inoculation of the movement against electoral antisemitism by the 1890s (Austrian socialism fares less well on this score than German socialism), the openness of the Socialist Party at the highest levels to Jews, and the aggressive anti-antisemitism of the KPD until its destruction by Hitler.[4] The target of hostile legislation from 1878 to 1890, socialism offered a natural breeding ground for sympathy toward other "deviants." The novelists Emil Felden and Heinrich Siemer were socialists; Rudolf Schay was a socialist; Karl Lamprecht, Gustav Schmoller, and Hajo Holborn, privileged academicians, were socialists and among those university professors ready to condemn antisemitism. The writers of the *Weltbühne*, though often unaffiliated with the Socialist Party, were left-wingers who consistently opposed antisemitism. True, many *Weltbühne* writers were Jewish and fall outside the rubric philosemitism. Nevertheless, one may assume some affinity of ideas between the journal's authors and its readership. Socialism was no guarantee of philosemitism: it was often a point of departure.

The introduction to this book addressed the objections of several scholars to the use of the term philosemitism. Philosemitism in Imperial and Weimar Germany *was* ambivalent, defensive, compromised by residual antisemitic prejudices, the by-product of conflicting agendas, and based on certain misunderstandings about the nature of Jews and Judaism. That German philosemites were ambivalent seems so obvious that no investigation would have been needed to demonstrate it. German liberals, possessing no concept of twentieth-century cultural pluralism or even a nineteenth-century concept of national identity as the product of political loyalty, regarded the disappearance of the Jews through conversion and intermarriage as the ultimate resolution of the Jewish question. Missionary Protestants saw the acceptance of Jesus as the Savior as the ultimate end of German Jewry. This inability to see religious pluralism as positive or even neutral remained a stumbling block to forming more than a tactical alliance with Jewry—a reality that Jews then and now well appreciate. Sympathetic "segregationists" saw Zionism as the natural response for those Jews possessed of a self-respecting concept of nationhood. Despite these qualifications, a conscientious attempt to defend Jews and Judaism did take place in Imperial and Weimar Germany.

One objection remains, however, to the term philosemitism, and it is a critical one that transcends the particular period and place under discussion, namely, that philosemitism is an inherently problematic posture for a non-Jew.[5] (That Jews ought to have a positive relationship with their own culture is, I hope, beyond dispute.) Ernst Bloch's bitter and sarcastic "The So-Called Jewish Question" first appeared in the *Frankfurter Allgemeine Zeitung* in 1963. Years before Frank Stern's study, Bloch pointed to the hollow sound of the mandatory affirmations of the Jews' humanity and good citizenship. While Bloch conceded that philosemitism in the salon period was indeed "a spiritual discovery," its post–World War II counterpart was only "a patronizing way of making amends."[6] Bloch's distinction, which recognizes that the content of terms depends on their context, is abandoned in the rest of this essay. Relying exclusively on his reading of post-Holocaust Germany, Bloch issued a blanket condemnation of philosemitism as inherently antisemitic. That his judgment has passed into the category of truism may be seen in Christopher Clark's approving summary of Bloch's view: "A philosemite is an antisemite that loves Jews."[7] More strident is the Jewish journalist Fritz Sänger's "Philosemitismus— nutzlos und gefährlich" (Philosemitism—useless and dangerous), which opposes all generalizations of any people whatsoever.[8] This essay has one advantage over Bloch's more refined approach: it demonstrates through a reductio ad absurdum just how impossible it is to avoid generalization and stereotype. This seems especially true when the people under consideration come as weighted with baggage as Jewry—baggage that in European lands before the Holocaust was presumed to be filled with old clothes.

Yet Bloch's verdict was similar to the one broached in the period under discussion in this volume—by Jews and friendly non-Jews alike. An article in the *Israelitische Wochenschrift* in 1890 pronounced itself satisfied with the minister of religion's declaration, "I am neither inclined nor disinclined toward the Jews. I will protect their rights and guard against injustice done to them." Writing as if one could maintain a cordon sanitaire between what one thinks about a group and how one acts toward them, the *Israelitische Wochenschrift* loftily proclaimed itself indifferent to German public opinion.[9] Most anti-antisemitic activists showed more sense than this, but they shared the presumption that society sought an undifferentiated humanity as its legitimate goal. No one would dispute that the overall thrust of the liberal apologetic was to deny Jewish difference, what the philosopher Michel Foucault called annihilating sympathy. This was exactly the point of Gershom Scholem's famous complaint that non-Jews failed to accept Jews qua Jews as partners in dialogue—a verdict Michael Brenner endorses.[10]

Bloch's celebration of working-class socialists and left-wing intellectuals as being indifferent to the distinction between Jew and non-Jew captures the limitations of his modernist goal. For the enemies of these two groups—despite their inflated assertions about "Jewish socialism" or the "Jewish press"—correctly recognized that Jews played a disproportionately large role in both groups. Tactically, socialists and left-wingers placed themselves at a considerable disadvantage by proclaiming as irrelevant a blatant reality. Strategically, the inability to affirm *any* Jewish role in such a movement shows the limits of leftist politics of that era. The "idea" of taking this approach existed: the socialist Rudolf Schay wrote an entire book celebrating the role of Jews in German politics. Bruce Frye cites a letter in which a Deutsche demokratische Partei (DDP) activist proudly championed his party as a Judenpartei. This posture was, of course, rejected.

For the Polish Jewish sociologist Zygmunt Bauman, the true culprit is allosemitism: supercharging the construct "Jew" or "semite" with too many and self-contradictory significations. Bauman posits that Jews in the Christian West occupied a special place not as pagan yet somehow more pagan than the pagans. Medieval people perceived Jews as "an awkward and unpleasant yet indispensable part of the Divine Chain of Being." Resolving the ambivalence of the Jew became more critical in the modern world with its desire to weed out of the garden any growth disturbing class, nation, or society. "To summarize, modern anti-Semitism was a constant yield of the modern ordering flurry. . . . The Holocaust was but the most extreme, wanton and unbridled—indeed, the most literal—expression of that tendency to burn ambivalence and uncertainty in effigy."[11]

Although evidence of the Enlightenment's limitations continues to mount, Bauman's prediction that in our postmodern era allosemitism will lose the unique position it occupied in premodern and modern history has yet to come true.[12] Both diaspora Jewry and Israel continue to exert a fascination out of proportion to numbers or influence. The Holocaust, while discrediting some kinds of anti-semitism, has become a new signifier of Jewish uniqueness. The state of Israel has become a lightning rod of hatred for much of the Arab world and substantial sections of the European intelligentsia. This anti-Israeli stance slides all too easily into antisemitism. (How Bauman, a critic of modernity's totalizing tendencies, can expect a restoration of natural communities without an increase in attention being paid to those very communities is beyond me.)

As long as the world insists on constructing meanings of "Jewishness" or "semitism," prudence dictates that positive constructions of "Jewishness" or "semitism" be encouraged, not condemned. A distinguished (Jewish) professor of literature writes, "We must stamp out philosemitism, wherever it rears its ugly head." This sentence could have been written a century ago—it appeared in a recent edition of *The Forward*.[13] I am not breathlessly awaiting Madonna's insights on Kabbala, nor am I proposing that the Jewish community marshal resources to fund philosemitic training workshops. But perhaps the scholarly world should temper its dismissive attitude toward this phenomenon, for malign neglect has proven remarkably ineffective.

Notes

Preface

1. The historiography on philosemitism has been reviewed by Kinzig, "Philosemitismus: Zur Geschichte des Begriffs" and "Philosemitismus: Zur historiographischen Verwendung des Begriffs."

2. Even English philosemitism may be better described as periodic bursts of sympathy or interest. What, after all, did the Fifth Monarchy men of Cromwell's day have to do with the novelistic representations of Walter Scott or George Eliot? See H. R. Trevor-Roper, "Europe's Brief Flood Tide of Philo-Semitism," *Horizon* 3 (1960): 100–103, 124–25. In Germany, the baroque period displayed clear philosemitic tendencies. See Hans-Joachim Schoeps, *Philosemitismus im Barock* (Tübingen: J. C. B. Mohr, 1952). Martin Friedrich, *Zwischen Abkehr und Bekehrung. Die Stellung der deutschen evangelischen Theologie zum Judentum* (Tübingen: J. C. B. Mohr, 1988), 1–13, has argued against an overall characterization of this period as philosemitic. Friedrich's claim that since anti-Christian Enlightenment tendencies, Pietistic associations with Old Testament Jewry, and Old Testament *Kirchenlieder* are unrelated, they ought to be disqualified, as evidence of philosemitism is not convincing. No one doubts that those who attacked Jews as part of the Golden International and those who attacked Jews as part of the Red International both deserve to be categorized as antisemites. When it comes to attitudes and sensibilities, logical consistency is rare.

3. See Gilman, *Jewish Self-Hatred.* Gilman brought a more sophisticated approach to a topic dealt with in Theodor Lessing's *Der jüdische Selbsthass* (Berlin, 1930) and Sol Liptzin's *Germany's Stepchildren* (Philadelphia, 1944).

4. Endelman, *Jewish Apostasy*, contains several important essays on this theme. My reflections can be found in "Zionism and Radical Assimilation," *Studies in Zionism* 13, no. 1 (1992): 21–41; "Radical Assimilation and Radical Assimilationists," in Marc Lee Raphael, ed., *What Is Modern about the Modern Jewish Experience?* (Williamsburg VA: Department of Religion, College of William and Mary, 1997), 33–49; "The Conversionary Impulse in Fin de Siècle Jewry," *Leo Baeck Institute Yearbook* 40 (1995): 107–22.

5. Erspamer, *The Elusiveness of Tolerance*; Shulamit Volkov, "Minorities and the Nation-State: A Post-Modern Perspective," *Jewish Studies* 37 (1997): 69–88.

6. Deák, *Germany's Left-Wing Intellectuals*, 25.

7. Michael Marrus and Robert Paxton, *Vichy France and the Jews* (New York: Basic Books, 1981).

8. To cite a trio of Anglophone works tending toward this conclusion: Sarah Gordon, *Hitler, Germans and the "Jewish Question"* (Princeton NJ: Princeton University Press, 1984); Ian Kershaw, *Popular Opinion and Political Dissent in the Third Reich* (New York: Oxford University Press, 1984); and David Bankier, *The Germans and the Final Solution: Public Opinion under Nazism* (Oxford: Basil Blackwell, 1992).

9. Rose, *German Question/Jewish Question*; Goldhagen, *Hitler's Willing Executioners.*

10. Geoff Eley, "What Are the Contexts for German Antisemitism?" *Studies in Contemporary Jewry* 13 (1997): 100–132; Fritz Stern, *Einstein's German World* (Princeton NJ: Princeton University Press, 1999), 272–88.

11. Rose, *German Question/Jewish Question*, 392 (index); Jacob Katz, *Richard Wagner: The Darker Side of Genius* (Hanover NH: Brandeis University Press, 1986).

12. Goldhagen, *Hitler's Willing Executioners*, 58.

13. Goldhagen, *Hitler's Willing Executioners*, 106–7.

14. Jacob Katz, "Was the Holocaust Predictable?" *Commentary* (May 1975): 41–48.

15. Edelstein, *An Unacknowledged Harmony*, states: "In its weakest sense philo-Semitism entails anti-anti-Semitism; that is, philo-Semitism necessarily implies a rejection of anti-Semitism in all the latter's forms" (19). Were this standard to be applied, most examples adduced below would be disqualified as philosemitic.

16. Hoelzel, "Thomas Mann's Attitude."

17. Edelstein, *An Unacknowledged Harmony*. The same could be said about Rappaport, *Jew and Gentile*.

18. This language is borrowed from Schoeps, *Philosemitismus im Barock*. Both antisemitism and philosemitism predated the rise of Christianity. Louis Feldman has recently argued that pro-Jewish attitudes were more widespread in the Hellenistic world than previously assumed (*Jew and Gentile in the Ancient World: Attitudes and Interactions from Alexander to Justinian* [Princeton NJ: Princeton University Press, 1993]). Menachem Stern's three-volume *Greek and Latin Authors on Jews and Judaism* (Jerusalem: Israel Academy of Sciences and Humanities, 1974–80) provides ample evidence supporting Feldman's basic position.

19. Low, *Jews in the Eyes of the German*.

20. W. D. Rubinstein and Hilary Rubinstein, *Philosemitism: Admiration and Support in the English-Speaking World for Jews 1840–1939* (New York: St. Martin's Press, 1999); W. D. Rubinstein and Hilary Rubinstein, "Philosemitism in Britain and in the English-Speaking World, 1840–1939: Patterns and Typology," *Jewish Journal of Sociology* 40, nos. 1–2 (1998): 5–47. Since this is a recently appearing piece of scholarship, I cite an example of what I consider apologetic: "It was neither indifference, antisemitism, nor anti-Zionism which made it all but impossible for the Allies to rescue the Jews of Nazi-occupied Europe, but the fact that these Jews until 1945 were the unreachable prisoners of a dictator whose aim was to kill all of them" (26). This claim elides the fact that while millions could not have been saved, thousands more could have. As David Wyman, *The Abandonment of the Jews* (New York: Pantheon Books, 1984), demonstrates, anti-Jewish sentiment certainly did play a role in the feeble efforts of the Anglo American team to rescue Jews. Older but more balanced discussions of English philosemitism can be found in Todd Endelman, *The Jews of Georgian England, 1714–1830* (Philadelphia: Jewish Publication Society, 1979) and David Katz, *The Readmission of the Jews into England* (Oxford: Clarendon Press, 1982).

21. Edelstein, *An Unacknowledged Harmony*; Rappaport, *Jew and Gentile*; Rubinstein and Rubinstein, *Philosemitism*.

22. On the importance of the national context in understanding antisemitism, see the exchange between Todd Endelman and Jacob Katz in *Commentary* 76, no. 6 (December 1983): 30–33 and the earlier discussion noted therein.

23. Brenner, "Gott schützte uns vor unseren Freunden," deals with the same period as this book intelligently but sketchily.

24. Ingrid Belke, "Publizisten warnen vor Hitler," *Conditio Judaica* (Tübingen: Max Niemeyer, 1993), 3:116–76; Arnold Paucker, "'Gerechtigkeit,' by Friedrich Oppeln-Bronokowski: The Fate of a Pamphlet on the Jewish Question," *Leo Baeck Institute Yearbook* 8 (1963): 238–51; Nathan Stolzfuss, *Resistance of the Heart: Intermarriage and the Rosenstrasse Protest in Nazi Germany* (New York: W. W. Norton, 1996).

25. See, for examples, Nechama Tec, *When Light Pierced the Darkness* (New York: Oxford, 1986); Samuel and Pearl Oliner, *The Altruistic Personality* (New York: Oxford, 1988); Philip Hallie, *Lest Innocent Blood Be Shed* (New York: Harper, 1980). Whether the heroic acts described by these works are philosemitic is not easily resolvable.

26. Herzog, *Intimacy and Exclusion.*

27. Frank Stern, *The Whitewashing.*

28. By the turn of the century, both *Meyers Konversations=Lexikon* and the *Brockhaus Konversations=Lexikon* listed "Philosemitismus," in both cases stressing the issues of political equality, tolerance, and opposition to antisemitism. The *Jüdisches Lexikon* (1927) defined the term as "opposition to antisemitism."

29. On this preference for "objective" over "subjective" criteria for philosemitism, see Celia Heller, "Philosemites Counter Antisemites in Catholic Poland during the Nineteenth and Twentieth Centuries," in Marvin Perry and Frederick Schweitzer, eds., *Jewish-Christian Encounters over the Centuries* (New York: Peter Lang, 1994), 269–90.

30. Kinzig, "Philosemitismus: Zur historiographischen Verwendung des Begriffs," calls this "secondary philosemitism" (364).

31. As will be seen from my adoption of his terminology, I agree with the sociologist Zygmunt Bauman's view that the phenomenon of "allosemitism," loosely understood as supercharging the construct "semitism" with intense, conflicting, and ambivalent meanings, lies at the root of both antisemitism and philosemitism. See Bauman, "Allosemitism." For an application of Bauman's insight that sees the postulating of a semitic essence as inevitably pernicious, see Cheyette, *Construction of "the Jew."*

32. The Centralverein deutscher Staatsburger jüdischen Glaubens (Central Organization of German Citizens of Jewish Faith, or cv) was probably the most effective anti-antisemitic organization in this period. By 1914 the cv represented roughly two thirds of German Jewry through individual or affiliated membership. As a Jewish organization, however, it falls outside the parameters of this study.

33. Franz Mehring, "Anti- und Philosemitisches," *Neue Zeit* 9, no. 2 (1890–91): 585–88.

34. Deák, *Germany's Left-Wing Intellectuals*; Shlomo Na'aman and Walter Grab, eds., *Juden und jüdische Aspekte in der deutschen Arbeiterbewegung* (Tel Aviv, 1976); Donald Niewyck, *Socialist, Anti-Semite and Jew* (Baton Rouge: Louisiana State University Press, 1971); Martin Jay, *Permanent Exiles* (New York: Columbia University Press, 1986); Shlomo Na'aman, "Social Democracy on the Ambiguous Ground between Antipathy and Antisemitism," *Leo Baeck Institute Yearbook* 36 (1991): 221–40; Robert Wistrich, "Socialism and Judeophobia—Antisemitism in Europe before 1914," *Leo Baeck Institute Yearbook* 37 (1992): 111–46; Jack Jacobs, *On Socialists and "the Jewish Question" after Marx* (New York: New York University Press, 1992); Philip Mendes, "Left Attitudes towards Jews: Antisemitism and Philo-Semitism," *Australian Journal of Jewish Studies* 9, nos. 1–2 (1995): 7–44.

35. The title of Rudolf Schay's *Die Juden in der deutschen Politik. Deutschlands Weg seit 1815* (Berlin: Welt, 1929) hints at Jewish domination and conspiracy. The substance of Schay's book, however, credits Jews with playing a decisive role in Germany's progress. Schay was a little overeager to claim his subjects (including Marx and Rathenau) for a German Jewish pantheon, but his inclusive maneuver was unmistakably philosemitic.

36. Eduard Lamparter's most important statements are *Das Judentum und seiner kultur- und religionsgeschichtliche Erscheinung* (Gotha: Leopold Klotz, 1928) and *Evangelische Kirche und Judentum* (Stuttgart, 1928). Lamparter is briefly mentioned in Maria Zelzer, *Weg und Schicksal der Stuttgarter Juden* (Stuttgart: Ernsty Klett, 1964) and Suchy, "The Verein zur Abwehr des Antisemitismus. II," 99–100.

37. Ignaz von Döllinger, *Heidentum und Judentum* (1857) and *Die Juden in Europa* (Linz: Carl von Kissling, 1891; rpt., Berlin: Philo, 1924), originally delivered as speeches to the Munich Academy in July 1881.

38. Jacques Kornberg, "Ignaz von Döllinger's *Die Juden in Europa*: A Catholic Polemic against Antisemitism," *Journal for the History of Modern Theology* 6 (1999): 233–45, 244.

39. As with that of Heinrich Rickert, Döllinger's philosemitic stance was a by-product of other battles, although Döllinger's *Heidentum und Judentum* (1857) already demonstrated his pro-Jewish inclinations.

40. Helmut Walser Smith, "Religion and Conflict: Protestants, Catholics and Anti-Semitism in the State of Baden in the Era of Wilhelm II," *Central European History* 27, no. 3 (1994): 312–13. See also the collection of essays in Helmut Walser Smith, ed., *Protestants, Catholics and Jews in Germany, 1800–1914* (Oxford: Berg, 2001).

41. Mosse, *German Jews beyond Judaism*, 44–46. Consider the following judgment by Fritz Stern: "Einstein's German world was one in which Christians and Jews (or individuals of Jewish descent) lived and worked together in the relatively protected realm of science, [and] prejudice against Jews yielded to a recognition of talent and of shared values" (*Einstein's German World*, 7). Alan Rocke, *The Quiet Revolution: Hermann Kolbe and the Science of Organic Chemistry* (Berkeley: University of California Press, 1993), 350–63, bears out Stern's observation.

42. Kirsten Meiring, *Die christlich-jüdische Mischehe in Deutschland, 1840–1933* (Hamburg, 1998); and Till van Rahden, *Juden und andere Breslauer: Die Beziehungen zwischen Juden Protestanten und Katholiken in einer deutschen Grosstadt von 1860 bis 1925* (Göttingen, 2000).

1. Philosemitic Discourse in Imperial Germany

1. Helmut Schmidt, "The Terms of Emancipation," *Leo Baeck Institute Yearbook* 1 (1956): 28–47; Jacob Toury, "The Jewish Question: A Semantic Approach," *Leo Baeck Institute Yearbook* 11 (1966): 85–93.

2. Erspamer, *The Elusiveness of Tolerance*, 154. On Dohm, see Robert Liberles, "Dohm's Treatise on the Jews: A Defense of the Enlightenment," *Leo Baeck Institute Yearbook* 33 (1988): 29–42.

3. Pulzer, *Jews and the German State*, 324.

4. Volkov, "Antisemitism as a Cultural Code."

5. For an influential challenge to the notion of a German *Sonderweg*, see David Blackbourn and Geoffrey Eley, *The Particularities of German History* (New York: Oxford University Press, 1984). This revision ignores the Jewish question almost entirely.

6. Samuel Oliner and Pearl Oliner, *The Altruistic Personality* (New York, 1986); Nechama Tec, *When Light Pierced the Darkness* (New York, 1986).

7. My persistent use of the German term Judentum reflects the fact that this word translates alternately as "Judaism" (the religion), "Jewry" (the community or nation of Jews), or "Jewishness" (specific qualities inhering in either Judaism or Jewry). This linguistic factor helped obfuscate the exact subject under discussion.

8. Peter Pulzer, "The Crisis of Liberalism," in Pulzer, *Jews and the German State*, 336. Assessing the situation in Weimar Germany, Donald Niewyck judges similarly: "The defenders of Jews were perhaps more numerous than their detractors, but they were less well organized simply because they could not regard the Jewish question as a central issue" (*The Jews in Weimar Germany*, 80).

9. By aggressively titling their journals *Der Jude*, both Gabriel Reisser (1806–62) and Martin Buber (1878–1965) intended to meet that prejudice head-on.

10. Nietzsche, *Beyond Good and Evil*, par. 251.

11. Freytag, *Über den Antisemitismus*, 14. The original reads: "Im Sinne seiner Broschüre erscheint er selbst als der gröste Jude." See Freytag, "Der Streit über das Judenthum," 1:325.

12. Max Weber to Carl Petersen (German Democratic Party), quoted in Bruce Frye, "A Letter from Max Weber," *Journal of Modern History* 39 (June 1967): 123. See Gary Abraham, *Max Weber and the Jewish Question: A Study of the Social Outlook of His Sociology* (Urbana-Champaign: University of Illinois Press, 1992).

13. Frye, "A Letter from Max Weber," 123; Marianne Weber, *Max Weber: A Biography* (New Brunswick NJ: Rutgers University Press, 1988), 648–49.

14. Coudenhove-Kalergi, *Das Wesen des Antisemitismus*, 45.

15. Gerlach, *Von Recht nach Links*, 26.

16. Coudenhove-Kalergi, *Das Wesen des Antisemitismus*, 45.

17. Friedrich Engels, cited in Low, *Jews in the Eyes of the German*, 403. Of course, many Jews would rather have been born "Herr von." The German environment contributed to both the stark dichotomy between German and Jew and the preference for the former.

18. This electoral policy suggested a certain failure of nerve. When Heinrich Gerland proclaimed that the Deutsche demokratische Partei was the Judenpartei and should be proud of the distinction, he was censured by local DDP organizations (Bruce Frye, "The German Democratic Party and the Jewish Problem," *Leo Baeck Institute Yearbook* 21 [1976]: 151). The following verdict seems apologetic: "The socialists could not be unambiguously pro-Jewish, because the largest part of Jewry belonged to the bourgeoisie, and philosemitism could easily be considered a bourgeois-friendly posture" (Hans Hellmuth Knütter, *Die Juden und die deutsche Linke in der Weimarer Republik, 1918–1933* [Düsseldorf, 1971], 154).

19. Suchy, "The Verein zur Abwehr des Antisemitismus. I"; Suchy, "The Verein zur Abwehr des Antisemitismus. II"; Lindner, "Philosemitismus im Krieg"; Kornberg, "Vienna in the 1890s." Another impediment to collaboration between the two groups was the growing assertiveness with which the Centralverein (CV) advocated continued Jewish existence within Germany.

20. Scholl, *Der Antisemitismus*, 4–5. Scholl, like Gerlach and others, engaged in a point-by-point explanation of Jewish stereotypes, attributing them to Christian oppression but not querying whether the stereotypes were still true. See also Bertha von Suttner's preface to James Simon, *Wehrt Euch! Ein Mahnwort an die Juden*. The original reads: "Die Hauptsache ist: ahem Meinungskampf muss—in Names der Vernunft und in Names des Gesetzes—das vor beiden unhaltbare Terrain 'Jude oder Nichtjude' entzogen werden" (vi).

21. See also Ernst von Wildrenbruch, cited in Franz Kobler, *Juden und Judentum in deutschen Briefen aus drei Jahrhunderten* (Vienna: Im Saturn, 1935), 322–23.

22. Dr. M. G. Conrad, in Klopfer, *Zur Judenfrage*, 9. I am palpably betraying a late-twentieth-century American perspective. For an American of any cultural group to display a mania for Chinese food or African American music may raise bemused smiles in Liberal circles; however, it is not seen as worthy of reproach.

23. Cited in Männchen, *Gustaf Dahlmans Leben und Wirken*, 109; Dalman, *Christentum und Judentum*, 13.

24. Theodor Mommsen, "Auch ein Wort über unser Judentum," in Böhlich, ed., *Der berliner Antisemitismusstreit*, 227; Stanley Zucker, "Theodor Mommsen and Antisemitism," *Leo Baeck Institute Yearbook* 17 (1972): 237–41.

25. Ingrid Belke, "Liberal Voices on Antisemitism," *Leo Baeck Institute Yearbook* 23 (1978): 82. One wonders if Hillebrand considered the Posen-born Lazarus more than "half-Germanized"?

26. Coudenhove-Kalergi, *Das Wesen des Antisemitismus*, 278. As Nietzsche wrote, "If a people is suffering and wants to suffer from nationalistic nervous fever and political ambition, it must

be expected that all sorts of clouds and disturbances—in short, little attacks of stupidity—will pass over its spirit into the bargain: now the anti-French stupidity, now the anti-Jewish, now the anti-Polish" (*Beyond Good and Evil*, par. 250). A comparative study of Liberalism's posture toward German minorities is beyond my scope. See the discussion in Volker R. Berghahn, *Imperial Germany, 1871–1914* (Providence RI: Berghahn, 1994), 96–123.

27. Pfarrer Wilhelm Schirmer, *Ahasver. Ein Mahnruf in der Judenfrage* (Danzig: A. W. Kasemann, 1891), 8.

28. Wilhelm Georg, *Hinter den Coulissen. Mein Austritt aus der antisemitischen Partei* (Hannover, 1895), 31.

29. Wagner, "Das Judentum in das Musik," cited in Rose, *German Question/Jewish Question*, 364. See also Reinhard Rürup's essay "German Liberalism and the Emancipation of the Jews," *Leo Baeck Institute Yearbook* 29 (1965): 59–68; Leonard Krieger, *The German Idea of Freedom: History of a Political Tradition* (Chicago, 1957).

30. Heinrich Rickert, cited in *Antisemiten-Spiegel. Die Antisemiten im Lichte des Christentums, des Rechtes und der Moral* (Danzig, 1890), 8–9.

31. Robert Max, *Nationale Pflichten zur Lösung der Judenfrage* (Kiel, 1893).

32. Ismar Schorsch writes, "A basic change in the character of German anti-Semitism, which became increasingly evident during the first decade of the twentieth century, decidedly altered the substance and tone of the Centralverein's message to German Jewry. At the very time when anti-Semitism was becoming less of a political factor, its social significance rose ominously" (*Jewish Reactions*, 137). The Christian missionary Johannes de Le Roi noted, "The great majority of the Christian population is far removed from the anti-Semitic parties, but anti-Semitic feeling, as the Jews themselves can attest to, is not decreasing but rather is on the rise" (*Nathanael* l3 [1897]: 14). The changing nature of antisemitism clearly prompted a more aggressive Jewish response.

33. Spangenberg, *Der Standpunkt*, 17–35.

34. Spangenberg, *Der Standpunkt*, 20. On the Freien wissenschaftlichen Vereinigung, see Pickus, *Constructing Modern Identities*, esp. 73–80.

35. Christian Wilhelm von Dohm, *Über die bürgerliche Verbesserung der Juden*, 2 vols. (Berlin: Stettin, 1781–83), cited in Uwe Eissig, "Der Juden und die Vision einer Judenfreien' Welt," *Leo Baeck Institute Yearbook* 88 (1991): 38; Salo Baron, "Ghetto and Emancipation," in *The Menorah Treasury* (Philadelphia, 1964), 50–63; Salo Baron, "Emphases in Jewish History," in *History and Jewish Historians* (Philadelphia, 1965), 65–89.

36. Treitzschke, in Boehlich, ed., *Der Berliner Antisemitismusstreit*, 79. Significantly, when philosemites referred to only one example of Jewish creativity, they inevitably chose Spinoza. Unlike Maimonides, who confronted a Gentile world intellectually and yet remained an important figure within Jewish life, Spinoza left the community of his birth.

37. Gustav Freytag's "Über den Antisemitismus" first appeared in the *Neue freie Presse* on 21 May 1893. The CV reprinted this essay in 1910. At the time, Freytag optimistically projected that "in a few generations without great trouble, the full incorporation [of the Jews] into our people will be completed not only in office and profession but also in heart and family."

38. Delitzsch, *Rohling's Talmudjude*, 85–86.

39. William Schoppe, *Die neutesten alwardtschen Judenflinten betreffend* (Dresden, 1892).

40. Steven T. Katz, "1918 and After: The Role of Racial Antisemitism in the Nazi Analysis of the Weimar Republic," in Sander L. Gilman and Steven T. Katz, eds., *Anti-Semitism in Times of Crisis* (New York, 1991), 245.

41. German Liberals looked frequently to England and America as exemplars of tolerance. In this work, the exclusion of Jews from the German diplomatic core was pronounced a cause of "deep shame" (*Der Juden Anteil am Fortschritt der Kultur* [Berlin, 1911], 21).

42. *Der Philosemit* (Prague, 1932).

43. Gerlach, *Von Recht nach Links*, 117. See also Helmut von Gerlach, "Antisemitismus," *Die Weltbühne* 16, no. 1 (January 1920): 7–11.

44. Empress Augusta, cited in *Antisemiten-Spiegel*, 29–30.

45. Sartre, *Anti-Semite and Jew*, 7–58.

46. Suttner, preface to Simon, *Wehrt Euch!* i–xii; Chaim Bloch, "Herzl's First Years of Struggle," *Herzl Year Book* 3 (1960): 77–90.

47. Walter Pohlmann, *Das Judentum und sein Recht* (Neuwied-Leipzig: Heuser, 1893), 8–9.

48. Schirmer, *Ahasver*, 11.

49. Adalbert Haffner, *Was d'Frau Waberl über den Antisemitismus sagt*, 37, Germania Judaica Collection, Stadtbibliothek, Cologne.

50. This declaration seems to have been specifically designed to prevent the clergy from participating in antisemitic agitation ("Rundschreiben," Das Ober-consistorium von Hessen, 3 October 1890, cited in Schrattenholz, *Antisemiten Hammer*, 573).

51. Schrattenholz, *Antisemiten Hammer*, 505. Did the proclivity to wish the theological death of Judaism serve to desensitize Germans to the physical death of Jewry? See Amy Newman, "The Death of Judaism in German Protestant Thought from Luther to Hegel," *Journal of the American Academy of Religion* 61, no. 3 (fall 1993): 455–84.

52. Schirmer, *Ahasver*, 4.

53. Klopfer, *Zur Judenfrage*, 33.

54. Theodor Mommsen's entry in *Antisemiten Hammer* proclaimed: "In the Jewish Question I am of the opinion that the calamity of antisemitism is an organized disgrace of our nation which can only be cured by the growing humanization of the Germans" (512–13).

55. Max Kalbeck, in Schrattenholz, *Antisemiten Hammer*, 510.

56. Schirmer, *Ahasver*, 4; Max Marcuse, "Die Assimilation der Juden in Deutschland," *Diskussion: Kultur Parlament* (July 1913): 13.

57. Gershom Scholem, "Against the Myth of a German Jewish Dialogue," cited in Werner Dannhauser, ed., *On Jews and Judaism in Crisis* (New York: Schocken, 1976), 63.

58. Nietzsche, *Beyond Good and Evil*, par. 251. Nietzsche never loses sight of the true power relations between German and Jew; he realizes that the Jews' entry into German society turns on the receptivity of the host culture.

59. Sander Gilman, *Nietzsche, Heine, and the Otherness of the Jews*, University of North Carolina Studies in Literature (Charlotte: University of North Carolina Press, 1974), 206–25.

60. Schoppe, *Die neutesten alwardtschen Judenflinten betreffend*, 37. I have seen this substitution of another Other worked with blacks, Arabs, Armenians, Ostjuden, and Orthodox (as opposed to Reform, hence Germanized) Jews.

61. Heman, *Das Erwachen*, 70, 110.

62. See, for instance, *Mitteilungen* 3, no. 2 (January 1893). In another instance, the author noted that while antisemites claimed Jews are universally hated, the English explorer Stanley referred to Germans as the Chinese (coolies) of Europe (*Mitteilungen* 4, no. 29 [July 1894]).

63. Döllinger, *Die Juden in Europa*. Döllinger's tract was originally presented to the Munich Academy of Science in 1881 (26).

64. Döllinger, *Die Juden in Europa*.

65. Professor Otto Caspari, in Klopfer, *Zur Judenfrage*, 12.

66. On the use and abuse of the Ahasveros legend, see the response of Martin Buber to the theologian Gerhard Kittel, who defended the expulsion of Jews from all university positions in 1933 (Frank Talmadge, *Disputation and Dialogue* [New York: KTAV, 1965], 51–54).

67. Mayer, *Aussenseiter*, 386–91. This classic was translated into English by Dennis Sweet as *Outsiders* (New York: Cambridge University Press, 1982; rpt., Cambridge: MIT Press, 1984). Mayer's

preface, "Note for the American Edition," explains why the word *Aussenseiter* is basically untranslatable. See Mosse, "The Image of the Jew."

68. Heinrich von Treitschke, *Politics* (New York: Harcourt, Brace and World, 1963), 126–27. Elsewhere, Treitschke lists three Jews—Mendelssohn, Reisser, and Veit—who became good Germans. Tellingly, all three were dead.

69. Eduard Bernstein, "Wie ich als Jude in der Diaspora aufwuchs," *Der Jude* 2 (1917–18): 186–95.

70. Jan Cronje, *Ich werde nie Antisemit*, Germania Judaica Collection, Stadbibliothek, Cologne.

71. Franz Kramer, *Wie Ich die Juden sah. Aus den Erinnerungen eines 78 jahrigen Katholiken*, Germania Judaica Collection, Stadbibliothek, Cologne. Himmler's 1943 speech to the ss in Posen is translated in Lucy Dawidowicz, *A Holocaust Reader* (New York: Behrman, 1976), 133.

72. Döllinger, *Die Juden in Europa*, 26. Reinhold Niebuhr, the eminent Protestant theologian, wrote in the 1940s: "When a minority group is hated for its virtues as well as its vices, and when its vices are hated not so much because they are vices but because they bear the stamp of uniqueness, we are obviously dealing with a collective psychology that is not easily altered by a little more enlightenment" (cited in Michael Morgan, ed., *The Jewish Thought of Emil Fackenheim* [Detroit: Wayne State University Press, 1987], 271).

73. Döllinger, *Die Juden in Europa*, 26–27.

74. Eisenhower's famous comment on civil religion is cited in Sydney Ahlstrom, *A Religious History of the American People* (Garden City NJ: Image, 1975), 2:450.

75. Many Liberals shared Döllinger's view of positive Jewish qualities being conducive to Deutschtum. Hofrath Maximillian Schmidt, for instance, praised the Jews' religious and family life as well as their sense of indebtedness for kind acts (Schrattenholz, *Antisemiten Hammer*, 516). There were undoubtedly many philosemites who left no record. An otherwise unknown university student from Darmstadt wrote: "I've traveled in largely Jewish circles in a German university and have observed that the Jewish students exceed the Christian ones in respect to talent, spirit, and also in introspection. While the Christian students spend their time drinking, their Jewish comrades are occupied with music, poetry, and philosophy" (Schrattenholz, *Antisemiten Hammer*, 509). This is obviously a romanticized portrait but nonetheless interesting.

2. The German Peace Movement and the Jews

1. Gordon Scott Clark, national executive director of Peace Action (1996–2001) and a peace activist for the last twenty years, estimates Jewish participants in this organization as approaching 20 percent.

2. On the Jewish Society for Jewish History and Literature, see Jacob Borut, "A New Spirit among Our Brethren in Ashkenaz": German Jewry's Change in Direction at the End of the 19th Century (Hebrew) (Jerusalem: Magnes Press of the Hebrew University, 1999).

3. Suttner, *Lebenserinnerungen*, 306–7.

4. Holl, *Pazifismus*, 84, 204–5. Significantly, Jews were deeply involved in the German Peace Society both at the beginning and end of its existence. Unlike groups that started out as integrated and became entirely Jewish (e.g., the Freie wissenschaftliche Vereine), the German Peace Society remained a meeting ground of Christian and Jew.

5. Richard Cohen, "The German League for Human Rights in the Weimar Republic," Ph.D. diss., SUNY-Buffalo, 1989, 50, passim.

6. Chickering, *Imperial Germany*, 74. Chickering takes issue with Istvan Deák's characterization of the prewar peace society as comprising well-heeled professors, journalists, and Jews but demonstrates only that Deák overestimates the economic status of peace activists. Chickering offers no explanation why salesmen in general should be inclined to pacifism.

7. Holl, *Pazifismus*, 54.

8. Holl, *Pazifismus*, 83–94; Deiter Riesenberger, *Geschichte der Friedensbewegung in Deutschland, von den Anfängen bis 1933* (Göttingen: Vandenhoeck und Ruprecht, 1985), 246.

9. Alan Levenson, "Theodor Herzl and Bertha von Suttner: Criticism, Collaboration and Utopianism," *Journal of Israeli History* 15, no. 2 (1994): 213–22.

10. Steve Beller, *Vienna and the Jews: A Cultural History* (Cambridge: Cambridge University Press, 1989).

11. Suttner, preface to Simon, *Wehrt Euch!* This tract played a significant role in galvanizing the Centralverein (CV), a Jewish self-defense organization. The scholarly literature on the CV is immense, but the best treatments of it during the Imperial and Weimar periods remain, respectively, Schorsch, *Jewish Reactions*, 117–48, and Paucker, *Der jüdische Abwehrkampf*.

12. Suttner, preface to Simon, *Wehrt Euch!* vi.

13. Bertha von Suttner, *Memoiren* (Bremen, 1965), 176; Hamann, *Bertha von Suttner*, 194–321.

14. Cited in Leopold Schaffer, ed., *Vermächtnis und Mahnung zum 50. Todestag Bertha von Suttners* (Bonn, 1964), 71–72.

15. Cited in Hamann, *Bertha von Suttner*, 212–13.

16. On the German Abwehrverein, see chapter 1, note 19. Jacques Kornberg, "The Response to Antisemitism in the 1890s: The Austrian Verein zur Abwehr des Antisemitismus," *Leo Baeck Institute Yearbook* 41 (1996): 161–96, contends that the failure of the Austrian branch to ally itself closely with the Left-Liberal Party in Austria doomed it to relative impotence. The German branch dissolved itself in the summer of 1933; the Austrian branch had fizzled out by the end of the 1890s.

17. Hamann, *Bertha von Suttner*, 202–3.

18. Konrad Jarausch, *Students, Society and Politics in Imperial Germany* (Princeton NJ: Princeton University Press, 1982), 271. On the Freie wissenschaftliche Vereinigungen, see Pickus, *Constructing Modern Identities*, 75–80.

19. Quidde, *Die Antisemitenagitation*.

20. Briggite Maria Goldstein, "Ludwig Quidde and the Struggle for Democratic Pacifism in Germany, 1914–1930," Ph.D. diss., New York University, 1984, 17–18.

21. Quidde, *Die Antisemitenagitation*, 11–12. Quidde was both right and wrong on this point. The failure of the antisemite petition to find any response from Bismarck doomed that particular form of initiative. The political demands of the antisemitic parties also met with failure. On the other hand, antisemites certainly succeeded in broaching a variety of radical solutions incomparably more violent and extreme than in the opening salvos of Treitschke and Stoecker.

22. Quidde, *Die Antisemitenagitation*, 5.

23. These statements are found in Quidde, *Die Antisemitenagitation*, 5, 7, 18.

24. Pickus, *Constructing Modern Identities*, 71.

25. Julius Jacobson, Quidde's Jewish father-in-law, is mentioned in Siegmund Kaznelson, *Juden in deutschen Kulturbereich*, 2nd ed. (Berlin: Jüdischer Verlag, 1959), 513.

26. Margarethe Quidde became a noted musicologist and animal rights activist.

27. Karl Holl, introduction to Quidde, *Der deutsche Pazifismus*.

28. Ullstein, Mosse, and Sonnemann were all liberal Jewish newspaper magnates sympathetic to the peace movement. The prominence of Jews in the press was a perpetual antisemitic target; newspapers such as the liberal, business-oriented *Frankfurter Zeitung* were derided as "Jew papers."

29. Goldstein, "Ludwig Quidde," 20.

30. "Interview mit Ludwig Quidde," *Wahrheit*, 15 May 1928, cited in Goldstein, "Ludwig Quidde," 18–19.

31. Sandi Cooper, "The Re-Invention of the 'Just War' among European Pacifists before the First World War," in Harvey Dyck, ed., *The Pacifist Impulse in Historical Perspective* (Toronto: Toronto University Press, 1996), 387.

32. Goldstein neglects to mention the fact of Quidde's marriage to a Jewish woman and relegates his essay on antisemitism to a footnote.

33. Kessler, *Tagebücher*, 714.

34. The Quidde-Einstein correspondence is located in the Albert Einstein Archive at the National and University Libraries, Jerusalem.

35. Otto Nathan and Heinz Norden, eds., *Einstein on Peace* (New York: Simon and Schuster, 1960), 1–7.

36. Foerster, *Erlebte Weltgeschichte,* 211–14.

37. Foerster, *Mein Kampf*, 10.

38. Foerster, *The Jews,* ix–x. Foerster's *Erlebte Weltgeschichte* notes a humorous interchange between himself and a relative, then Reichskanzler Michaelis. The latter chided Foerster for publishing his articles in a "Jewish paper." Foerster responded that he had long held these ideas and that the Jewish papers were better than the antisemitic rags favored by the reactionaries (275).

39. Foerster, *Politische Ethik.*

40. Foerster, *Politische Ethik*, 384.

41. Foerster, *Politische Ethik*, 370.

42. Foerster, *Mein Kampf,* 255. The original reads: "Nur durch Christus und in Christus wird die Judenfrage gelöst. Weder Ausstosung und Aussperrung, noch blosse Assimilierung und äusserliches taufen kann den ungeheureren inneres Schwerigkeiten des Problems irgendwie gerecht werden. Ernst wenn beide, der Jude und der Christ, sich von ganzer Seele dem Geist Christi 'assimilieren,' ist die wirkliche Assimilierung des jüdischen Volkes mit den arischen Rassen möglich und lebensfähig."

43. Foerster, *Mein Kampf*, 252–53.

44. Foerster, *Mein Kampf*, 254.

45. Tacitly, this acknowledged just how foreign the Ostjuden were, creating a zone of Jewish difference that could be affirmed despite the assimilation of German Jews.

46. Frank Stern, *The Whitewashing.*

47. Foerster, *Erlebte Weltgeschichte,* 642; Foerster, *Deutsche Geschichte und politische Ethik* (Nuremberg: Glock und Lutz, 1961), 198.

48. Foerster, *The Jews,* viii.

49. Foerster either neglects to mention or simply does not know that the Hasidim were an elitist, sectarian, and ascetic group extremely critical of the Jewish mainstream. They were also far more concerned with legal matters than Foerster assumes.

50. Foerster, *The Jews,* x.

51. Foerster still insisted in 1920 that "only through Christ and in Christ" could the Jewish problem be solved. See *Mein Kampf*, 255.

52. Einstein to Foerster, 13 March 1938, document 53–085, Foerster and Einstein correspondence.

53. Foerster, *The Jews,* 124.

54. Foerster continued to regard Jews as the spiritual wellspring of Western civilization, as a people chosen by God for a special mission. Richard Rubinstein's *After Auschwitz* (Indianapolis: Bobbs-Merrill, 1966) forcefully exposed the dark underside of this evaluation. Rubinstein contends that the idea of Chosenness, an idea initiated by ancient Israel and adopted by both Christianity and rabbinic Judaism, lay at the source of the Jews' special treatment through the ages. It provided a theological explanation for the Jews' long history of suffering. For devout Christians the Jews'

suffering somehow had to be part of the divine scheme of redemption. Rubinstein concluded, in light of Auschwitz, that the myth of Chosenness needed to be dispensed with altogether.

55. Foerster, *The Jews*, 126. Did penguins subconsciously remind Foerster of the Orthodox Jewish males of Eastern Europe who dressed only in black and white and (at least in stereotype) walked with a waddle?

56. Bauman, "Allosemitism." See also Zygmunt Bauman, *Modernity and the Holocaust* (Ithaca NY: Cornell University Press, 1991), 31–60.

57. Foerster, *The Jews*, 132.

58. Foerster discussed Ballin in Rathenau twice: in *Erlebte Weltgeschichte*, 272–73, and in *The Jews*, 132–34. In the latter treatment, Foerster juxtaposed Ballin and Rathenau with the orthodox Jewish businessman R. E. May, whose annual report Foerster described as "quite as much an annual of ethics as it was a survey of trade." By adding May's example I suspect that Foerster was trying to ameliorate the judgment on Jewish complicity on the rise of German nationalism in *Erlebte Weltgeschichte*. Regrettably, he does this by simply reverting to the "bad Jew" versus "good Jew" model.

59. Foerster, *The Jews*, 145.

60. Foerster, *The Jews*, 146, 145–53.

61. Foerster, *The Jews*, 139.

62. Richard Coudenhove-Kalergi, "Biographie," in Heinrich Graf Coudenhove-Kalergi, *Anti-semitismus* (Vienna: Amalthea, 1992), 43–44.

63. Coudenhove-Kalergi, *Anti-Semitism throughout the Ages*, 21. All quotes, unless otherwise noted, are from this translation.

64. Coudenhove-Kalergi, *Anti-Semitism throughout the Ages*, 222.

65. Coudenhove-Kalergi, *Ein Leben für Europa*, 44.

66. Coudenhove-Kalergi, *Anti-Semitism throughout the Ages*, 157.

67. Coudenhove-Kalergi, *Anti-Semitism throughout the Ages*, 195.

68. Coudenhove-Kalergi, *Anti-Semitism throughout the Ages*, 91–97.

69. Coudenhove-Kalergi, *Anti-Semitism throughout the Ages*, 104.

70. Coudenhove-Kalergi, *Anti-Semitism throughout the Ages*, 21–22.

71. Heinrich Graf Coudenhove-Kalergi, *Antisemitismus. Von den Zeiten der Bibel bis Ende des 19. Jahrhunderts* (Vienna: Amalthea, 1992), 291.

72. Coudenhove-Kalergi, *Anti-Semitism throughout the Ages*, 219–20.

73. Coudenhove-Kalergi, *Anti-Semitism throughout the Ages*, 208–9.

74. Richard Coudenhove-Kalergi, "Judentum," in Kurt Lenz and Walter Fabian, *Die Friedensbe-wegung* (Berlin: C. A. Schwetschke und Sohn, 1922), 74.

75. Karl Holl introduces the pivotal figure of Alfred Fried as "einen jungen, ehrgeizigen Österre-ichen, der soeben in Berlin sein Glück als Journalist und Verleger versuchte, zur Nachahmung an" (*Pazifismus*, 42). Only one pertinent fact remains unstated.

76. Arthur von Suttner in the Abwehrverein circular, *Freies Blatt*, 15 May 1894, cited in Hamann, *Bertha von Suttner*, 194.

77. Gerlach, *Von Recht nach Links*, 261.

78. Mosse, *German Jews beyond Judaism*.

79. Pickus, *Constructing Modern Identities*, 75–80; Herzog, *Intimacy and Exclusion*, esp. 112–15.

80. In a self-revision well known to students of German Jewish history, the late Jacob Katz abandoned the term "neutral society," employed in his path-breaking *Out of the Ghetto* (Cambridge: Harvard University Press, 1973), for the term "semi-neutral society." Katz thus intended to highlight

the majoritarian impulse of the emancipationist view of the future. Katz was generally correct—I refer here to exceptions to the rule.

3. The Problematics of Philosemitic Fiction

1. The popularity of Dinter's work peaked in the 1920s, but he enjoyed a wide readership into the Nazi period. On Dinter, see Michael Schmidt, "Im Westen eine 'Wissenschaft' . . . Antisemitismus im völkisch-fascistischen Roman der Weimarer Republik," in Hans Otto Horch and Horst Denkler, eds., *Conditio Judaica* (Tübingen: Max Niemeyer, 1993), 3:96. Hans Reimann's hilarious *Die Dinte wider das Blut* (1922) imagines a thinly veiled Dinter (Dr. Hermann Stänker) engaged in the creation and re-Aryanization of a semitic bunny rabbit. Reimann's parody offers an example of an anti-antisemitic work that should not be termed philosemitic.

2. The literature on Freytag is ably discussed in Gubser, *Literarischer Antisemitismus*. Gubser concludes that despite Freytag's personal liberation from antisemitic sentiments and his later positive portrayals of Jewish life, "[d]as alles macht aber der betreffende Werk [*Soll und Haben*] nicht weniger antisemitisch" (287).

3. The exceptions to this rule deserve mention: Erspamer, *The Elusiveness of Tolerance*, 98–112; Ritchie Robertson, *The "Jewish Question" in German Literature, 1749–1939* (Oxford: Oxford University Press, 1999); Roddler F. Morris, "Philosemitism on the German Right: The Case of the Novelist Walter Bloem," *Simon Wiesenthal Center Annual* 4 (1987): 203–59.

4. Additional works that touch on Jewish themes favorably but fleetingly could have expanded this discussion considerably. I am sure that I missed many pro-Jewish themes in German literature and probably other pro-Jewish works. I hope these pages will be read as an invitation to undertake a more systematic investigation of pro-Jewish themes—an able doctoral candidate would find plenty to write about. I stumbled upon the novels discussed here in Cologne's Germania Judaica, Tel Aviv's Weiner Library, and Jerusalem's National and University Libraries.

5. Mark Gelber, "What Is Literary Antisemitism?" *Jewish Social Studies* 47, no. 1 (winter 1985): 1–20.

6. Bauman, "Allosemitism," 143–56.

7. Antisemitism is condemned in most of these works but without any striking reconsideration of the phenomenon from either a political or a literary standpoint. Knobloch's Michael Eli Lesser offers an instance where antisemitism causes surprise but is overcome. In Siemer's *Juda und die Andern*, Felden's *Die Sunde wider das Volk*, and Pueschel's *Die Juden von Kronburg*, antisemitism is a foreign and destructive growth that is un-German and, in all three cases, destroys a positive Jewish figure.

8. Pulzer, *Jews and the German State*, 15.

9. Celia Applegate, *A Nation of Provincials: The German Idea of Heimat* (Berkeley: University of California Press, 1990).

10. German Jews were also stymied in taking a clear approach to intermarriage, which offered a superb proof of Jewish willingness to integrate but also threatened complete (and morally painless) disintegration of the community. On the emancipatory period, see Erspamer, *The Elusiveness of Tolerance*, 106–9.

11. Ruth Klüger, "Die Leiche unterm Tisch," in *Katastrophen. Über deutsche Literatur* (Göttingen: Wallstein, 1994), 83–105.

12. Michael Foucault, *Discipline and Punish: The Birth of the Prison* (New York: Vintage Books, 1995); Gavin Rendall and Gary Wickham, *Using Foucault's Method* (London: Sage, 1999).

13. In the interest of keeping this study to a reasonable length, I exclude discussion of other works, including those listed in the appendix. To take but one example, I offer Emil Scholl's (1875–

1932) massive seven-hundred-page novel *Arnold Bach* (Berlin-Leipzig, 1908). In this novel, Scholl, a member of a renowned Liberal family, produced one of the few "philosemitic" works in German fiction to imagine a happy ending.

14. Siemer was the author of the following works: *Maja Orbinska in Hamburg*; *Meine fünf Klosterjahre*; *Weltbund der Auslanddeutschen*; *Die Zukunft der Deutschen in Ausland*, 3rd ed. (1921).

15. Siemer, *Juda und die Andern*, 6–7. The opposition between Hansgeorg and Samuel is repeated consistently throughout the book, sometimes in violent imagery. On page 33, for instance, Siemer contrasts the North German and the Jew: pride versus pride, brain versus brain, blood versus blood.

16. Siemer, *Juda und die Andern*, 222. See Florian Krobb, *Jüdische Frauengestalten in der deutschsprachigen Erzahlliteratur* (Tübingen: M. Niemeyer, 1993).

17. Siemer, *Juda und die Andern*, 260 ff.

18. Siemer, *Juda und die Andern*, 84.

19. Siemer, *Juda und die Andern*, 263.

20. Siemer, *Juda und die Andern*, 44.

21. Siemer tells us in the frontispiece, "Der Verfasser ist kein Jude und hat kein jüdisches Blut, er stammt aus niedersächschich-friesischer Familie mit rheinisch-westfälischem Einschlag."

22. Although this drive to educate informs the entire novel, the principal excurses are as follows: Goldstein muses to himself on the lachrymose course of Jewish history (65–79); Goldstein lectures the receptive Gerd on Judaica (93–109); Gerd and Benno attend a debate between rival factions within the Berlin Jewish community (235–42).

23. Siemer, *Juda und die Andern*, 245.

24. Siemer, *Juda und die Andern*, 39.

25. Suchy, "The Verein zur Abwehr des Antisemitismus. II," 90.

26. Felden, *Die Sünde wider das Volk*, 16: "Certainly, the Jew was here and there mocked, just as in the best marriages the husband mocks the wife and the wife mocks the husband. Overall, however, the Jew was respected."

27. Felden, *Die Sünde wider das Volk*, 50.

28. Felden, *Die Sünde wider das Volk*, 60–63.

29. Felden, *Die Sünde wider das Volk*, 64.

30. The curious reader may consult my tedious doctoral dissertation, "Jewish Reactions to Intermarriage in Nineteenth Century Germany," Ohio State University, 1990.

31. Artenburg writes: "Studien die ich seitdem getrieben haben, brachten mir zur Überzeugung, dass eine Ehe für uns beide—für beide Elfriede—verhängnisvoll werden und uns nur Leid und Unglück bringen würde." Friedrich's comment, clearly Felden's own viewpoint, is to decry the fact that racial hatred could overcome the love for a man and a woman (Felden, *Die Sünde wider das Volk*, 211).

32. Felden, *Die Sünde wider das Volk*, 259, 279.

33. For examples, see Felden, *Die Sünde wider das Volk*, 35–36, 142, 272–74.

34. Presumably, Knobloch uses these two names to evoke the German (Michael) and Jewish (Eli) components of Lesser's identity.

35. The native absence of friction is asserted by several of these philosemitic authors.

36. This comparison with Cahan and Richler should not be pushed too far. Knobloch is a Christian with philosemitic tendencies. On the one hand, he is much more positive in his portrayal of the Jewry that Lesser has left behind than either Cahan or Richler. On the other hand, his novel lacks the in-depth familiarity with Jewish circumstances, exactly that which gives Cahan's and Richler's works their power.

37. Knobloch, *Gläserne Wände*, 38. Pfeiffer is probably based on Maj. Meno Burg, the highest-ranking Jewish officer in the Prussian army in the nineteenth century.

38. Knobloch, *Gläserne Wände*, 127.

39. Knobloch, *Gläserne Wände*, 14–15, 61–62.

40. Knobloch, *Gläserne Wände*, 104, 154.

41. Knobloch, *Gläserne Wände*, 193.

42. Knobloch, *Gläserne Wände*, 222–23.

43. Knobloch, *Gläserne Wände*, 219.

44. Knobloch, *Gläserne Wände*, 194.

45. Knobloch, *Gläserne Wände*, 231–32.

46. Knobloch, *Gläserne Wände*, 287.

47. Knobloch, *Gläserne Wände*, 255–56.

48. Knobloch, *Gläserne Wände*, 311.

49. Pueschel seems to have been a member of the nationalist camp, offering another example (in addition to Walter Bloem [see note 3]) of philosemitism on the German Right. See Pueschel in *Centralverein-Zeitung*, 4 December 1924, 769.

50. Pueschel, *Die Juden von Kronburg*.

51. Pueschel, *Die Juden von Kronburg*, 28.

52. Pueschel, *Die Juden von Kronburg*, 10.

53. Pueschel, *Die Juden von Kronburg*, 83. Note that Luther's and Bismarck's ambiguous legacies regarding Jews are not confronted; similarly, Pueschel praises Father Jahn as the champion of the family, asserts that only a return to "family values" will bring the cessation of civil unrest, but turns a blind eye to the fact that Father Jahn was very antisemitic (117).

54. Pueschel, *Die Juden von Kronburg*, 16–22.

55. Pueschel, *Die Juden von Kronburg*, 51.

56. Pueschel, *Die Juden von Kronburg*, 173.

57. See the discussion in Erspamer, *The Elusiveness of Tolerance*, 98–112.

58. Pueschel, *Die Juden von Kronburg*, 134. Cf. Gustav Levenstein, *Zur Ehre des Judentums* (Berlin, 1911).

59. Pueschel, *Die Juden von Kronburg*, 204.

60. Pueschel, *Die Juden von Kronburg*, 130–35.

61. Pueschel, *Die Juden von Kronburg*, 223.

62. Pueschel, *Die Juden von Kronburg*, 259.

63. Pueschel, *Die Juden von Kronburg*, 264.

64. Scholz, *Der Jude von Konstanz*, 18, 34.

65. Scholz, *Der Jude von Konstanz*, 73–74; see 36 for further blood imagery.

66. Scholz, *Der Jude von Konstanz*, 40.

67. Scholz, *Der Jude von Konstanz*, 99–100.

68. Scholz, *Der Jude von Konstanz*, 42.

69. Scholz, *Der Jude von Konstanz*, 106–7.

70. Scholz, *Der Jude von Konstanz*, 52.

71. Scholz, *Der Jude von Konstanz*, 126.

72. Nachshon, not Nasson. Bellet and Simlai sound Hebraic, but are they actually names? The man who will marry Bellet if Nasson fails to return to Judaism is improbably named Simon ben Gamaliel, a name from the early rabbinic era familiar to readers of the New Testament as the erstwhile teacher of Paul.

73. Scholz, *Der Jude von Konstanz*, 134.

74. Scholz, *Der Jude von Konstanz*, 124.
75. Scholz, *Der Jude von Konstanz*, 175–84.
76. Jaques, *Das Kreuz des Juden*, 4.
77. Jaques, *Das Kreuz des Juden*, 96.
78. Jaques, *Das Kreuz des Juden*, 32.
79. Jaques, *Das Kreuz des Juden*, 39.
80. Jaques, *Das Kreuz des Juden*, 170–74.
81. Jaques, *Das Kreuz des Juden*, 145.
82. Jaques, *Das Kreuz des Juden*, 144–52.
83. Ferch, *Mensch*, 46, 60.
84. Ferch, *Mensch*, 46–48, 79.
85. Ferch, *Mensch*, 201, 202.
86. Ferch, *Mensch*, 243.
87. Ferch, *Mensch*, 100.
88. Susan Suleiman, "The Jew in Jean-Paul Sartre's *Réflexions sur la question juive:* An Exercise in Historical Reading," in Linda Nochlin and Tamar Garb, eds., *The Jew in the Text* (London: Thames and Hudson, 1995), 210–18.
89. Lessing's Jewish characters are also problematic. See Jo-Jacqueline Eckhardt, *Lessing's "Nathan der Weise" and the Critics* (Columbia: Camden House, 1993).
90. Excepting Johann Ferch's cardboard couple, Hermann Jaques's Moritz Hardenstein, on a sea cruise to nowhere, is the sole survivor of their German Jewish encounters. The paucity of happy endings to these German Jewish encounters is unnerving considering the Liberal role as the standard-bearers of "cultural optimism," to invert a phrase from Fritz Stern, *The Politics of Cultural Despair* (New York, 1964).
91. What is called for here is an effort at "sideshadowing," exploring the full range of literary constructions of Jewishness in place of incessant "backshadowing" that merely confirms the demonization of the Jew in German fiction. See Michael André Bernstein, *Foregone Conclusions: Against Apocalyptic History* (Berkeley: University of California Press, 1994).

4. Missionary Protestants and Judaism

1. On German pietism, see Koppel S. Pinson, *Pietism as a Factor in the Rise of German Nationalism* (New York: Columbia University Press, 1934), and, more recently, Christopher Clark, *The Politics of Conversion: Missionary Protestantism and the Jews in Prussia, 1728–1941* (Oxford: Clarendon, 1995).
2. Schorsch, *Jewish Reactions*, mentions Strack's appeal to the Berlin public prosecutor in 1893. No mention of either Delitzsch or Strack can be found in Paucker, *Der jüdische Abwehrkampf,* or Marjorie Lamberti, *Jewish Activism in Imperial Germany* (New Haven CT: Yale University Press, 1978). Brief discussions of both Delitzsch and Strack can be found in Michael Meyer, ed., *German-Jewish History in Modern Times*, 4 vols. (New York: Columbia University Press, 1998), 2:175, 3:217, 253, 4:168; and Jacob Borut, *"A New Spirit among Our Brethren in Ashkenaz": German Jewry's Change in Direction at the End of the 19th Century* (Hebrew) (Jerusalem: Magnes Press of the Hebrew University, 1999).
3. Tal, *Christians and Jews*; Kusche, *Die unterlegene Religion*; Engelmann, *Kirche am Abgrund*.
4. Wagner, *Franz Delitzsch*; Golling and Osten-Sacken, eds., *Hermann L. Strack*.
5. Frank Putnam defines compartmentalization as "the separation of areas of awareness and memory from each other. Compartmentalization may be alternatively conceptualized as a failure of integration of experience and knowledge" (*Dissociation in Children and Adolescents* [New York: Guilford Press, 1997], 71).

6. Yehuda Amir, "Contact Hypothesis in Ethnic Relations," *Psychological Bulletin* 71 (1969): 319–42; Hilde Weiss, "On the Significance of Personal Contact to Jews," in Herbert Strauss, ed., *Error without Trial: Current Research on Antisemitism*, vol. 2 (Berlin: De Gruyter, 1988).

7. Josef Wohlgemuth, "Hermann L. Strack," *Jeschurun* 9 (1922): 384.

8. Garb, "Introduction," 20–21.

9. An apologetic and decontextualized approach also mars works in the sphere of Anglo-American relations where philosemitism (missionary and otherwise) was admittedly more widespread than in Germany.

10. Clark, *Politics of Conversion*, 281.

11. Bauman, "Allosemitism," 143–56; Zygmunt Bauman, *Modernity and the Holocaust* (Ithaca NY: Cornell University Press, 1991), 31–60.

12. Tal, *Christians and Jews*, 160–222.

13. Heschel, *Abraham Geiger*.

14. George Foot Moore, "Christian Writers on Judaism," *Harvard Theological Review* 14 (1921): 197–254; E. P. Sanders, *Paul and Palestinian Judaism* (London: SCM, 1977); Kusche, *Die unterlegene Religion*, 144–45.

15. See the introduction to the newer editions of Emil Schürer, *Geschichte des jüdischen Volkes im Zeitalter Jesu Christi* (Leipzig: Hinrichs, 1886), xi–xii; Moore, "Christian Writers on Judaism," 137–40. See E. P. Sanders's polemic with Ben Meyer over Joachim Jeremias's legacy in *Journal of Biblical Literature* 110 (1991): 451–62, 463–77.

16. Heschel, *Abraham Geiger*, fairly summarizes Delitzsch's standpoint: "Delitzsch adopted a sympathetic posture toward Judaism, portraying it as Christianity's inferior but genuine precursor" (195). Delitzsch himself commented, "Die Vorgeschichte Israels ist auch die Vorgeschichte Christentums" (*Christentum und jüdische Presse*, 3).

17. Franz Delitzsch, *Zur Geschichte der jüdischer Poësie* (Leipzig: Karl Tauchnitz, 1836).

18. Leopold Zunz's seminal *Über jüdische Literatur* appeared only in 1818, his study of Jewish preaching in 1836, the same year as Delitzsch's work.

19. Franz Delitzsch, *Zur Geschichte der jüdischen Poësie*. Leipzig: Karl Tauchnitz, 1836.

20. David Kaufmann, "Obituary on Franz Delitzsch," in Franz Delitzsch, *Gesammelte Schriften* (Frankfurt am Main: J. Kaufmann, 1908), 1:290–306; in English, *Jewish Quarterly Review* (1890): 386–99.

21. Delitzsch, *Jüdisches Handwerkleben*. The missionary movement as a whole expressed a consistent preference for skilled workers over the free professions, academia, journalism, etc. The missionary world disapproved of the Jewish occupational structure. Wolfgang Heinrichs finds Delitzsch more critical of the Jewish role in the contemporary economy than his teacher, Julius Fürst. Perhaps Fürst's Jewish origins, like Paulus Cassel's, help explain their resistance to Jewish stereotypes.

22. Delitzsch, *Jewish Artisan Life*, 17.

23. Delitzsch, *Jewish Artisan Life*, 19.

24. Delitzsch's selection of rabbinic materials is not careful with respect to dating. Yalkutim (midrashic collections) and the tanhumas (early medieval Palestinian midrashim) from a much later period are used indiscriminately. This conflation of rabbinic literature irrespective of period and place was common in scholarship of that era. Neither Strack nor the English Presbyterian George Foot Moore nor even most Jewish researchers were preoccupied with questions regarding the dating of rabbinic texts, the attribution of rabbinic sayings, the ideology of individual rabbinic works, or the intertextual relationship between discrete texts.

25. Delitzsch, *Ein Tag in Capernaum*, 83–84. In contrast to Rosemary Reuther's famous thesis about patristic literature, here we have Christology without Jewish denigration.

26. Delitzsch, *Jesus und Hillel*, 52.

27. Delitzsch, *Christentum und jüdische Presse*, 40.

28. Delitzsch, *The Old Testament History of Salvation*, 190–93, 195–96.

29. Delitzsch, *Jesus und Hillel*, 25.

30. Delitzsch, *Christentum und jüdische Presse*, 33. Compare James Charlesworth, ed., *Hillel and Jesus* (Minneapolis: Fortress Press, 1997).

31. Delitzsch, *Christentum und jüdische Presse*, 24.

32. Arthur Wiessmann, *Ernste Antworten auf Ernste Fragen. Franz Delitzsch's neueste Schrift* (Vienna: Kloepflmacher, 1888), 15, passim; A. Blumenthal, *Offener Briefe* (1889), cited in Wagner, *Franz Delitzsch*, 164.

33. On the connection between these two works, see Strack's introduction in *Einleitung*, 5th ed., and Strack and Billerbeck's introduction in *Kommentar*, v–vi. Delitzsch's influence on this choice of topics is undeniable. In his *Iggeret paulus ha-shaliach el haromayim/Paulus des Apostels Brief an die Römer aus dem griechischen Urtext auf Grund des Sinai-Codes in das Hebräische Übersetz und aus Talmud und Midrasch Erläuterte* (Leipzig: Dörffling und Frank, 1870), Delitzsch's explicit motive is to show the superiority of Christianity. On the other hand, the idea that rabbinic literature could shed light on the New Testament was more than most German Protestant scholars would have conceded.

34. Strack, *Introduction*, ix.

35. Strack, *Einleitung*.

36. Jacob Neusner, *The Study of Ancient Judaism* (Leiden: E. J. Brill, 1981), x–xi.

37. Reviews of *Einleitung* can be found in Alexander Marx, *Jewish Quarterly Review* 13 (1922): 352–65; S. Poznanaski, *Revue des Études Juives* 72 (1921): 102–7; and Josef Wohlgemuth, *Jeschurun* 9 (1922): 381–84.

38. Strack, *Introduction*, 202.

39. Delitzsch, *Paulus des Apostels Brief*, 7–11.

40. Sanders, *Paul and Palestinian Judaism*, 42–43, 58–59, 234–35. Francis Watson, *Paul, Judaism and the Gentiles* (New York: Cambridge University Press, 1986), 1–22, gives a good overview of Protestant scholarship since the Reformation.

41. Samuel Sandmel, "Parallelomania," *Journal of Biblical Literature* 81, no. 1 (March 1962): 1–13.

42. Sandmel, "Parallelomania," 9.

43. Sandmel, "Parallelomania," 10.

44. Strack and Billerbeck, *Kommentar*, v–vi.

45. Lamparter, *Evangelische Kirche und Judentum*, 45. Solomon Rappaport also regarded the *Kommentar* as philosemitic (*Jew and Gentile*, 61).

46. Delitzsch, *Zur Geschichte der jüdischen Poësie*.

47. Wolfgang Heinrichs, "Das Bild in der protestantischen Judenmission des deutschen Kaiserreichs," *Zeitschrift für Religions—und Geistesgeschichte* 44, no. 3 (1992): 195–220; Clark, *Politics of Conversion*.

48. Johann F. A. de Le Roi, *Geschichte der evangelischen Judenmission*, 2nd ed. (Leipzig: Hinrich'sche Buchhandlung, 1899); Johann F. A. de Le Roi, "Die neuere Litteratur über die Judenfrage," *Nathanael* 3, no. 3 (1897): 65–89. This article contains one of the earliest juxtapositions of "antisemitic" and "philosemitic." De Le Roi commented that the philosemitic works outnumber the antisemitic 295 to 186 but that "die philosemitischen aber stammen zum allergrössten Teil aus

jüdischen Federn" (79). On de Le Roi, see Clark, *Politics of Conversion*, 252–81; Engelmann, *Kirche am Abgrund*, 51–61.

49. Gustaf Dalman, report to the Generalversammlung des Centralvereins, *Saat auf Hoffnung* 26 (1889): 9.

50. Michael Meyer, "The Great Debate on Antisemitism," *Leo Baeck Institute Yearbook* 12 (1966): 137–70.

51. Since "Old Testament" is the term used exclusively by Christians and mainly by contemporary Jews who entered the polemical fray, I will use it here despite its patently problematic nature.

52. Michael Baumgarten (Liberal Protestant) and Ignaz Johann Döllinger (Catholic) are exceptions.

53. Hermann Strack, "Geschichte und Wesen des Antisemitismus," *Nathanael* 25 (1909): 99–120, esp. 119.

54. I do not consider the Jewish press here because they had a very limited non-Jewish reading audience. How many Christians, after all, subscribed to the *Allgemeine Zeitung des Judentums*?

55. It should be noted that most of the material in the missionary journals is neutral in its presentation of Jews and Judaism. Local reports, appeals for financial aid, lead articles on the New Testament with an evangelical slant, and biographical sketches of great missionary figures (especially Jewish apostates) comprised a considerable part of any given issue.

56. On Strack, see Golling and Osten-Sacken, eds., *Hermann L. Strack*, 12–52. On Delitzsch, whose friendships with Jews was proverbial, see Elizabeth Delitzsch, *Franz Delitzsch als Freund Israels: Ein Gedenkblatt* (Leipzig: Evangelisch-luth. Zentralvereins, 1910); Wagner, *Franz Delitzsch*, esp. 149–66.

57. On Rabinovitch, see Steven Zipperstein, "Heresy, Apostasy and the Transformation of Joseph Rabinovitch," in Endelman, ed., *Jewish Apostasy*, 206–31.

58. I am not suggesting that Jews could have turned to missionaries as an alternative to Liberalism. The Left-Liberals represented a real political force and an overall agenda supported by most German Jews. But a supplementary tactical alliance with missionaries was ruled out by ideological not practical considerations.

59. Franz Delitzsch to Moritz Lazarus, 5 January 1883, Moritz Lazarus Archive, VAR 298/94.

60. Engelmann, *Kirche am Abgrund*, 51–61.

61. See note 2.

62. Delitzsch, *Wissenschaft*.

63. Franz Delitzsch to Moritz Lazarus, 5 January 1883, Moritz Lazarus Archive, VAR 298/94.

64. Delitzsch, *Rohling's Talmudjude*, 4–6.

65. Delitzsch, *Rohling's Talmudjude*, 6.

66. Delitzsch, *Rohling's Talmudjude*, 10.

67. Delitzsch, *Rohling's Talmudjude*, 5.

68. Franz Delitzsch to Salomon Buber, 1885, in Hans-Joachim Barkenings, "Delitzsch," in Wolf-Dieter Marchen and Karl Thieme, eds., *Christen und Juden* (Mainz: Matthias Grünewald, 1961), 210.

69. "In tiefster Seele unsympathetisch ist mir jener Antisemitismus welcher nur für die Schattenseiten des jüdischen Volkes offene Augen hat, und nicht für dessen Tugenden" (Delitzsch, *Christentum und jüdische Presse*, 3).

70. Delitzsch, *Christentum und jüdische Presse*, 52; Hermann Strack, "Sie eifern um Gott, aber mit Unverstand," *Nathanael* 2 (1886): 129–44. According to both Delitzsch and Strack, Jewish egotism (*Selbstgerechtigkeit*) was a major failing.

71. Clark, *Politics of Conversion*, esp. chap. 7.

72. Delitzsch, *Christentum und jüdische Presse*, 19–20, 42.

73. Clark, *Politics of Conversion*, 147–63; Heinrichs, "Das Bild," 201–2.

74. Franz Delitzsch, *Welche Anforderungen stellt die Gegenwart an die Missions-Arbeit unter den Juden? Vortrag gehalten zu Berlin, am 28 April 1870* (Erlangen: Deichert, 1870), 5; Franz Delitzsch, *Ernste Fragen* (Leipzig: Schriften des Institutum Judaicum zu Leipzig, 1888), 38.

75. Delitzsch, *Ernste Fragen*, 38.

76. I must disagree with Wolfgang Heinrichs's view that the missionary perspective on Reform Judaism was unconditionally negative ("Das Bild," 201–2).

77. Delitzsch, *Christentum und jüdische Presse*, 57.

78. See, for instance, *Allgemeine Zeitung des Judentums* 52 (1888): 594–96, 609–11.

79. Paul Gerhard Aring, *Christen und Juden heute—und die "Judenmission"?* (Frankfurt am Main: Haag und Herchen, 1987), 228.

80. Delitzsch, *Welche Anforderungen*, 5.

81. Hermann Strack, "Die 'Jüdische Presse' und die Judenmission," *Nathanael* 13 (1897): 115–22.

82. Hermann Strack, "Geschichte und Wesen des Antisemitismus," *Nathanael* 25 (1909): 99–120.

83. Strack returned to this theme in nearly every one of his works on the Jewish question. Take, for instance, the first sentence in the eighth edition of Strack, *Jews and Human Sacrifice*: "Untruth does not become truth by frequent repetition. But as long as it is repeated, it is a duty incumbent on him who claims to be a champion of truth, knowledge and justice, to be continually exposing the falsehoods of his opponents' assertions, and to state the real truth of the matter" (xii).

84. Strack, *Jews and Human Sacrifice*, xvi.

85. The Wissenschaft des Judentums was clearly moving in a less apologetic direction by the turn of the century.

86. See Elisheva Carlebach, "Attribution of Secrecy and Perceptions of Jewry," *Jewish Social Studies* 2, no. 3 (spring 1996): 115–36.

87. Strack quotes Dalman's comment approvingly in *Die Juden, dürfen sie "verbrecher von Religions wegen" genannt werden?* (Berlin: Hermann Walther, 1893), 22.

88. Heinrich Laible, "Jesus Christus im Thalmud," *Nathanael* 6, nos. 1–2 (1890): 3–128.

89. Delitzsch, *Welche Anforderungen*, 7.

90. "Mauscheln" was used to refer either to Yiddish or to German as spoken by Jews who had not achieved complete linguistic assimilation. The literature on the contempt for Yiddish is immense, but the best place to start is Gilman, *Jewish Self-Hatred*.

91. Heinrich Laible, in *Theologisches Literaturblatt* 37 (1916): 484, cited in Ralf Golling, "Der Beitrag H. L. Stracks zur Erschliessung des Judentums," in Golling and Osten-Sacken, eds., *Hermann Strack*, 49.

92. Hermann Strack, *Das Wesen des Judentums* (Leipzig: J. C. Hinrich'sche, 1906), 23. This address was given at a conference for the Jewish mission in Amsterdam and represents Strack's contribution to the "Essence of Judaism" instigated by Harnack's *Essence of Christianity*. See Tal, *Christians and Jews*, 204–28. Strack began his address by claiming that anyone who sees his religion as true must wish it to be the religion of all. Clearly, Strack has read his Talmud with more care than his Mendelssohn!

93. See Clark, *Politics of Conversion*, 270.

94. Strack, *Jews and Human Sacrifice*, xvii.

95. Strack, *Herr Adolf Stoecker*, 1–10; Hermann Strack, *Die Juden, sind sie Religions Verbrecher?* (Berlin: H. Walther, 1893), 5.

96. Hermann Strack, "Meine Stellung zum Judentum," in *Herr Adolf Stoecker*, 1–6.

97. Kusche, *Die unterlegene Religion*, 137–45.

98. Rappaport, *Jew and Gentile*, 62.

99. Aring, *Christen und Juden heute*, 231–32.

100. Moore wrote of Ferdinand Weber, *System der altsynagogalen palästinischen Theologie*: "The fundamental criticism to be made of Weber's 'system' is precisely that it is a system of theology and not an ancient Jewish system but a modern German system" ("Christian Writers on Judaism," 229).

101. The story of the mission's closure is told in the final chapter of Clark, *Politics of Conversion*, 282–303.

102. On Strack, Josef Wohlgemuth is cited in Golling and Osten-Sacken, eds., *Hermann Strack*, 14–15. On Delitzsch, see Kaufmann, "Franz Delitzsch"; and Chaim Bloch, "Franz Delitzsch— Deutscher und Judenfreund," *Israelitisches Familienblatt*, 8 September 1932, 8.

5. The Gentile Reception of Herzlian Zionism

1. Nahum Sokolow, *A History of Zionism, 1600–1918*, 2 vols. (London: Longmans, 1911, 1919); Nathan M. Gelber, *Vorgeschichte des Zionismus* (1917; rpt. Vienna: Phaedon, 1927); Nussenblatt, *Ein Volk*; and Adolf Boehm, *Die zionistische Bewegung*, 2 vols. (Tel Aviv: Hozaah Ivrit, 1935). In Sokolow's second volume, eleven of the twelve illustrations are of non-Jews. A reverse supersessionism operates in these works, treating Christian proto-Zionism as the precursor for which Jewish Zionism served as the fulfillment. See especially Boehm: "Long before the end of the nineteenth century the Zionist idea was formulated in theory—mainly conceptualized by non-Jews [*Nichtjuden*]" (*Die zionistische Bewegung*, 1:62). See Willehad Eckert's assessment in Martin Stöhr, ed., *Zionismus* (Munich: Chr. Kaiser, 1980), 121.

2. Hermann Ellern and Bessi Ellern, eds., *Herzl, Hechler, the Grand Duke of Baden and the German Emperor, 1896–1904* (Tel Aviv: Ellern's Bank, 1961). These documents provide a sense of Herzl's reception by the German regime.

3. Norman Rose, *The Gentile Zionists* (London: Frank Cass, 1973); Michael J. Pragai, *Faith and Fulfillment: Christians and the Return to the Promised Land* (London: Vallentine-Mitchell, 1985); Daniel Dratwa, "Emile Vanaervelde on Zionism and the 'Jewish Question,'" *Studies in Zionism* 10, no. 1 (spring 1989); Eyal Naveh, "Unconventional Christian Zionist: The Theologian Reinhold Niebuhr," *Studies in Zionism* 11, no. 2 (autumn 1990); Moshe Davis, *America and the Holy Land* (Westport CT: Praeger, 1995); Paul Charles Merkley, *The Politics of Christian Zionism* (London: Frank Cass, 1998); Mark H. Gelber, *Melancholy Pride: Nation, Race and Gender in the German Literature of Cultural Zionism* (Tübingen: Max Niemeyer, 2000).

4. "On the basis of the Zionist idea of Herzl a new relationship between the nations of the world and the Jewish people was created. Rather than the relationship that has existed until now, which even among our friends among the nations was a relationship of tolerance and sympathy . . . [there is] an entirely different relationship to a living Hebrew nation awakening to a national life, and an aspiration toward redemption, to a nation that is revealed in the eyes of the nations in the greatness of its suffering and the brightness of its hope" (Leib Jaffe, ed., "Ha-notzrim ba-kongress ha-rishon," in *Sefer ha-kongress* [n.d., 1922–23], 155). Written from very different perspectives, Almog, *Zionism and History*, and Berkowitz, *Zionist Culture*, emphasize the creation of a new Jewish consciousness.

5. German was the language of the early congresses and of important Zionist periodicals, and it was the native language of the movement's first two presidents.

6. For a justification for treating the years 1896–1906 as a discrete unit, see Almog, *Zionism and History*, 18. Max Aram, "Die Philosemiten und das wahre Interesses der Juden," *Die Welt* 3, no. 39 (29 September 1899), proclaimed that Zionism intends to cure the patient (world Jewry), rendering the palliative measures of philosemitic "physicians" unnecessary. We shall see that these palliatives were much sought after.

7. Salo Baron, "World Dimensions of Jewish History," in *Jewish History and Jewish Historians* (Philadelphia: Jewish Publication Society, 1964), 23–42.

8. See Joseph Walk, "Das 'Deutsche Komitee Pro Palästina,'" *Bulletin des Leo Baeck Instituts* 52 (1976): 162–93.

9. Katz, "Zionism versus Anti-Semitism," 140–52.

10. On Börries von Münchhausen, see Brenner, "Gott schütze uns," 174–99.

11. Yakov Rabi, "The Image of Seer of the State as Foreign Correspondent," *Kesher* 21 (May 1997): 1–10; Mordechai Naor, "Herzl and the Media," *Kesher* 3 (May 1988): 32–38; Ohed David, "The 'King of the Jews' as Media Magician," *Kesher* 27 (May 2000): 49–58.

12. Ernst Pawel, *The Labyrinth of Exile* (London: Collins Harville, 1990), 322–26; Avner Falk, *Herzl, King of the Jews* (Lanham MD: University Press of America, 1993), 546. See also Siegmund Werner, "Herzl und *Die Welt*," *Die Welt* 14, no. 20 (20 March 1910): 412–14.

13. *The Encyclopedia of Zionism and Israel* (New York: Herzl Press–McGraw-Hill), 1213.

14. *Die Welt* ceased publication in 1914. By that time *Jüdische Rundschau* and less prominent journals had expanded the range and reach of the Zionist press in the German language.

15. "Christen über die Judenfrage," *Die Welt* 1, no. 1 (4 June 1897).

16. On Friedrich Fuerst Wrede's novel *Die Goldschilds*, serialized in *Die Welt*, see Gelber, *Melancholy Pride*, 250.

17. Zionist Emil Kronburger gathered these Gentile testimonies together in *Zionisten und Christen* (Leipzig: M. W. Kaufmann, 1900).

18. Emile Zola, "Für die Juden," *Die Welt* 2, no. 5 (4 February 1898): 4–6. Zola's "Pour les juifs" originally appeared in *Le Figaro*, 16 May 1896.

19. Zola, "Für die Juden," 4.

20. Zola, "Für die Juden," 5.

21. Georges Clemenceau, "Und was thun die Juden?" *Die Welt* 2, no. 21 (27 May 1898), originally in *Aurore*. Clemenceau later claimed to have read *Der Judenstaat* and spoke warmly of Herzl as a genius. "Clemenceau Remembers Herzl," in Raphael Patai, ed., *Herzl Year Book* 3 (New York: Herzl Press, 1960), 117–23.

22. Clemenceau, "Und was thun die Juden?" As Jacob Katz emphasized in "Zionism versus Anti-Semitism," the intentions of a particular line of arguments count for more than similarities in analysis. Ha'Am Ahad said very similar things about Jewish subservience, and no one questioned his commitment to the Jewish people.

23. Clemenceau, "Und was thun die Juden?" 7.

24. "Lord Salisbury über den Zionismus," *Die Welt* 2, no. 41 (14 October 1898).

25. There are a couple of ironies worth noting. First, Salisbury is wrong when he claims that it depends "entirely on the Jews" and the Zionists themselves knew it, for why else would they even bother to publish his opinion? Second, Salisbury failed to imagine a reason why the sultan should object to founding of an autonomous Jewish state in Palestine. His political judgment, therefore, leaves much to be desired.

26. "Lord Salisbury über den Zionismus," *Die Welt* 4, no. 44 (2 November 1900), 5.

27. "Minister Chamberlain über die Judenfrage," *Die Welt* 6, no. 40 (October 1902).

28. The following list is by no means exhaustive: "Der Zionismus im englischen Parlament," *Die Welt* 4, no. 41 (12 October 1900); Sir Clement Hill to Mr. L. J. Greenberg, "Einer Erklärung der englischen Regierung," *Die Welt* 7, no. 1 (27 August 1903); Sidney Whitman (*Contemporary Review*), "Theodor Herzl," *Die Welt* 8, no. 37 (9 September 1904); "Sir Harry Johnston über das Ostafrikaprojekt," *Die Welt* 8, no. 42 (4 October 1904); "Eine Interview with Lord Hindlip," *Die Welt* 8, no. 50 (9 December 1904); "Ein englischer Sozialist über den Zionismus," *Die Welt* 8, no. 7 (12 February 1904).

29. The following list is by no means exhaustive: "Senator Sakrewskij über die Affaire Dreyfus und den Antisemitismus in Frankreich," *Die Welt* 2, no. 7 (18 February 1898); "Russische Schrift-steller über den Zionismus," *Die Welt* 6, no. 35 (29 August 1902); "Maxim Gorki und Tolstoi über Kischenew," *Die Welt* 7, no. 22 (29 May 1903); "Zionismus und Staatsbürgertum," *Die Welt* 11, no. 8 (1907): 6–7.

30. See, for instance, "Graf Witte über die Judenfrage," *Die Welt* 10, no. 10 (9 March 1906).

31. Arthur Hertzberg, "Introduction," in *The Zionist Idea* (New York: Athenaeum, 1973), 49.

32. Johannes Heinrich Dunant, *Die Welt* 1, no. 22 (29 October 1897).

33. Paula Winkler-Buber, "Betrachtungen einer Philozionistin," *Die Welt* 4, no. 36 (6 September 1901): 4–6.

34. Baron Maxim Manteuffel, Christen über die Judenfrage Series *Die Welt* 1, no. 21 (22 October 1897).

35. *Jüdische Rundschau* 14, no. 50 (15 December 1911).

36. See John Efron, *Defenders of the Race* (New Haven CT: Yale University Press, 1994).

37. Camilla Theimer, *Antisemitismus und Nationaljudentum. Ein arischer Beitrag zur Lösung der Judenfrage,* 43, Germania Judaica Collection, Stadbibliothek, Cologne. For another work combining antisemitism and Zionism, see Friedrich Siebert, *Der völkische Gedanke und die Verwirklichung des Zionismus* (Munich: Lehmanns, 1916).

38. Theodor Herzl, "Die Verein zur Abwehr," *Die Welt* 1, no. 2 (11 June 1897).

39. Baron Arthur Gundaccar von Suttner, *Die Welt* 1, no. 4 (25 June 1897).

40. "Antwort der Baronin Bertha von Suttner," *Die Welt* 1, no. 3 (18 June 1897): 6.

41. Anonymous obituary, "Mathias Jakob Schleiden," *Die Welt* 8, no. 15 (8 April 1904): 6–7.

42. "Bjoernson und der Jude," *Die Welt* 7, no. 3 (16 January 1903); reprinted on the death of Björnson in *Die Welt* 14, no. 18 (6 May 1910).

43. Pastor Friedrich Naumann, "Der Zionismus," *Die Welt* 38, no. 6 (19 September 1902).

44. "Karl Kautsky über Judentum und jüdisches Proletariat," *Die Welt* 9, no. 50 (15 December 1905).

45. Adolf Friedemann's obituary of Eugen Richter complained that Richter's Freisinnige Volkspartei seated no self-conscious Jews (*zielbewussten Juden*) on the national level, allowed occasional disparaging remarks (*antisemitelnde*) to go unchallenged in the Prussian Landtag, and did not field local Jewish candidates. Friedemann bemoaned Jewish loyalty to Left-Liberalism and attacked the "childish" hope in "our Christian friends" ("Eugen Richter," *Die Welt* 10, no. 11 [16 March 1906]). On Friedemann, see Steven Poppel, *Zionism in Germany, 1897–1933* (Philadelphia: Jewish Publication Society, 1976), 24–25.

46. Heman, *Die historische Weltstellung,* 60–61.

47. Clark, *Politics of Conversion,* 250–52.

48. Edward Browne to Herzl, 29 August 1897, in Theodor Herzl correspondence, Central Zionist Archives (hereafter CZA), H VIII 1068.

49. Ernst Rohmer to Herzl, in CZA, H VIII 690.

50. H. d. Ablaing to Herzl, 26 April 1904, in CZA, H VIII 1.

51. Almog, *Zionism and History,* 60–61, esp. n. 47.

52. Heman, *Das Erwachen,* 23.

53. Heman, *Das Erwachen,* 113, 48, 112.

54. Heman, *Das Erwachen,* 83. Compare to Heman [pseudonymously: Schelomo ben David ha-Esrachi], "Die Mission des jüdisches Volkes," *Die Welt* 1, nos. 45–48 (1897); Heman [anonymous], "Was soll man vom Zionismus halten?" in Kronburger, *Christen über Zionismus,* 54–55.

55. Heman, *Das Erwachen*, 23.

56. Heman, *Das Erwachen*, 98.

57. Heman's hostility to Reform Judaism reflects a growing trend within missionary Protestants.

58. Heman, *Das Erwachen*, 70.

59. Heman to Herzl, 19 December 1897, in CZA, H VIII 344.

60. Heman to Herzl, 27 August 1903, in CZA, H VIII 344.

61. Herzl to Heman, 1 October 1899, cited in Bein et al., eds., *Theodor Herzl*, 5:221; Heman to Herzl, 8 October 1899, in CZA H VIII 344.

62. Herzl to Heman, 11 October 1899, in Bein et al., eds., *Theodor Herzl*, 5:226.

63. C. F. Heman, *Geschichte des jüdischen Volkes seit der Zerstörung Jerusalems* (Callu: Vereins-buchhandlung, 1908); C. F. Heman, *Die religiose Widergebürt der jüdische Volk* (Basel: Verlag der Vereinsbuchhandlung, 1909).

64. On Bahr, see Gelber, *Melancholy Pride*, 254–55.

65. Bahr, *Der Antisemitismus*.

66. Bahr, *Der Antisemitismus*, 15.

67. Moritz Czaky, ed., *Hermann Bahr: Tagebücher, Skizzenbüche, Notizhefte*, 3 vols. (Vienna: Boehlau, 1994–97).

68. See Donald Davaiau, *Der Mann von Übermorgen. Hermann Bahr 1863–1934* (Vienna: Öster-reicher, 1984), 184–89.

69. Czaky, ed., *Hermann Bahr*, 2:216 (2 March 1896). See also Bein et al., eds., *Theodor Herzl*, 4:75–76.

70. Hermann Bahr, "The Fateful Moment," in Meyer Weisgal, *Theodor Herzl: A Memorial* (New York: New Palestine, 1929), 66–67.

71. Hermann Bahr, "Erinnerungen," *Die Welt* 18, no. 27 (3 July 1914): 693.

72. Bahr's view of the psychological benefit for Western Zionists recalls Ahad Ha'Am's critical evaluation of Western Zionism penned after the First Zionist Congress, "The Jewish State and the 'Jewish Question,'" translated and reprinted in Hertzberg, *The Zionist Idea*.

73. Hermann Bahr, *Die Welt* 1, no. 25 (19 December 1897): 8.

74. Hermann Bahr, "Das Judenproblem," *Die Welt* 15, no. 8 (24 December 1911): 166–69. This same audience would soon be galvanized by Martin Buber's epochal "Three Addresses on Judaism."

75. In Bahr's *Die Zeit* he described Herzl's *Das neue Ghetto* as follows: "It is no drama. Drama placates us—here, we are agitated. The piece wants to show that we have never let the Jews out of their ghetto." Herzl responded with thanks to this review, sensing agreement with the analysis of the Jewish question and overlooking Bahr's judgment as to his play's theatrical worth. ("It is no play.") This play, the last before Herzl's breakthrough to Zionism, was replete with anti-Jewish sentiment. Cited in Bein et al., eds., *Theodor Herzl*, 4:409 and notes.

76. Bahr, "Das Judenproblem," 168.

77. Bahr's conclusion has much in common with a view of Zionism that Michael Berkowitz has termed "supplemental nationalism."

78. Bertha von Suttner, *Memoiren* (Bremen: C. Schünemann, 1965 reprinted as *Lebenserrinerun-gen*), 45.

79. See Nussenblatt, *Ein Volk*, 138–44.

80. Harry Zohn, ed., *The Complete Diaries of Theodor Herzl* (New York, 1960), 1:837; Nussenblatt, *Ein Volk*, 112–34; Herzl to Suttner, 16 January 1899, in CZA, H VIII 344.

81. Steven Beller, *Herzl* (New York: George Weidenfeld, 1991).

82. In her letter of condolence to Julie Herzl, Bertha von Suttner described Herzl as the fallen king of Zion and noted, "Alt-Neuland war das letzte Buch, das ich meinem armen kranken Manne

vorgelesen und das ihn (wie ich) begesitert hat" (Tulo Nussenblatt, *Zeitgenossen über Herzl* [Brünn: Reinhold, 1929], 271).

83. Cited in Nussenblatt, *Ein Volk*, 133.

84. Bertha von Suttner, "Nach dem Haag!" *Die Welt* 3, no. 21 (26 May 1899): 1–2; Bertha von Suttner, "Gespräche über den Zionismus und dem Haag," *Die Welt* 3, no. 28 (14 July 1899): 1–2.

85. To Maxim von Manteuffel (1864–1950) Herzl wrote: "Das Ziel ist hoch, der Weg ist weit, und *mes bons Juifs* sind zuweilen recht muthlos—von den *mauvais Juifs* gar nicht zu reden" (Bein et al., eds., *Theodor Herzl*, 4:250 [7 May 1897]).

6. Christian Author, Jewish Book?

1. See, respectively, Henry Hatfield, *From the Magic Mountain: Mann's Later Masterpieces* (Ithaca NY: Cornell University Press, 1979), 68 (to Hatfield's credit, he recognizes that it is "by no means easy to decide" to which genre *Joseph* belongs); Ruth Klüger, "Thomas Manns jüdische Gestalten," in *Katastrophen. Über deutsche Literatur* (Göttingen: Wallstein, 1994), 39–58; T. J. Reed, *The Uses of Tradition* (Oxford: Clarendon, 1974), and Ronald Hayman, *Thomas Mann: A Biography* (New York: Scribner, 1995); Hermann Kurzke, *Mondwanderungen* (Frankfurt: Fischer, 1993), and earlier essays; and Anthony Heilbut, *Eros and Literature* (New York: Alfred A. Knopf, 1996).

2. Two excellent examples are Aviva Zornberg, *Genesis: The Beginning of Desire* (Philadelphia: Jewish Publication Society, 1995); and Josipovici, *Book of God*.

3. Mark Van Doren estimates the work as 45 times as long as the section of Genesis that deals with the hero alone and 125 times as long as the section that covers in addition, as Mann himself does, the careers of Abraham, Isaac, and Jacob ("Joseph and His Brothers, a Comedy in Four Parts," in Henry Hatfield, ed., *Thomas Mann: A Collection of Critical Essays* [Englewood NJ: Prentice-Hall, 1964], 99).

4. Hence Ignaz Feuerlicht, *Thomas Mann* (New York: Twayne, 1968), could write: "[H]e was humorously engaged in the parody of a Bible commentary" (47). By "excavative and atomizing" I mean especially the intense focus on the various authorial strands of the Bible. A review of trends in Bible criticism may be found in Rolf Knierim, "Criticism of Literary Features, Form, Tradition and Redaction," in Douglas Knight, ed., *The Hebrew Bible and Its Modern Interpreters* (Chico CA: Scholars Press, 1985), 123–65.

5. Knight, ed., *The Hebrew Bible*, 165.

6. Ludwig Lewisohn, *New Palestine*, 15 September 1944, 519–20.

7. Doris Sommer, "Mann, Midrash and Mimesis," Ph.D. diss., Rutgers University, 1978.

8. Heftrich, *Geträumte Taten*, 516 n. 10, 393–401.

9. Marc Bregman, *Serah bat Asher: Biblical Origins, Ancient Aggadah and Contemporary Folklore*, Bilgray Lectures (Tucson: University of Arizona Press, 1996), 1.

10. On midrash as a category of modern literature, see Steven D. Fraade, "Interpreting Midrash 2: Midrash and Its Literary Contexts," *Prooftexts* 7, no. 3 (September 1987): 292.

11. I have abstracted this short list of midrashic features from David Stern, "Midrash," in Paul Mendes-Flohr and Arthur Cohen, eds., *Contemporary Jewish Religious Thought* (New York: Scribner's, 1987), 613–19.

12. Koelb, " Mann's 'Coat of Many Colors,' " 475. These words are "untranslatable" because they are ambiguous (tam), because their exact meaning is unknown (ketonet pasim), or because in a particular usage they are hapax legomena (aron).

13. In a letter to Joseph Angell, Mann lists among the eight books he used most in preparing Joseph "[d]ie Sagen der Juden, drei Bande, gesammelt und bearbeitet von Micha Josef bin Gorion,

deutsch erschienen bei Ruetten und Loening" (*Briefe 1937–1944* [Frankfurt am Main: S. Fisher, 1963], 24–25).

14. Sommer, "Mann, Midrash and Mimesis," chap. 4.

15. Mann to Rabbi Jakob Horovits, 2 June 1927, in *Thomas Mann's Briefe* (Frankfurt am Main: S. Fischer, 1963).

16. Thomas Mann, "Joseph und seine Brüder: Ein Vortrag," in *Gesammelte Werke*, vol. 11 (Frankfurt: S. Fischer, 1960), 472–84.

17. See, most recently, Hoelzel, "Thomas Mann's Attitude."

18. Josipovici, *Book of God*, 287.

19. Mann, *Joseph and His Brothers*, 4:1207. Hereafter cited in text as *Joseph*.

20. This is a brilliant touch on Mann's part. He feels that "opportunity" alone does not explain why the brothers conspire to kill him before Joseph has even had a chance to speak (Genesis 37:18). By having Joseph arrive dressed in the provocative garment, ample motive exists.

21. Josipovici is relying here on Erich Auerbach's luminous essay "Odysseus' Scar," in *Mimesis* (Princeton NJ: Princeton University Press, 1953), 3–23.

22. Josipovici, *Book of God*, 293.

23. Josipovici claims that readings of the New Testament (Mark 14:51–52) that turn the unnamed man in the sidon (garment) into a fulfillment of Genesis 37:15 are typical Christian fulfillment (pleroma) misreadings.

24. Josipovici, *Book of God*, 294.

25. Josipovici, *Book of God*, 298.

26. Josipovici, *Book of God*, 20.

27. The rabbis' awareness of whether the Bible's language ought to be treated as merely human or as a divine encoding is captured in the conflict between Rabbi Eliezer and Rabbi Akiva over the dictum "The Torah speaks in the language of human beings." Josipovici's blanket statement that the words of the Bible are merely well-ordered words but not pieces of a crossword puzzle reflects Rabbi Eliezer's view; Jewish tradition has generally sided with Rabbi Akiva's view.

28. In Judaic terms, one could express this dual commitment to biblical certainty and uncertainty easily: Halachah (law) and Haggadah (lore).

29. Klüger, "Thomas Manns jüdische Gestalten," esp. 54–57. These three pages offer a penetrating look at the philosemitic dimension of Mann's Joseph, including the observation that the hero is functionally a Diaspora Jew for most of the tetralogy, that Jacob is a model of balancing religious ideals with the demands of the day, and that the Jews in this story are the principal representatives of humanity. Klüger, however, fails to recognize how Jewish readings of the Bible influence Mann's own narrative.

30. Robert Alter, *The Art of Biblical Narrative* (New York: Basic Books, 1981). The opening chapter, a close reading of Genesis 38, acknowledges that rabbinic midrash had commented on many of the same connections Alter notes.

31. An example: The Soncino Chumash, still widely used in synagogues in the United States and Great Britain, excuses Tamar, explaining, "To prevent detection by Judah, she resorts to a disguise and a stratagem that must have appeared quite honorable in her Canaanite eyes." The Stone Chumash, increasingly favored by modern Orthodox congregations, insists, "As someone who was to play such a significant role in the destiny of Israel, it is inconceivable that she was of Canaanite descent." While these views are incompatible on one level, on another they both find Tamar laudable.

32. Benno Jacob, *The First Book of the Bible*, ed. Ernest and Walter Jacob (New York: KTAV, 1974), 261, first published as *Das erste Buch der Tora* (Berlin: Schocken, 1934).

33. Gerhard von Rad, *Genesis: A Commentary* (Philadelphia: Westminster, 1972).

34. Pau1 Pahl, ed., *Martin Luther: Lectures on Genesis* (St. Louis: Concordia, 1965), chaps. 38–44, 9–10.

35. Mann wrote Meno Spann on 16 June 1942: "On female greatness: the last volume has a female figure who does not actually lack greatness: Tamar, the daughter-in-law of Judah, who will intervene in the salvation history [*Heilsgeschichte*] at any price. You will see" (*Briefe 1937–1944*, 261).

36. In rabbinic Judaism, every person possesses a yetzer (inclination) for both good and bad.

37. An example: Joseph in Jewish tradition is criticized for his vanity, insensitivity to Jacob, and inappropriate behavior with women. In Christian tradition, Joseph becomes the very model of chastity.

38. Mann to Agnes Meyer, 17 February 1943, in Mann, *Briefe 1937–1944*, 299.

39. Mann was heavily influenced by the Nietzschean notion of eternal recurrence and liberally alludes to earlier figures in subsequent characterizations. In Mann's usage, eternal recurrence is quite close to that facet of midrash that sees Noah as the prototype for all future examples of animal husbandry and drunkenness, Jacob as the prototype for the nexus of sickness and aging, etc.

40. *Go'el* means "redeemer"; in the book of Ruth, the man willing to fulfill the obligations of Levirite marriage with Ruth is also called *go'el*.

41. This conscious neglect of narrative order is also found in rabbinic literature, justified by the dictum "There is no before or after in Torah."

42. Through ingenious exegesis, rabbinic tradition finds seven prophetesses in the Bible (Babylonian Talmud, Megillah, 14a).

43. Klüger, "Thomas Manns jüdische Gestalten," 57.

44. Josipovici, *Book of God*, 297.

45. I am indebted to Stanley Brodwin, "Notes on a New Letter by Thomas Mann: The Passover in Young Joseph," *Modern Fiction Studies* 30, no. 2 (summer 1984): 257–65, for bringing these passages to my attention.

46. Compare to Hoelzel, "Thomas Mann's Attitude," 238.

47. Cited in Nigel Hamilton, *The Brothers Mann* (New Haven CT: Yale University Press, 1978), 221.

48. I am not arguing that Mann's approach is identical to the rabbis'. I note only that his narrative style owes more to the midrashim than to Augustine, Aquinas, or Luther.

7. An Adventure in Otherness

1. Nahida Remy's *Das jüdische Weib* went through at least four editions in German between 1891 and 1922 and was twice published in English. All citations are from Louise Mannheimer's translation, *The Jewish Woman*.

2. Remy, *The Jewish Woman*, 63–64.

3. Remy, *The Jewish Woman*, 90.

4. Remy, *The Jewish Woman*, 249.

5. Richard J. Evans, *The Feminist Movement in Germany, 1894–1933* (London: Sage, 1976), 130.

6. Evans, *Feminist Movement in Germany*, 26.

7. Cited in Amy Hackett, "The Politics of Feminism in Wilhelmine Germany, 1890–1918," Ph.D. diss., Columbia University, 1976, 333. Helene Lange, one of the leaders of German feminism, also emphasized occupational training as a means of improving mothering skills (Evans, *Feminist Movement in Germany*, 27–28).

8. Hackett, " Politics of Feminism," xvii; Susannah Heschel, "Introduction," in *On Being a Jewish Feminist* (New York: Schocken, 1983), 13–36.

9. Wolfgang Paulsen, "Theodor Fontane—The Philosemitic Antisemite," *Leo Baeck Institute Yearbook* 26 (1981): 312–13.

10. Paulsen, "Theodor Fontane."

11. Quoted in Paul Mendes-Flohr, "Werner Sombart's *The Jews and Modern Capitalism*," *Leo Baeck Institute Yearbook* 21 (1976): 87–107.

12. Paula Winkler, "Betrachtungen einer Philozionistin," *Die Welt* 36, no. 6 (6 September 1901). See also Maurice Friedman, *Martin Buber's Life and Work: The Early Years, 1878–1923* (Detroit: Wayne State University Press, 1988), 50–52.

13. Nahida Ruth Lazarus, *Ich suchte dich. Biographische Erzählung* (Berlin: Siegfried Cronbach, 1898). The name Nahida Remy appears in parentheses beneath Nahida Ruth Lazarus. This autobiography was translated into Hebrew (*Bikashtikha,* 1932) and into Polish (Moritz Lazarus Archive, VAR 298/138c). The title reflects the roots of Remy's quest. Putatively, the "dich" is God; psychologically, the "dich" seems also to be her mother. Remy's *The Jewish Woman* initially lacked a chapter on the Jewish mother. Remy needed to be prompted by Moritz Lazarus to rectify this oversight, his sole substantive criticism of her work.

14. Lazarus, *Ich suchte dich,* 10–11; Remy, *The Jewish Woman,* 247.

15. Remy always refers to "Die Gräfin" by her title, never her proper name.

16. Lazarus, *Ich suchte dich,* 66–67.

17. The 3 March 1898 letter to Sophie Pataky, editor of *Lexicon der deutschen und österreichen Schriftstellerin der Gegenwart,* and the short sketch of Nahida Sturmhöffel's life are found in the Moritz Lazarus Archive, VAR 298/120.

18. Lazarus, *Ich suchte dich,* 168–69.

19. Nahida's first meeting with Max Remy contains an interesting detail: Remy's mother was at his office, and the conversation took place between the two women—the evident affection at this meeting was between Nahida and Mrs. Remy, not between Nahida and Max. It was also at this meeting that we learn two more interesting family facts: that Nahida's mother was also named Nahida, a name taken from a novel; Nahida tells Mrs. Remy that she "never speaks of her father" because he "made my mother very unhappy" (Lazarus, *Ich suchte dich,* 180). See also "Warum ich Jüdin wurde," *Israelitisches Wochenblatt* 3, no. 22 (11 June 1897).

20. Patricia Herminghouse, "Women and the Literary Enterprise in Nineteenth-Century Germany," in Ruth-Ellen Joeres, ed., *German Women in the Eighteenth and Nineteenth Centuries* (Bloomington: Indiana University Press, 1986), 78–93.

21. Lazarus, *Ich suchte dich,* 194; Nahida Remy to Zerline Meyer, Sunday evening, 19th [September], 1892, Moritz Lazarus Archive, VAR 298/115a.

22. Lazarus, *Ich suchte dich,* 207.

23. Lazarus, *Ich suchte dich,* 211.

24. On the Jewish salons of Berlin, see Deborah Hertz, *Jewish High Society in Old Regime Berlin* (New Haven CT: Yale University Press, 1988).

25. Nahida Remy was not the only contemporary to lay the blame for Jewish apostasy at the feet of Jewish women. See Hertz, *Jewish High Society,* 7–22.

26. "Sittenlehre als Gottesdienst" is a phrase Remy used in her *Culturstudien über das Judenthum* (Berlin: C. Dunker, 1893). Only the first volume of Moritz Lazarus's massive two-volume work on Jewish philosophy, *The Ethics of Judaism* (Philadelphia: Jewish Publication Society, 1899), appeared during his lifetime. The second volume appeared posthumously in 1911, thanks largely to Remy's efforts. See David Baumgardt, "The Ethics of Lazarus and Steinthal," *Leo Baeck Institute Yearbook* 2 (1957): 205–17.

27. Lazarus's attention to popular culture for a Jewish thinker in the German *Kulturbereich* whether liberal (Hermann Cohen) or Orthodox (Samson Raphael Hirsch).

28. Yosef Hayim Yerushalmi, *From Spanish Court to Italian Ghetto* (New York: Columbia University Press, 1972), 266. As Baumgardt, "The Ethics of Lazarus and Steinthal," noted many years ago, Lazarus was the first Jewish scholar to alert the non-Jewish world to humor contained within traditional sources.

29. Nahida Remy, *Prayer in the Bible and the Talmud* (New York, 1894), 6–20.

30. See, for instance, Gustav Karpeles, *Die Frauen in der jüdischen Literatur. Ein Vortrage* (Berlin, 1889); Meyer Kayserling, *Die jüdischen Frauen in der Geschichte, Literatur and Kunst* (Leipzig, 1879).

31. Remy, *The Jewish Woman*, 156.

32. Remy, *The Jewish Woman*, 160.

33. Lazarus, *Ich suchte dich*, 204–5. On Bertha Pappenheim, see Marion Kaplan, *The Jewish Feminist Movement in Germany: The Campaigns of the Jüdischer Frauenbund, 1904–1938* (Westport CT: Greenwood, 1979).

34. Remy, *The Jewish Woman*, 50.

35. Remy, *The Jewish Woman*, 50–51.

36. Remy, *The Jewish Woman*, 251.

37. That Ruth was happy in her second marriage seems clear from her devotion to publishing Lazarus's posthumous works. In a letter to his cousin Johanna Berendt, Moritz Lazarus wrote: "Taken all in all—this excellent woman is my light and my life. That she is a talented, successful writer, you know; but she is also a highly cultivated soul, and enthusiastic. . . . How can I describe her? Take a look at Song of Solomon 31:31" (Belke, *Moritz Lazarus und Heymann Steinthal*, 1:242–43).

38. Julius Brodnitz, "Nahida Remy. Ein Wort der Erinnerung und des Dankes," cv *Zeitung,* 20 January 1928, 28–29.

8. The Apostate as Philosemite

1. "As medieval civilization was expressed almost entirely in religious terms, it is very likely that a Jew who was captivated by the values of Christian society experienced this process in the form of religious conversion" (Katz, *Exclusiveness and Tolerance*, 76).

2. Apostate translates into Hebrew as *meshumad* or *mumar*.

3. I am skeptical about Endelman's useful but overly neat division between "sincere" and "opportunistic" converts, as I have explained in "The Conversionary Impulse in Fin-de-Siècle Germany," *Leo Baeck Institute Yearbook* 50 (1995): 107–22.

4. Hermann Strack admitted that it was unclear what induced Cassel to join the Church but contended that the reasons were obviously not mercenary.

5. Quoted in Paulus Cassel, "Wie ich über Judenmission denke," *Nathanael* 13, no. 5 (1897): 132–33.

6. Cassel's final "head count" of converts was placed at 262 by Reverend W. T. Gidney, *The History of the London Society for Promoting Christianity amongst the Jews, from 1809–1908* (London: Society for Promoting Christianity amongst the Jews, 1908).

7. Cassel, "Wie ich über Judenmission denke," tells us that he was brought to Christianity not by missionary activity but by his own reading of history—Jewish history in particular.

8. Cassel, *Martyrdom of Christ Church.*

9. Cassel, "Wie ich über Judenmission denke," 131–32.

10. Cassel, *Die Antisemiten*; Johann F. A. de Le Roi, *Geschichte der evangelischen Judenmission*, 2nd ed. (Leipzig: Hinrich'sche Buchhandlung, 1899). Cassel did complain about a trip to England:

"I was hospitably received every-where—but not by any members of the committee, not one of whom had the time to invite me to his house" (*Martyrdom of Christ Church*, 14).

11. Paulus Cassel, *Der Judengott und Richard Wagner* (Berlin: Wohlgemut, 1881), 32. For opposing views of Richard Wagner's developing antisemitism, see Katz, *Darker Side of Genius*; and Rose, *German Question/Jewish Question*.

12. Cassel, *Der Judengott und Richard Wagner*, 32–34.

13. Cassel, *Der Judengott und Richard Wagner*, 42.

14. Cassel, *Der Judengott und Richard Wagner*, 44. Cassel's political quietism, his aggressive attack on antisemites, and his extreme biblicism no doubt were contributing reasons for the fact that many educated, well-off Jews were willing to attend the lectures of this apostate.

15. Clark, *Politics of Conversion,* shows that the Prussian government oscillated between expressing a considerable interest in converting Jews and practicing the tolerance of *Realpolitik*.

16. Cassel, *Wider Heinrich von Treitschke*, 8–9.

17. Cassel, *Wider Heinrich von Treitschke*, 22–24. Cassel seems unaware or unconcerned that this could easily become an argument for Jewish Orthodoxy, which was beginning to regard the emancipation with ambivalence on exactly this point.

18. Cassel, *Wider Heinrich von Treitschke*, 27–28.

19. Cassel's position may be influenced by the Tübingen school and F. C. Baur, who proclaimed that "Christianity developed within Jewish soil, grew out of Judaism, and wants nothing more than to be a spiritualized Judaism." See Heschel, *Abraham Geiger*, 106–26.

20. Cassel, *Christus und das Judenthum* (Berlin: Walther und Appolant, 1883), 14.

21. Cassel's critique of Catholicism centered on its tendency to incorporate the Old Testament into practice (i.e., Judaizing). Cassel considered even Catholics too quick to equate Judaism with the Old Testament and inadequately aware of the Old Testament as a prophecy wholly fulfilled by the advent of Jesus. Cassel pointed to the New Testament (*Israel in der Weltgeschichte*, 8). In other words, its purpose was fulfilled, and no Old Testament–New Testament integration was required.

22. Cassel, *Israel in der Weltgeschichte*, 8.

23. Ragussis, *Figures of Conversion*, discusses the role that reading (albeit secret reading) played in the conversionary autobiographies. With Stein, we have an example from the German context.

24. Stein's conversionist methods raise the question of gender roles in the postconversionary careers of baptized Jews.

25. Rachel Feldhay-Brenner, "Ethical Convergence in Religious Conversion," in Harry J. Cargas, ed., *The Unnecessary Problem of Edith Stein* (Washington DC: United States Holocaust Memorial Council, 1994), 77–102; "Edith Stein, the Jew and the Christian: An Impossible Synthesis," in Frank Littell and Alan Berger, eds., *What Have We Learned* (Lewiston ME: Edwin Mellen, 1995).

26. Stein, *Aus dem Leben*.

27. As Rosenzweig wrote his mother on the occasion of his cousin's baptism: "In Germany today the Jewish religion cannot be 'accepted,' it has to be grafted on by circumcision, dietary observance, Bar Mitzvah. Christianity has a tremendous advantage over Judaism: it would have been entirely out of the question for Hans to become a Jew. . . . A Christian, however, he can become" (quoted in Nahum Glatzer, *Franz Rosenzweig: His Life and Thought* [New York: Schocken, 1961], 19). Note that two thirds of the items mentioned by Rosenzweig apply only to males. The Jewish home and family, important vehicles for transmitting Judaism, proved inadequate again and again in the case of intellectuals, male or female.

28. When Feldhay-Brenner writes that Stein "continued to fulfill" the Mishnaic tenet "All Israel are responsible to one another," she implies this dictum would be recognizable to Stein ("Ethical

Convergence," 78). I see no evidence to support that; indeed, I doubt that Stein would even know the difference between Mishnah and Talmud.

29. Stein, by the way, was more careful than her biographers in distinguishing "traditional" from "Orthodox." She describes Metis as a "strengglaubiger und gesetzestreuer Jude" (*Aus dem Leben*, 140–42).

30. Stein, *Aus dem Leben*, 142.

31. Levenson, "The Conversionary Impulse." Franz Kafka, *Brief an den Vater* (Frankfurt am Main: Fischer, 1995), expresses this alienation most forcefully. (Kafka wrote the letter in 1919 but never sent it.)

32. Although Teresa of Avila had some Marrano roots, this common ancestry does not seem to have elicited any comment from Edith, an interesting contrast to Cassel's insistence on the Jewish roots of the first Christians. Biographies of Stein tend toward hagiography. See Freda Mary Oben, "Edith Stein the Woman," in John Sullivan, ed., *Carmelite Studies* (Washington DC: ICS, 1987), 333. Oben, not surprisingly, is herself a Jewish-born Catholic. See Waltraud Herbstrith, *Edith Stein*, 5th ed. (San Francisco: Harper and Row, 1985).

33. Herbstrith, *Edith Stein*, 63. As the Nazi assault mounted, Stein spoke often of her willingness to "bear the Cross" for the Jewish people. While this represents a desire for solidarity, the notion of expiatory human suffering is foreign to Judaism. The willingness to die for God's glory (martyrdom) differs from the Jewish concept of *kiddush hashem*. The latter is not something to be sought after, desired, or anticipated; it is a necessary response when faced with the choice of death or the desecration of God's name through murder, incest, or public idolatry.

34. Karl Jacob Hirsch, *Quintessenz meines Lebens* (Mainz: Haase und Koehler, 1990), 238–42.

35. Edith Stein, *Life of a Jewish Family*, ed. Josephine Koeppel (Washington DC: ICS, 1986), 24.

36. Edith Stein to Gertrud von Le Fort, 17 October 1933, in Josephine Koeppel, ed., *Edith Stein: Self Portrait in Letters, 1916–1942* (Washington DC: ICS, 1993), 159–60; Stein, *Aus dem Leben*, foreword.

37. I have been unable to locate a copy of Stein's letter to Pius XI or even a reasonable description of its contents. The setting is described in Herbstrith, *Edith Stein*, 64–65. The papal encyclical "Mit brennender Sorge," issued in 1937, condemned racism but did not single out the Nazi persecution of the Jews.

38. Herbstrith, *Edith Stein*, 103. Stein's self-perception as a "Jewish" martyr, obviously, is problematic from a Jewish perspective. That it represents Stein's self-perception is beyond doubt.

Appendix

1. On the nature of antisemitism and philosemitism in the German scientific community, see Alan Rocke, *The Quiet Revolution: Hermann Kolbe and the Science of Organic Chemistry* (Berkeley: University of California Press, 1993), esp. 34–35; and Fritz Stern, *Einstein's German World*.

2. For an excellent historiographic overview, see Robert Wistrich, "Socialism and Judeophobia— Antisemitism in Europe before 1914," *Leo Baeck Institute Yearbook* 37 (1992): 111–45; Philip Mendes, "Left Attitudes towards Jews: Antisemitism and Philosemitism," *Australian Journal of Jewish Studies* 9, nos. 1–2 (1995): 7–44.

3. This group would include Edmund Silberner, Richard Lichtheim, and, with qualifications, Robert Wistrich.

4. This group would include Paul Massing, Donald Niewyck, and Shulamit Volkov.

5. As the epigraph from Michael Brenner's article indicates, he considers the dialogue between Jews and philosemites for Imperial and Weimar Germany a failure. It is by no means obvious, however, that successful intergroup dialogue necessitates the abandonment of all preconceptions.

6. Ernst Bloch, "The So-Called Jewish Question," in *Literary Essays* (Stanford CA: Stanford University Press, 1998), 490, uses the terms Judeophilia and philosemitism interchangeably.

7. Clark, *Politics of Conversion*, an excellent monograph on the conversionary movements in Prussia, takes Bloch's dictum too much to heart.

8. Fritz Sänger, "Philosemitismus—nutzlos und gefährlich," in Axel Silenius, ed., *Antisemitismus, Antizionismus—Analyze, Funktionen, Wirkung* (Frankfurt am Main: Tribüne, 1973).

9. Dr. Fritz Rothschild, "Unsere Freunde und Feinde," *Israelitische Wochenschrift* 24 (1890).

10. Gershom Scholem, "Against the Myth of the German-Jewish Dialogue," in Dannhauser, ed., *On Jews and Judaism in Crisis* (New York: Schocken, 1976), 63.

11. Bauman, "Allosemitism," 154.

12. Bauman, "Allosemitism," 155.

13. Melvin Jules Bunkiet, "Quick Crush This Philosemitism before It Gets Out of Hand," *Forward*, 31 January 2003, 12.

Selected Bibliography

Unpublished Sources

Delitzsch, Franz, and Moritz Lazarus. Correspondence. Moritz Lazarus Archive, VAR 298/94. Manuscript Division, National and University Libraries, Jerusalem.

Foerster, Friedrich Wilhelm, and Albert Einstein. Correspondence. Documents 53–070 through 53–085. Albert Einstein Archive, Manuscript Division, National and University Libraries, Jerusalem.

Herzl, Theodor. Correspondence. Theodor Herzl Papers, Central Zionist Archives, Jerusalem.

Quidde, Ludwig, and Albert Einstein. Correspondence. Documents 48–052 through 48–054. Albert Einstein Archive, Manuscript Division, National and University Libraries, Jerusalem.

Remy, Nahida. Correspondence. Moritz Lazarus Archive, VAR 298/120–40. Manuscript Division, National and University Libraries, Jerusalem.

Primary Works

Antisemiten-Spiegel. Die Antisemiten im Lichte des Christentums, des Rechtes und der Moral. Danzig: A. W. Kasemann, 1890.

Bahr, Hermann. *Der Antisemitismus. Ein International Interview.* Konigstein: Jüdischer, 1979.

———. *Die Rotte Korahs. Roman.* Vienna: H. Bauer Verlag, 1948.

Belke, Ingrid. *Moritz Lazarus und Heymann Steinthal: Die Begründer der Völkerpsychologie in ihren Briefen.* 2 vols. Tübingen: J. C. B. Mohr, 1971.

Cassel, Paulus. *Die Antisemiten und die evangelische Kirche.* Berlin: J. A. Wohlgemut, 1881.

———. *Israel in der Weltgeschichte.* Berlin: Beck, 1886.

———. *The Martyrdom of Christ Church in Berlin by the London Society.* Berlin: Buchhandlung des Lesecabinets, 1891.

———. *Wider Heinrich von Treitschke und für die Juden.* Berlin: Stahn, 1880.

Coudenhove-Kalergi, Heinrich Graf. *Anti-Semitism throughout the Ages.* Authorized English translation by Angelo S. Rappoport. London: Hutchinson, 1935.

———. *Antisemitismus.* Munich: Amalthea, 1992.

———. *Das Wesen des Antisemitismus.* Vienna: Paneuropa, 1929.

Coudenhove-Kalergi, Richard. *Ein Leben für Europa*. Cologne: Kieppenheuer und Witsch, 1966.

Dalman, Gustaf. *Christentum und Judentum*. Leipzig: Schriften des Institutum Judaicum in Berlin, no. 24, 1898.

Delitzsch, Franz. *Christentum und jüdische Presse. Selbsterlebtes*. Erlangen: Deichert, 1882.

———. *Jesus und Hillel. Mit Rücksicht auf Renan und Geiger*. 3rd ed. Erlangen: Deichert, 1875.

———. *Jewish Artisan Life in the Time of Jesus*. London: Hutchinson, 1906.

———. *Jüdisches Handwerkleben zur Zeit Jesu. Ein Beitrag zur neutestamentlichen Zeitgeschichte*. Erlangen: Andreas Deichert, 1868.

———. *Rohling's Talmudjude beleuchtet*. Leipzig: Dörffling und Frank, 1881.

———. *Ein Tag in Capernaum*. Leipzig: Justus Naumann, 1871.

———. *Wissenschaft, Kunst und Judentum*. Grimma: Gabhart, 1838.

Döllinger, Ignaz von. *Die Juden in Europa*. Berlin: Philo, 1924.

Felden, Emil. *Die Sünde wider das Volk*. Berlin: Oldenburg, 1921.

Ferch, Johann. *Mensch, nicht Jude! Roman*. Leipzig: Oldenburg, 1924.

Foerster, Friedrich Wilhelm. *Erlebte Weltgeschichte, 1869–1953*. Nurnberg: Glock und Lutz, 1953.

———. *The Jews*. Trans. Brian Battershaw. London: Hollis and Carter, 1961.

———. *Mein Kampf gegen des militaristische und nationalistische Deutschland*. Stuttgart: Friede durch Recht, 1920.

———. *Memoiren*. Nuremberg: Glock und Lutz, 1953.

———. *Politische Ethik und politische Pedagogik*. 4th ed. Munich: Ernst Reinhardt, 1920.

Freytag, Gustav. *Briefe an seine Gattin*. Berlin: Wilhelm Borngräber, n.d.

———. "Der Streit über das Judenthum in der Musik," 1869. Reprint in *Gesammelte Aufsätze*. Vol. 2. Leipzig: Verlag von S. Hirzel, 1888.

———. *Über den Antisemitismus*. 1893; rpt. Berlin: Central-Verein deutscher Staatsbürger jüdischen Glaubens, 1910.

Gerlach, Hellmut von. *Von Recht nach Links*. Zurich: Europa, 1937.

Heman, Carl Friedrich. *Das Erwachen der jüdischen Nation*. Basel: J. C. Hinrichs, 1897.

———. *Die historische Weltstellung der Juden und der moderne Judenfrage*. 2nd ed. Leipzig: J. C. Hinrichs, 1882.

Hermann, Jaques. *Das Kreuz des Juden*. Dresden: Carl Reissner, n.d.

Herzl, Theodor. *Altneuland*. Leipzig: R. Löwit, 1902.

Kessler, Harry Graf. *Tagebücher, 1918–1937*. Frankfurt am Main: Insel, 1961.

Klopfer, Carl Edward, ed. *Zur Judenfrage*. Munich: I. F. Lehrmann, 1891.

Knobloch, Alfred. *Gläserne Wände*. Berlin: Morawe und Scheffelt, 1914.

Kronburger, Emil. *Zionisten und Christen.* Leipzig: M. W. Kaufmann, 1900.

Mann, Thomas. *Briefe, 1937–1944.* Frankfurt am Main: S. Fisher, 1963.

———. *Joseph and His Brothers.* Trans. H. T. Lowe-Porter. New York: Alfred A. Knopf, 1948.

———. "Joseph und seine Brüder: Ein Vortrag." In *Gesammelte Werke.* Vol. 11. Frankfurt am Main: S. Fischer, 1960.

Nietzsche, Friedrich. *Beyond Good and Evil.* Trans. R. J. Hollingdale. London: Penguin, 1973.

Pueschel, Ernst. *Die Juden von Kronburg. Ein Buch von deutschem Volks- und Menschentums.* Neudietendorf: E. W. Pueschel, 1924.

Quidde, Ludwig. *Die Antisemitenagitation und die deutsche Studentenschaft.* Göttingen: Peippmüller, 1881.

———. *Der deutsche Pazifismus während des Weltkrieges, 1914–1918.* Boppard am Rhein: Harald Boldt, 1979.

Remy, Nahida (Ruth Lazarus). *Ich suchte Dich. Biographische Erzählung.* Berlin: Siegfried Cronbach, 1898.

———. *The Jewish Woman.* Trans. Louise Mannheimer. Cincinnati: C. J. Krehbiel, 1895.

———. *Das jüdische Weib.* 3rd ed. Leipzig: G. Laudin, 1892.

Sartre, Jean-Paul. *Anti-Semite and Jew.* Trans. George Becker. New York: Schocken, 1948.

Scholl, Carl. *Der Antisemitismus vom sittlichen Standpunkt aus betrachtet.* Bamberg: Verlag der Handelsdruckerei, 1894.

Scholz, Wilhelm von. *Der Jude von Konstanz. Trauerspiel in fünf Aufzeugen.* 2nd ed. Munich: Georg Müller, 1913.

Schrattenholz, Josef, ed. *Antisemiten Hammer. Eine Anthologie aus der Weltlitteratur.* Düsseldorf: E. Lintz, 1894.

Siemer, Heinrich. *Juda und die Andern.* Berlin: Gebrüder Pätel, 1928.

Singer, J., ed. *Briefe berühmte christlicher Zeitgenossen über die Judenfrage.* Vienna: Oskar Frank, 1885.

Spangenberg, Max. *Der Standpunkt der Freien wissenschaftlichen Vereinigung und der Universität Berlin zur Judenfrage und der Wissenschaft.* Berlin, 1882.

Stein, Edith. *Aus dem Leben einer jüdischen Familie.* Louvain: E. Nauwelärts, 1965.

Strack, Hermann. *Einleitung in Talmud und Midrasch.* Munich: C. H. Beck, 1921.

———. *Herr Adolf Stoecker, christliche Liebe und Wahrhaftigkeit.* Karlsruhe: H. Renther, 1885.

———. *Introduction to the Talmud and Midrash.* New York: Athenaeum, 1978.

———. *The Jews and Human Sacrifice.* 8th ed. Trans. Henry Blanchamp. New York: B. Blom, 1921.

Strack, Hermann, and Paul Billerbeck. *Kommentar zum neuen Testament aus Talmud und Midrasch Erlautet.* Munich: C. H. Beck, 1922.

Suttner, Bertha von. *Lebenserinnerungen.* Berlin: Verlag der Nation, 1970.

———. Preface to *Wehrt Euch! Ein Mahnwort an die Juden* by James Simon. Berlin, 1893.

———. *Die Waffen nieder!* 12th ed. Dresden: G. Pearson's, 1895. Published in English as *Lay Down Your Arms!* Trans. T. Holmes. New York: Longmans, Green, 1908.

Secondary Works

Almog, Shmuel. *Zionism and History: The Rise of a New Jewish Consciousness.* Jerusalem: Magnes Press of the Hebrew University, 1987.

Bauman, Zygmunt. "Allosemitism: Premodern, Modern, Postmodern." In Bryan Cheyette and Laura Marcus, eds., *Modernity, Culture and "the Jew."* New York: Polity, 1993. 143–56.

———. *Modernity and Ambivalence.* Ithaca NY: Cornell University Press, 1991.

Bein, Alex, et al., eds. *Theodor Herzl. Briefe und Tagebücher.* Vol. 5. Berlin: Ullstein-Propylaen, 1983.

Belke, Ingrid. "Liberal Voices on Antisemitism." *Leo Baeck Institute Yearbook* 23 (1978): 61–88.

Berkowitz, Michael. *Zionist Culture and Western European Jewry before the First World War.* Cambridge: Cambridge University Press, 1993.

Boehlich, Walter, ed. *Der berliner Antisemitismusstreit.* Frankfurt am Main: Insel, 1965.

Brenner, Michael. "Gott schützte uns vor unseren Freunden—Zur Ambivalenz des Philosemitismus im Kaiserreich." *Jahrbuch für Antisemitismusforschung* 2 (1993): 173–99. Offprint.

Cheyette, Bryan. *The Construction of "the Jew" in English Literature and Society: Racial Representations, 1875–1945.* New York: Cambridge University Press, 1993.

Chickering, Roger. *Imperial Germany and a World without War: The Peace Movement and German Society, 1892–1914.* Princeton NJ: Princeton University Press, 1975.

Clark, Christopher. *The Politics of Conversion.* Oxford: Clarendon, 1995.

Deák, Istvan. *Germany's Left-Wing Intellectuals: A Political History of the Weltbühne and Its Circle.* Berkeley: University of California Press, 1968.

Edelstein, Alan. *An Unacknowledged Harmony: Philo-Semitism and the Survival of European Jewry.* Westport CT: Greenwood, 1982.

Endelman, Todd, ed. *Jewish Apostasy in the Modern World.* New York: Holmes and Meier, 1987.

Engelmann, Hans. *Kirche am Abgrund. Adolf Stoecker und seine antijüdische Bewegung.* Berlin: Institut Kirche und Judentum, 1984.

Erspamer, Peter. *The Elusiveness of Tolerance: The "Jewish Question" from Lessing to the Napoleonic Wars.* Chapel Hill: University of North Carolina Press, 1997.

Garb, Tamar. "Introduction: Modernity, Identity, Textuality." In Linda Nochlin and Tamar Garb, eds., *The Jew in the Text: Modernity and the Construction of Identity.* London: Thames and Hudson, 1995. 7–19.

Gelber, Mark H. *Melancholy Pride: Nation, Race and Gender in the German Literature of Cultural Zionism.* Tübingen: Max Niemeyer Verlag, 2000.

Gilman, Sander. *Jewish Self-Hatred.* Baltimore MD: Johns Hopkins University Press, 1986.

Goldhagen, Daniel Jonah. *Hitler's Willing Executioners: Ordinary Germans and the Holocaust.* New York: Vintage, 1996.

Golling, Ralf, and Peter von der Osten-Sacken, eds. *Hermann L. Strack und das Institutum Judaicum in Berlin.* Berlin: Institut Kirche und Judentum, 1996.

Gubser, Martin. *Literarischer Antisemitismus. Untersuchungen zu Gustav Freytag und anderen bürgerlichen Schriftstellern des 19. Jahrhunderts.* Göttingen: Wallstein, 1998.

Hamann, Brigitte. *Bertha von Suttner. Ein Leben für den Frieden.* Munich: Piper, 1986.

Heftrich, Eckhard. *Geträumte Taten: Joseph und seine Brüder.* Frankfurt am Main: Klostermann, 1993.

Herbstrith, Waltraud. *Edith Stein.* 5th ed. San Francisco: Harper and Row, 1985.

Herzog, Dagmar. *Intimacy and Exclusion: Religious Politics in Pre-Revolutionary Baden.* Princeton NJ: Princeton University Press, 1996.

Heschel, Susannah. *Abraham Geiger and the Jewish Jesus.* Chicago: University of Chicago Press, 1998.

Hoelzel, Alfred. "Thomas Mann's Attitude toward Jews and Judaism: An Investigation of Biography and Oeuvre." *Studies in Contemporary Jewry.* Vol. 6. New York: Oxford University Press, 1990.

Holl, Karl. *Pazifismus in Deutschland.* Frankfurt am Main: Suhrkamp, l988.

Josipovici, Gabriel. *The Book of God.* New Haven CT: Yale University Press, 1988.

Katz, Jacob. *Exclusiveness and Tolerance.* New York: Behrman, 1961.

———. *Out of the Ghetto.* New York: Schocken, 1978.

———. "Zionism versus Anti-Semitism." In *Jewish Emancipation and Self-Emancipation.* Philadelphia: JPS, 1986. 141–52.

Kinzig, Wolfram. "Philosemitismus: Zur Geschichte des Begriffs." *Zeitschrift für Kirchengeschichte* 105, nos. 2–3 (1994): 202–28.

———. "Philosemitismus: Zur historiographischen Verwendung des Begriffs." *Zeitschrift für Kirchengeschichte* 3 (1994): 360–83.

Koelb, Clayton. "Thomas Mann's 'Coat of Many Colors.'" *German Quarterly* 49, no. 4 (1976): 472–84.

Kornberg, Jacques. "Vienna in the 1890s. The Austrian Opposition to Antisemitism. The Verein zur Abwehr des Antisemitismus: An Analysis of a Failure." *Leo Baeck Institute Yearbook* 41 (1996): 161–98.

Kusche, Ulrich. *Die unterlegene Religion. Urteil deutscher Alttestamentler*. Berlin: Institut Kirche und Judentum, 1991.

Lindner, Erik. "Philosemitismus im Krieg. Programmatik and Argumentation der Zeitschrift 'Mitteilungen aus dem Verein zur Abwehr des Antisemitismus.'" Master's thesis, Westphälischen Wilhelms-Universität, 1989.

Low, Alfred D. *Jews in the Eyes of the German*. Philadelphia: Institute for the Study of Human Issues, 1979.

Männchen, Julia. *Gustaf Dahlmans Leben und Wirken in der Brüdergemeinde Universität Leipzig*. Wiesbaden: Otto Harrassowitz, 1987.

Mayer, Hans. *Aussenseiter*. Frankfurt am Main: Suhrkamp, 1975.

Meyer, Michael. "The Great Debate on Antisemitism." *Leo Baeck Institute Yearbook* 12 (1966): 137–70.

Mosse, George. *German Jews beyond Judaism*. Cincinnati: Hebrew Union College, 1985.

———. "The Image of the Jew in German Popular Culture." *Leo Baeck Institute Yearbook* 2 (1957): 218–27.

Niewyck, Donald. *The Jews in Weimar Germany*. Baton Rouge: Louisiana State University Press, 1980.

Nussenblatt, Tulo. *Ein Volk unterwegs zum Frieden*. Vienna: Reinhold, 1933.

Paucker, Arnold. *Der jüdische Abwehrkampf gegen Antisemitismus und Nationalsozialismus in dem letzten Jahren der Weimarer Republik*. Hamburg: Leibniz, 1968.

Pickus, Keith. *Constructing Modern Identities: Jewish University Students in Germany, 1815–1914*. Detroit MI: Wayne State University Press, 1999.

Pulzer, Peter. *Jews and the German State: The Political History of a Minority, 1848–1933*. Oxford and Cambridge: Blackwell, 1992.

Ragussis, Michael. *Figures of Conversion: "The Jewish Question" and English National Identity*. Durham NC: Duke University Press, 1995.

Rappaport, Solomon. *Jew and Gentile: The Philosemitic Aspect*. New York: Philosophical Library, 1980.

Rengstorf, Karl Heinrich, and Siegfried von Kortzfleisch, eds. *Kirche und Synagoge*. Stuttgart: Ernst Klett, 1970.

Rose, Paul Lawrence. *German Question/Jewish Question: Revolutionary Antisemitism from Kant to Wagner*. 2nd ed. Princeton NJ: Princeton University Press, 1990.

Sandmel, Samuel. "Parallelomania." *Journal of Biblical Literature* 81, no. 1 (March 1962): 1–13.

Sartre, Jean-Paul. *Réflexions sur la question juive.* Trans. George Becker. New York: Schocken, 1948.

Schorsch, Ismar. *Jewish Reactions to German Antisemitism, 1870–1914.* New York: Columbia University Press, 1972.

Schürer, Emil. *Geschichte des jüdischen Volkes im Zeitalter Jesu Christi.* Leipzig: Hinrichs, 1886.

Stern, Frank. *The Whitewashing of the Yellow Badge.* Oxford: Pergamon, 1992.

Suchy, Barbara. "The Verein zur Abwehr des Antisemitismus. I." *Leo Baeck Institute Yearbook* 28 (1983): 205–39.

———. "The Verein zur Abwehr des Antisemitismus. II." *Leo Baeck Institute Yearbook* 30 (1985): 67–103.

Tal, Uriel. *Christians and Jews in Germany: Religion, Politics, and Ideology in the Second Reich, 1870–1914.* Ithaca NY: Cornell University Press, 1975.

Volkov, Shulamit. "Antisemitism as a Cultural Code." *Leo Baeck Institute Yearbook* 23 (1978): 25–46.

Wagner, Siegfried. *Franz Delitzsch. Leben und Werk.* Munich: Kaiser, 1978.

Wiese, Christian. *Wissenschaft des Judentums und protestantische Theologie im wilhelminischen Deutschland.* Tübingen: Mohr-Siebeck, 1999.

Source Acknowledgments

The author gratefully acknowledges permission to reprint different or earlier versions of the following articles and book chapters:

Chapter 1: "Philosemitic Discourse in Imperial Germany," in *Jewish Social Studies* 2, no. 3 (summer 1996): 25–35, courtesy of Indiana University Press.

Chapter 2: "The German Peace Movement and the Jews: An Unexplored Nexus," *Leo Baeck Institute Yearbook* 46 (2001): 277–304, courtesy of the Leo Baeck Institute.

Chapter 3: "The Problematics of Philosemitic Fiction," *German Quarterly* 75, no. 4 (fall 2002): 379–93.

Chapter 4: "Missionary Protestants as Defenders and Detractors of Judaism: Franz Delitzsch and Hermann Strack," *The Jewish Quarterly Review* 92, nos. 3–4 (January–April 2002): 383–420.

Chapter 5: "The Gentile Reception of Herzlian Zionism Reconsidered," *Jewish History* 16, no. 2 (2002): 187–211. (c) Kluwer Academic Publishers. Reprinted with kind permission of Kluwer Academic Publishers.

Chapter 6: "Christian Author, Jewish Book? Thomas Mann's *Joseph und seine Brüder*," *The German Quarterly* 71, no. 2 (spring 1998): 166–178.

Chapter 7: "An Adventure in Otherness," in Tamar Rudavsky, ed., *Gender and Judaism* (New York: New York University Press, 1995), 99–111.

Chapter 8: "The Apostate as Philosemite: Selig Paulus Cassel and Edith Stein," in Dagmar Lorenz and Renate Posthafen, eds., *Transforming the Center, Eroding the Margins* (Columbia SC: Camden House, 1998), 132–145.

Index

Abwehrverein (Society for the Defense against Antisemitism), ix, xiii; Coudenhove's rejection of, 36; defense tactics of, 7–9; in *Die Welt*, 99; and emancipation, 4; and German Peace Society, 25, 78; Herzl and Austrian branch of, 107–8; on Jewish failings and contributions, 16–17; liberals' attack of, 12–26; *Mitteilungen* (Reports), 12; Quidde's rejection of, 25–28

Ahad Ha'Am (Asher Zvi Ginzburg), Zionism unlike Herzl's, 103–5, 108

antisemitism, vii, xi–xii; in Berliner Antisemitismusstreit (1879–81), 4–5; Coudenhove's rejection of, 36; and German politics in Kaiserreich, 9–11; Herzl's view of, 98; liberals' attack of, 12–16; Quidde's rejection of, 25–28; in Pueschel's novel, 54–56; and philosemitism, 150n18, 151n28, 151n29, 154n32. *See also* Die Judenfrage (The Jewish question)

Der Antisemitismus. Ein International Interview (Antisemitism. An international interview), 105

Augusta, Empress, 12–13

Bahr, Hermann: author of *Der Antisemitismus*, 105; and Herzl, 104–6

Ballin, Albert, 34

Baron, Salo, 10, 94

Baumann, Zygmunt, and allosemitism, 33–34; application to Delitzsch and Strack, 66, 143, 151n31

Beller, Steve, 24

Bernstein, Eduard: as pacifist, 27–28; upbringing, 17–18

Billerbeck, Paul, 74–76

Bloch, Ernst, 147

Brenner, Michael, 143, 147, 150n23, 176n5

Buber, Paula Winkler, as philozionist, 125

Bund neues Vaterland (League for a new fatherland), 27

Caspari, Otto, 17

Cassel, (Paulus) Selig: as Christian triumphalist, 136; and Heinrich von Treitschke, 134–35; and London Society for Promotion of Christianity, 133–34; in *Nathanael*, 133; path toward missionary life, 133–36; upbringing, 132; and Wagner, 134

Chickering, Roger, 22

Christentum und jüdische Presse (*Christianity and Jewish Press*, 1882), 71–72

Clark, Christopher, 77, 179n9

Clemenceau, Georges, 96–97

conversion, religious, 56–58; and Missionary Protestants, 64, 133; Nahida Remy's attack on, 177n27; number in 1914, 132, 146

Corda, Benjamin (Alfred Knobloch), 51–54

Coudenhove-Kalergi, Heinrich von, 6–7; on antisemitism and philosemites, 36; author of *Wesen des Antisemitismus* (The essence of antisemitism), 35; on Catholics and Protestants, 37–38; as critic of race science, 37; and German Peace Society, 35–40; on Reform Judaism, 38–39; Spinoza's influence on, 38

Coudenhove-Kalergi, Richard von: continued father's pacifism, 39–40; on Jewish pacifism, 40; as pan-Europeanist, 40

Dalman, Gustaf, 8, 69, 77; editor of *Nathanael*, 86

Delitzsch, Franz, 11, 64; *Christentum und jüdische Presse*, 71–72, 82; early career of, 64–65; *Ein Tag in Capernaum*, 69–70;

Delitzsch, Franz (*continued*)
Ernste Fragen, 83; Jesus und Hillel, 72; as
Judaic scholar, 68–70; Jüdisches Handwerkleben zur zeit Jesu (*Jewish Artisan Life
in the Time of Jesus*), 69; as philosemite
and antisemite, 81–84; relationship with
Moritz Lazarus, 145; and Second Temple
period, 69–71; shortcomings as rabbinic
scholar, 70–71, 164n24
Deutsche Friedensgesellschaft (German Peace
Society), 21–43; and Abwehrverein and
Left Liberalism, 25; and anti-antisemitism,
25; Bertha von Suttner as member, 23–25;
Chickering's view of, 22; Coudenhove as
member, 35–39; Foerster as member, 29–
35; Jewish participation in, 21–22; Quidde
as member, 25–29; as vehicle of Jewish
identity, 42
Dinter, Arthur, 44
Dohm, Christian Wilhelm von, 3–4, 10, 45–46
Döllinger, Ignaz, xiii–xiv, 16; on Jewish
virtues, 18–19; on Ostjuden, 156n75
Dunant, Jean Henri, 98

East Africa project, 104
Edelstein, Alan, x
einheitskultur (unified, homogenous culture),
vs. mischkultur (mixed, heterogeneous
culture), 8–9
Einleitung in Talmud und Midrasch (Introduction to the Talmud and Midrash),
73–74
Ehrlich, Arnold Bogumil, 65
Einstein, Albert: as contributor to Die
Friedensbewegung (The peace movement),
39; and Foerster, 33; and Quidde, 27
Ernste Fragen (Serious questions) (Delitzsch),
83
Erspamer, Peter, and tolerance debates, 3

Felden, Emil, as author and Abwehrverein
member, 49
feminism, German and Jewish, 123–24, 130
Ferch, Johann, 61–63
Foerster, Friedrich Wilhelm: Die Juden, 30,
32–35; and Einstein, 33; and German
Peace Society, 29–35; on Judaism and
Christianity, 43, 145; and Ostjuden, 30–

31; as signer of Manifesto to Europeans,
29; supporter of Versailles Treaty, 29
Fontane, Theodor, 124
Freytag, Gustav, 6, 11, 44, 63
Fried, Alfred, 21, 41, 107–8

Gerlach, Hellmut von, 7, 12, 44, 145–46
Goldhagen, Daniel Jonah, viii–ix
Gressmann, Hugo, 88–89

Hamann, Brigitte, 24
Heftrich, Eckhard, on Mann's Joseph, 111
heimat (homeland), 45–63; in Ernst Pueschel,
54–65; in Heinrich Simer, 47–49; in Hermann Jaques, 60; in Wilhelm von Scholz,
57–58
Heman, Carl Friedrich: and Christian mes-
sianism, 102; and Das Erwachen der
jüdischen Nation (The awakening of
the Jewish nation), 103; denigration of
Muslims by, 16; and East Africa project,
104; and Herzl 101–4
Hempel, Johannes, 89
Hertzberg, Arthur, 98
Herzl, Theodor: analysis of antisemitism
by, 98, 102; and Austrian Abwehrverein,
99; and Bahr, 104–6; and contributions
to Zionism, 93–94; and Die Welt, 94;
and Heman, 101–4; and Islam, 103; and
Pinsker and gentile admirers, 101; and
Suttner, 107–8
Herzog, Dagmar, xi–xii, 42
Heschel, Susannah: on Geiger, 67; on Geiger
and Delitzsch, 71
Hoelzel, Alfred, discussion of Mann, ix–x
Holl, Karl, 22
Husserl, Edmund, and Edith Stein, 137–38

Ich Suchte Dich (I sought you) (Remy, 1898),
125–28
intermarriage, Jewish-Christian: in Felden's
novel, 49–50; as fictional theme, 45–63; in
Knobloch's novel, 53; number in 1914, 45;
in Scholz's play, 58; as solution to Jewish
Question, 5, 14
Der Israelit (German orthodox Jewish journal), 104

Jacob, Benno, as Bible scholar, 116

Jaques, Hermann, 59–61
Jesus und Hillel (Jesus and Hillel) (Delitzsch, 1875), 72
Jewry, American, peace activism of, 21
Joseph und seine Brüder (*Joseph and His Brothers*) (Mann, 1948), 110–22
Josipovici, Gabriel: on Jewish and Christian reading, 113–15; on Rashi, 114; on Thomas Mann, 113–15
Die Judenfrage (The Jewish question): in *Die Welt*, 99; and emancipation, xi, 3–5; Freytag's views on, 11; and liberal press, 27; liberals' role in, 10–20; and missionary Protestants, 77–80; in other lands, 95–98; role in German politics, 3–4; Schirmer's views on, 9; Schoppe's views on, 11; and Tivoli Program, 27; at universities, 26. *See also* antisemitism
Die Juden (*The Jews*) (Foerster, 1959), 32–35
Das jüdische Weib (*The Jewish Woman*) (Remy, 1891), 123, 125, 128–29
Jüdisches Handwerkleben zur zeit Jesu (*Jewish Artisan Life in the Time of Jesus*) (Delitzsch, 1868), 69

Katz, Jacob, viii, xi, 4; on "neutral" society, 42; on religious conversion, 132; on Zionism, 94
Kautsky, Karl, 100–101
Klüger, Ruth, 46, 51; on Mann's *Joseph*, 116, 120, 122
Kommentar zum neuen Testament aus Talmud und Midrasch Erlautet (Commentary to the New Testament) (Strack and Billerbeck, 1922), 75–87
Kramer, Franz, 18

Lamparter, Eduard, xiii
Aus dem Leben einer jüdischen Familie (Life of a Jewish family) (Stein, 1965), 137–39
Lazarus, Moritz: and Delitzsch, 145; and Nahida Remy (Lazarus), 127, 131, 145, 176n37
Lessing, Gotthold Ephraim, 3, 46, 63
Levy, Hirsch, 65
Lewisohn, Ludwig, 111
Liberals: ambivalence toward Jews, 3–20, 152n8, 152n19, 156n75, 165n75; and defense of Jews, 19, 27; and German Jewish identities, 42; and Left Liberal parties, xiii, 9–10, 27
Low, Alfred, x
Luther, Martin, verdict on Tamar, 116–17

Mann, Thomas: and Bible scholarship, 110–13; christology of, 120–21, 145; as evaluated by Hoelzel, ix–x; and Gabriel Josipovici, 113–15; and *Joseph und seine Brüder*, x, 111–22; and midrash 111–13, 122; and portrait of Tamar in Genesis, 38, 115–21
Mayer, Hans, 17, 44
Mehring, Franz, xiii

Nathanael (a missionary journal), 79, 85
Naumann, Friedrich, 100
Nazis: and Edith Stein, 140; fictional precursors of, 44; and Foerster, 33; and German Protestants, 89; and Quidde, 28; and Richard Coudenhove, 40; voters for, viii
Nietzsche, Friedrich: on causes for German antisemitism; 19, 40; on Judentum and Deutschtum, 15; on prevalence of German antisemitism, 5–6

Ostjuden (East European Jews): in Döllinger's view, 16, 31–32, 86–87; in Naumann's view, 100; in Nietzsche's analysis, 15

philosemitism: defined, vii; early scholarship on, x–xii; failure as political code, 20; as false category, ix; among gentile Zionists, 93–108; in German politics, 9–10; limitations of fictional, 44–45; Nahida Remy as proponent of, 131, 149nn1–2, 150n18, 151nn28–29; and the nature of liberals, 19–20; Salo Baron on, 94; three scholarly models of, 64–66; Zionist position on, 109
Pickus, Keith, on German-Jewish identity, 42
Pinsker, Leon (Lev), and Herzl's Zionism, 93, 101, 108
Protestants, liberal, xiii, 67–68
Protestants, missionary, x, xiii, 64; antisemitism of, 77; and Delitzsch, 64–65, 68–73, 77–81; and Selig Cassel, 133–36, 164n24, 165n33, 166n55; and Strack, 65–66, 73–81, 84–87
Pueschel, Ernst, 54–57

Quidde, Ludwig: and Einstein, 28; evaluation of antisemitism, 25–26; and German Peace Society, 25–29; and Göttingen University, 25–26; and Left Liberal parties, 27

Rad, Gerhard von, 116
Rathenau, Walter, 34
Rechtsstaat (civic equality and rule of law), xii, 9, 19, 78
Remy, Nahida (Ruth Lazarus) (née Nahida Sturmhöffel), 123–31; Das jüdische Weib, 125–28; as feminist, 123–24; and Ich Suchte Dich, 125–28; and Moritz Lazarus, 127, 131, 145, 176n37; upbringing, 126–27
Rickert, Heinrich, xii, 9
Rohling, Auguste, 81–82
Rose, Paul Lawrence, vii–x

Salisbury, Lord, 97
Sandmel, Samuel: on Strack-Billerbeck's Kommentar, 75–76
Schay, Rudolf, xiii, 151n35
Schirmer, Wilhelm, 9, 14
Scholem, Gershom, 14, 147
Scholz, Wilhelm von, 57–59
Schoppe, Wilhelm, 11; on Jews and Negroes, 16
Socialists, as discussed by Goldhagen, ix, xiii, 103, 146
Spangenberg, Max, 10
Spätjudentum (Late Judaism), as derogatory construct, 67–68
Stein, Edith, 132; and Edmund Husserl, 137–38; and Eduard Metis, 138; and Göttingen University circle, 138–39; Aus dem Leben einer jüdischen Familie (Life of a Jewish family, 1965), 139–41; and mother, Auguste, 137–38; upbringing, 136–41
Stern, Frank, xii
Strack, Hermann, 64–90; author of Das Wesen des Judentums (The essence of Judaism), 87; early career of, 65–66; and Jewish scholars, 66; as Judaic scholar, 73–74; as philosemite and antisemite, 84–85;

shortcomings of, 165n33; and Yiddish, 86–87
Suttner, Arthur Gundaccar von, and Austrian Abwehrverein, 99, 107
Suttner, Bertha von (née Kinsksy), 13; author of Die Waffen Nieder (Lay Down Your Arms) 23, 107; and German Peace Society, 23–25; as supporter of Herzl, 107–8

Ein Tag in Capernaum (A day in Capernaeum) (Delitzsch 1871), 69–70
Tamar: and christological themes, 120–21; in Genesis, 38, 115; and Jewish-Christian polemic, 120–21; in Mann's Joseph, 115–21; and other biblical women, 119–12
Treitschke, Heinrich von, 4; compared to Dohm, 10; on "exception Jews," 17

Volkov, Shulamit, 4, 149n5

Die Waffen Nieder! (Lay Down Your Arms!) (Suttner, 1889), 23, 107
Wagner, Richard: on Jewish emancipation, 134; path to antisemitism, viii, xii
Weber, Max, 6
Die Welt (Zionist journal), 94–101, 109
Die Weltbühne (Left-wing journal), xiii
Das Wesen des Antisemitismus (The essence of antisemitism) (H. von Coudenhove, 1901), 35–36
Das Wesen des Christentums (Strack, 1906), 87
Wider Heinrich von Treitschke and fur die Juden (Against Heinrich von Treitschke and for the Jews) (Cassel, 1880), 135–36

Yiddish: in Die Welt, 95; as Germanic language, 86–87

Zionism: Coudenhove's support of, 39; and Die Welt, 94–100; early history of, 93; gentile support for, 93–109; and Heman, 101–6; as represented in Jaques's novel, 61; supported by antisemites, 99
Zola, Emile, 96

DATE DUE

AUG 30 '04 S		